A
LITTLE
LATIN READER

A
LITTLE
LATIN READER

MARY C. ENGLISH

MONTCLAIR STATE UNIVERSITY

GEORGIA L. IRBY

THE COLLEGE OF WILLIAM AND MARY

New York   Oxford

OXFORD UNIVERSITY PRESS

Oxford University Press, Inc., publishes works that further Oxford University's objective of excellence in research, scholarship, and education.

Oxford New York
Auckland Cape Town Dar es Salaam Hong Kong Karachi
Kuala Lumpur Madrid Melbourne Mexico City Nairobi
New Delhi Shanghai Taipei Toronto

With offices in
Argentina Austria Brazil Chile Czech Republic France Greece
Guatemala Hungary Italy Japan Poland Portugal Singapore
South Korea Switzerland Thailand Turkey Ukraine Vietnam

For titles covered by Section 112 of the US Higher Education
Opportunity Act, please visit www.oup.com/us/he for the latest
information about pricing and alternate formats.

Published by Oxford University Press, Inc.
198 Madison Avenue, New York, New York, 10016
http://www.oup.com

Library of Congress Cataloging-in-Publication Data

English, Mary C.
A little Latin reader / Mary C. English, Georgia L. Irby
    p. cm.
  ISBN 978-0-19-984622-1
  1. Latin language—Readers. 2. Latin language—Grammar. I. Irby,
Georgia L. (Georgia Lynette), 1965– II. Title.
PA2095.E54 2012
478.6'421—dc23   2011031037

Printing number: 9 8 7 6 5

Printed in Canada
on acid-free paper

CONTENTS

PREFACE

Our goal for *A Little Latin Reader* is simple: we want students to read as much authentic Latin as possible in their first few years of study. Unfortunately, many of the Latin textbooks on the market do not emphasize reading extended passages of unadapted Latin at the earliest stages of Latin instruction. As a result, students become experts at "textbook Latin" but find the transition to classical authors difficult and frustrating. In direct response to seeing even our best students struggle at this stage of learning Latin, we have collected over 200 lively passages, 2–10 lines in length, suitable for elementary and intermediate students who are still solidifying their knowledge of Latin grammar and syntax. Students who work their way through the entire reader (or at least a good portion of it) can become acquainted with major Roman authors – Catullus, Caesar, Cicero, Horace, Livy, Martial, Ovid, and wonderful Latin inscriptions that record the first-hand testimony of everyday life in the Roman world, from Pompeii to Roman Britain.

We have arranged the selections in this reader to emphasize the points of Latin grammar and syntax that the individual texts highlight. In very general terms, the passages unfold in order of increasing difficulty; we present sentences that emphasize simple infinitives long before ones that feature subjunctive clauses and gerundives. That said, we do believe that students should be challenged to confront the realities of "authentic Latin" early in their study of the language, and they should be encouraged to tackle unadapted Latin passages even before they have met every form or vocabulary word as part of their formal instruction. We have provided brief introductions for all the passages to give students some narrative context as well as extensive running vocabulary notes so that students can read the entries without needing to look up unfamiliar words in a dictionary. We have also identified the meter for all of the poetry selections, and we hope that students and instructors consult Appendix B on Latin meter and scansion so as to appreciate the beauty and intricacy of Latin verse.

The arrangement of topics and the length of the passages are intended to provide the highest degree of flexibility in the classroom: a single selection can provide additional practice in syntax and translation during the first or last few minutes of a class session; a series of selections can provide the foundation of an entire class meeting; selections can be used for practice and/or testing in translating at sight; or the entire reader can be used as the core text of a comprehensive review of Latin grammar. The final sections of the reader feature twelve extended passages (six prose and six poetry) from authors that are typically categorized as "intermediate Latin" (Livy, Petronius, Pliny, Vergil, Sulpicia, and Ovid) and "advanced Latin" (Sallust, Tacitus, Suetonius, Horace, Germanicus, and Statius). These selections can be used as "sneak peaks" or "previews" of work to be done at the next level of Latin, or they can function as an extra challenge for especially talented Latin classes. We have also included an Index of Latin Grammar and Syntax as well as an Index of Roman Culture (Appendices D and E) so that instructors and students can use this book as a resource for whatever classes and assignments they envision (e.g., some instructors may want to use Appendix D to find extra passages that feature ablative constructions; others may want to use Appendix E to create lessons on the Roman family or ancient science).

In formatting the reader, we have used the *Oxford Classical Texts* (OCTs) for the Latin text. To aid students in pronunciation and the identification of forms, we have included macrons for almost all of the passages in the text (Sections 1–46) and in the glossary, which features words appearing in more than one selection. We have followed the governing principle of the *Oxford Latin Dictionary* and marked all of the vowels that are long by nature. For the intermediate and advanced passages (Sections 47–50), we have omitted the macrons because students at this level should be confident enough in their pronunciation and identification of forms to proceed without them. For the inscriptions, we have retained the texts as they have come down to us. We have expanded all abbreviations, indicated by parentheses (e.g., 6.1), we have supplied text that eroded or has been chiseled off, indicated by square brackets (e.g., 7.1), and we have provided notes for words rendered according to local pronunciation (e.g., *anc* for *hanc*, 34.4) as well as for all scribal errors in grammar and syntax. The major collections of inscriptions used in the Reader include *CIL* (*Corpus Inscriptionum Latinarum*), *ILS* (*Inscriptiones Latinae Selectae*), and *RIB* (*Roman Inscriptions of Britain*). We hope that students and instructors consult Appendix C on Latin Epigraphy for further information.

Finally, we would like to thank Charles Cavaliere, Shelby Peak, and Marie Flaherty-Jones, our editors at Oxford University Press, who provided many wonderful suggestions for this book. We would also like to thank Adam Hindin, William Hutton, and John Oakley for their advice and support. We owe a debt to our Latin students over the years who inspired us to undertake this project and who field-tested the selections in the reader (a special thanks to Georgia Irby's Intermediate Latin class at William and Mary, Fall 2010, who used an earlier draft of the reader as their primary text and provided us with crucial feedback, especially Tejas Aralere, Reese Kim, Tara Martin, Melissa McCue, Rebecca Obniski, Nicholas Reck, Michael Scuzzarella, Joshua Smith, Jessica Stayton, and Russel Walker). We would also like to thank the following people who reviewed the manuscript in various stages of development and provided invaluable feedback: Peter Anderson, Grand Valley State University; David Christensen, University of Arizona; Jane Crawford, University of Virginia; Victor A. Leuci, Westminster College; and Robert Luginbill, University of Louisville. Most of all, we would like to thank our families: Richard and Patricia Irby, Georgia Irby's parents, for their unceasing support and faith, and John Robinson, her nautical mentor and best friend; and Aditya and Theodore Arjuna Adarkar, loving husband and son of Mary English, and Howard and Mary English, her parents, who supported this project day after day and cheered it on to completion.

A Little Latin Reader provides a wonderful introduction to Latin literature and Roman history and culture. Enjoy these passages, read them aloud, and learn about ancient Rome from the Romans themselves!

1. NOMINATIVE AND ACCUSATIVE CASES

1.1. *CIL* IV 3117: Pompeii. Painted wall graffito. No love lost.

Serēna Isidōru(m) fastīdit.

Notes: **Serēna, -ae**, f: a woman's name, "clear, tranquil"; **Isidōrus, -ī**, m: a Greek man's name, "gift of Isis"; **fastīdiō, -īre, -īvī, -ītus**: loathe, dislike.

1.2. *CIL* IV 3794: Pompeii. Painted wall graffito. My home!

Aemilius Celer hīc habitat.

Notes: **Aemilius Celer, Aemiliī Celeris**, m: a man's name (the cognomen *Celer* means "swift"); **hīc**: here; **habitō, -āre, -āvī**: live.

1.3. *CIL* IV 7086: Pompeii. Painted wall graffito. Young love!

Marcus Spedūsa(m) amat.

Notes: **Marcus, -ī**, m: a man's name; **Spedūsa, -ae**, f: a woman's name; **amō, -āre, -āvī, -ātus**: like, love.

1.4.   *CIL* IV 275: Pompeii. An election poster.

> C(aium) Cuspium Pansam aed(īlem) Sāturnīnus cum
> discentēs rog(at).

Notes: **Caius Cuspius Pansa, Caiī Cuspiī Pansae**, m: a man's
name (the cognomen *Pansa* means "splay-footed," where the feet
are flat and turned out); **aedīlis, -is**, m: aedile, a Roman politician
in charge of streets, traffic, markets, and public games; **Sāturnīnus,
-ī**, m: a man's name, "belonging to Saturn"; **cum** + ablative: with;
discentēs = *discentibus* from *discens, discentis*, m: student; **rogō,
-āre, -āvī, -ātus**: endorse.

1.5.   Ovid, *Metamorphoses* 1.505–506: Apollo is in love with the beautiful nymph Daphne, who rejects his advances. Here, as Apollo literally runs after Daphne, he compares his chase with that of wild
animals as they hunt their prey. Meter: dactylic hexameter.

> "Nympha, manē, sīc agna lupum, sīc cerva leōnem,
> sīc aquilam pennā fugiunt trepidante columbae."

Notes: **nympha, -ae**, f: nymph, maiden; **maneō, -ēre, mansī, mansus**: stay, remain; **sīc**: thus, so, as; **agna, -ae**, f: lamb; **lupus, -ī**, m:
wolf; **cerva, -ae**, f: hind, deer; **leō, leōnis**, m: lion; **aquila, -ae**, f:
eagle; **pennā...trepidante**: "with its feather wavering" (ablative
absolute); **fugiō, -ere, fūgī**: flee, escape; **columba, -ae**, f: dove.

1.6.   Ovid, *Metamorphoses* 1.550: Ovid describes the moment when
Daphne turns into a tree. Meter: dactylic hexameter.

> In frondem crīnēs, in rāmōs bracchia crescunt.

Notes: **in** + accusative: into; **frons, frondis**, f: leaf, foliage; **crīnis,
-is**, m: hair; **rāmus, -ī**, m: branch; **bracchium, -iī**, n: arm; **crescō,
-ere, crēvī, crētus**: grow.

2.   SIMPLE INFINITIVES

2.1.   *CIL* VIII 17938: Timgad (Africa). What makes life worth living.

> Vēnārī, lavārī, lūdere, rīdēre: hoc est vīvere.

Notes: **vēnor, -ārī, -ātus sum**: hunt (deponent verb with passive forms but active meanings); **lavō, -āre, lāvī, lautus**: bathe (passive conveys reflexive sense of the verb, "to bathe oneself"); **lūdō, -ere, lūsī, lūsus**: play; **rīdeō, -ēre, rīsī, rīsus**: laugh; **hoc**: this; **vīvō, -ere, vixī, victus**: live.

2.2.   Horace, *Carmina* 3.2.13: Horace proclaims the ideal Roman citizen as tolerant of hardship and poverty, courageous, fearless, and virtuous. Meter: Alcaic strophe (here, the first line of a four-line stanza).

> Dulce et decōrum est prō patriā morī.

Notes: **dulcis, -e**: sweet; **decōrus, -a, -um**: beautiful, graceful, noble; **prō** + ablative: for, on behalf of; **patria, -ae, f**: country, fatherland; **morior, -ī, mortuus sum**: die (deponent verb).

2.3.   Horace, *Epistulae* 1.1.41–42: Horace writes about the virtues of moderation and simple living. Meter: dactylic hexameter.

> Virtūs est vitium fugere et sapientia prīma
> stultitiā caruisse.

Notes: **virtūs, virtūtis, f**: virtue; **vitium, -iī, n**: vice, sin; **fugiō, -ere, fūgī**: flee, escape; **sapientia, -ae, f**: wisdom; **prīmus, -a, -um**: first; **stultitia, -ae, f**: foolishness, silliness; **careō, -ēre, caruī** + ablative: be without, lack (*caruisse*: perfect active infinitive, "to have lacked").

3. SUM

3.1.   *CIL* IV 5279: Pompeii. Painted wall graffito. Life is fleeting.

> Tū mortu(u)s es; tū nūgas es.

Notes: **mortuus, -a, -um**: dead; **nūgas** = *nūgax, -ācis*: trifling, trivial.

3.2.   Ovid, *Metamorphoses* 1.512–514: Apollo tells Daphne what sort of man he is not. Meter: dactylic hexameter.

> "Nōn incola montis,
> nōn ego sum pastor, nōn hīc armenta gregēsque
> horridus observō."

Notes: **incola, -ae**, m: inhabitant, dweller; **mons, montis**, m: mountain; **pastor, -ōris**, m: shepherd; **hīc**: here; **armentum, -ī**, n: cattle, herd; **grex, gregis**, m: flock, herd; **-que**: and (enclitic coordinating conjunction connecting the word to the one before it); **horridus, -a, -um**: rough, shaggy, bristly; **observō, -āre, -āvī, -ātus**: watch, attend to.

3.3.   Ovid, *Metamorphoses* 1.517–518: Apollo explains to Daphne his parentage and his divine functions. Meter: dactylic hexameter.

> "Iuppiter est genitor. Per mē quod eritque fuitque
> estque patet; per mē concordant carmina nervīs."

Notes: **Iuppiter, Iovis**, m: Jupiter, the supreme god of the Romans; **genitor, -ōris**, m: father; **per** + accusative: through; **quod**: that, which; **pateō, -ēre, -uī**: open, be revealed; **concordō, -āre, -āvī, -ātus**: agree, be harmonious; **carmen, carminis**, n: song, poetry; **nervus, -ī**, m: string of a musical instrument.

3.4.   Ovid, *Metamorphoses* 1.557–559: Apollo honors Daphne by making her his sacred tree. Meter: dactylic hexameter.

> Cui deus "At quoniam coniunx mea nōn potes esse,
> arbor eris certē" dixit "mea. Semper habēbunt
> tē coma, tē citharae, tē nostrae, laure, pharetrae."

Notes: **cui**: to whom, referring back to Daphne, whom Apollo pursued but lost; **deus, -ī**, m: god; **at**: but, moreover; **quoniam**: since; **coniunx, coniugis**, m/f: spouse; **meus, -a, -um**: my; **arbor, -oris**, f: tree; **certē**: certainly; **dīcō, -ere, dixī, dictus**: say; **semper**: always; **habeō, -ēre, -uī, -itus**: have, "wear"; **coma, -ae**, f: hair; **cithara, -ae**, f: lyre, lute; **noster, nostra, nostrum**: our; **laurus, -ī**, f: laurel; **pharetra, -ae**, f: quiver.

4. VOCATIVE CASE

4.1.   Ovid, *Metamorphoses* 1.481–482: Daphne's father explains her filial obligations. Meter: dactylic hexameter.

> Saepe pater dixit "Generum mihi, filia, dēbēs,"
> saepe pater dixit "dēbēs mihi, nāta, nepōtēs."

Notes: **saepe:** often; **pater, patris,** m: father; **gener, generī,** m: son-in-law; **mihi:** to me; **fīlia, -ae,** f: daughter; **dēbeō, -ēre, -uī, -itus:** owe; **nāta, -ae,** f: daughter; **nepōs, -ōtis,** m: grandson.

4.2. Catullus 3.1–3: In this mock dirge, Catullus laments that his mistress's beloved pet has passed away. Meter: hendecasyllabics.

> Lūgēte, ō Venerēs Cupīdinēsque
> et quantum est hominum venustiōrum,
> passer mortuus est meae puellae.

Notes: **lūgeō, -ēre, luxī, luctus:** mourn (*lūgēte:* imperative plural); **Venus, Veneris,** f: Venus, goddess of love; **Cupīdō, Cupīdinis,** m: Cupid, son of Venus; **-que:** and (enclitic coordinating conjunction, see 3.2); **quantum:** however many, as many; **homō, hominis,** m: person; **venustus, -a, -um:** charming, pleasing (*venustiōrum:* comparative genitive plural: "rather charming"); **passer, passeris,** m: sparrow; **mortuus, -a, -um:** dead.

4.3. Catullus 101.1–2: Catullus writes this poem on the occasion of his brother's death. Meter: elegiac couplets.

> Multās per gentēs et multa per aequora vectus
> adveniō hās miserās, frāter, ad inferiās.

Notes: **per** + accusative: through; **gens, gentis,** f: nation, people, race; **aequor, -oris,** n: sea; **vehō, -ere, vexī, vectus:** carry, transport (*vectus:* perfect passive participle, "having been transported"); **adveniō, -īre, advēnī, adventus:** arrive; **hās miserās ... ad inferiās:** "at these miserable funeral rites"; **frāter, frātris,** m: brother.

5. IMPERATIVES

5.1. *CIL* IV 6702: Pompeii. Painted wall graffito. I was here.

> Aufidius hīc f(uit). Valē.

Notes: **Aufidius, -iī,** m: a man's name; **hīc:** here; **valeō, -ēre, valuī, valītus:** be well, prevail, farewell, good-bye.

5.2.   *CIL* X 874: Pompeii. Painted wall graffito. Business is good.

Salvē, lucru(m)!

Notes: **salveō, -ēre**: be well, greet; **lucrum, -ī**, n: profit.

5.3.   *CIL* X 876: Pompeii. Painted wall graffito. Business advice.

Lucru(m) accipe!

Notes: **accipiō, -ere, accēpī, acceptus**: take, receive.

5.4.   *CIL* X 877: Pompeii. Painted wall graffito. Good advice.

Cavē canem!

Notes: **caveō, -ēre, cāvī, cautus**: beware; **canis, -is**, m/f: dog.

5.5.   *CIL* IV 1864: Pompeii. Painted wall graffito. No love lost.

Samius Cornēliō, suspend(e)re!

Notes: **Samius, -iī**, m: a man's name, recalling Samos, an island in the eastern Aegean sea; **Cornēlius, -iī**, m: a man's name; **suspendō, -ere, suspendī, suspensus**: hang (*suspendere*: second person singular passive imperative).

5.6.   *ILS* 8730.1–4: Rome. Bronze plate with a pierced handle, worn as a collar by a slave with a history of running away.

Tenē mē et revocā mē in forō Martis ad Maximiānum antīquārium.

Notes: **teneō, -ēre, -uī, tentus**: hold, detain; **revocō, -āre, -āvī, -ātus**: recall, summon; **forum, -ī**, n: forum, open square, marketplace; **Mars, Martis**, m: Mars, the Roman god of war; **ad** + accusative: to; **Maximiānus, -ī**, m: a man's name, "the greatest"; **antīquārius, -ī**, m: someone who studies antiquities.

5.7.   Ovid, *Metamorphoses* 1.510–511: Apollo begs Daphne not to flee so enthusiastically. Meter: dactylic hexameter.

"Aspera, quā properās, loca sunt. Moderātius, ōrō,
curre fugamque inhibē: moderātius insequar ipse."

Notes: **asper, aspera, asperum**: rough, uneven; **quā**: where; **properō, -āre, -āvī, -ātus**: hasten, hurry; **locus, -ī, m**: region, area, place (this noun can be neuter in the plural); **moderātius**: with more restraint (comparative adverb); **ōrō, -āre, -āvī, -ātus**: beg; **currō, -ere, cucurrī, cursus**: run; **fuga, -ae, f**: flight; **inhibeō, -ēre, -uī, -itus**: hold back, restrain; **insequor, -ī, insecūtus sum**: pursue; **ipse, ipsa, ipsum**: here, "I myself."

5.8. *CIL* X 7697.6–7: Cagliari (Caralis, Sardinia). Part of a longer funerary inscription, cut into a rock, on the transitory nature of human life.

> Quī legis hunc titulum mortālem tē esse mementō.

Notes: **quī, quae, quod**: who, what (a relative pronoun referring to the addressee of *mementō*); **legō, -ere, lēgī, lectus**: read; **hic, haec, hoc**: this; **titulus, -ī, m**: inscription, notice; **mortālem...esse**: indirect statement with an accusative subject (*tē*) and infinitive verb (*esse*); **mortālis, -e**: mortal, transitory, subject to death; **mementō** from *meminī, -isse*: second person singular future imperative (*meminī* is a defective verb that takes all forms, except for the imperative, in the perfect system).

6. GENITIVE CASE

6.1. *CIL* VII 748, addit. 310 [*ILS* 2551; *RIB* 1778]: Carvoran, a Roman fort on Hadrian's Wall (Britannia). Altar with plain sides and a molded base found in the Bath House. A monumental inscription for Lucius Aelius Caesar, the adopted son and intended heir of Hadrian (reigned 117–138 CE).

> Fortūnae Aug(ustae) prō salūte L(ūcī) Aelī Caesaris ex vīsū T(itus) Flā(vius) Secundus praef(ectus) coh(ortis) I Hāmiōrum Sagittār(iōrum) v(ōtum) s(olvit) l(ibens) m(eritō).

Notes: **Fortūna, -ae, f**: Fortune, a personified goddess; **Augustus, -a, -um**: honorable, venerable, of the emperor, a title given by the Senate to Julius Caesar's nephew who reigned from 31 BCE to 14 CE; **prō** + ablative: for, on behalf of; **salūs, salūtis,** f: health, safety, welfare; **Lūcius Aelius Caesar, Lūciī Aeliī Caesaris,** m: a man's name (*Lūcius*: a Greek name recalling Lycia in Turkey and the Greek word for wolf; *Caesar*: from *caesariēs, -ēī*, f: a beautiful head of dark hair [ironically, Julius Caesar had thinning hair]; from Hadrian onward, *Caesar* was used as a title for the heir to the throne); **ex** + ablative: from; **vīsus, -ūs,** m: appearance, vision; **Titus Flāvius Secundus, Titī Flāviī Secundī,** m: a man's name (the nomen derives from *flāvus, -a, -um*: golden or reddish yellow – often referring to hair color; *Secundus*: favorable, next); **praefectus, -ī,** m: prefect, an officer in the Roman army; **cohors, cohortis,** f: troop, company, cohort; **Hāmius, -a, -um**: Hamian, a tribe of Syria; **Sagittārius, -iī,** m: archer; **vōtum solvit libēns meritō**: abbreviated as *v.s.l.m.* on the stone; **vōtum, -ī,** n: vow; **solvō, -ere, solvī, solūtus**: loosen, free, release, fulfill; **libēns, libentis**: willing, joyful; **meritō**: deservedly, rightly.

6.2.   Ovid, *Metamorphoses* 1.452–453: Ovid begins the story of Apollo and Daphne. Meter: dactylic hexameter.

> Prīmus amor Phoebī Daphnē Pēnēia, quem nōn
> fors ignāra dedit, sed saeva Cupīdinis īra.

Notes: **prīmus, -a, -um**: first; **amor, -ōris,** m: love; **Phoebus, -ī,** m: Phoebus, Apollo ("bright, radiant, pure"); **Daphnē, -ēs,** f: a Greek woman's name, "laurel"; **Pēnēius, -a, -um**: belonging to the river Peneus in Thessaly (Daphne's father was the river Peneus; the name derives from the Greek for a poor man or worker and emphasizes the rustic setting); **quem**: whom; **fors, fortis,** f: chance, luck; **ignārus, -a, -um**: inexperienced, ignorant; **dō, dare, dedī, datus**: give; **saevus, -a, -um**: fierce, violent, savage; **Cupīdō, Cupīdinis,** m: Cupid; **īra, -ae,** f: anger, wrath.

6.3.   Catullus 5.1–3: Catullus urges his mistress, Lesbia, to live life to the fullest and to discount the gossip of old men. Meter: hendecasyllabics.

> Vīvāmus, mea Lesbia, atque amēmus,
> rūmōrēsque senum sevēriōrum
> omnēs ūnius aestimēmus assis!

Notes: **vīvāmus…amēmus…aestimēmus:** "let us live…let us love…let us value" (hortatory subjunctives); **rūmor, -ōris,** m: rumor, murmuring; **senex, senis,** m: old man; **sevērus, -a, -um:** strict, stern, severe *(sevēriōrum:* comparative genitive plural, "rather strict"); **omnis, -e:** all; **ūnius…assis:** "as worth a penny" (genitive of value); **aestimō, -āre, -āvī, -ātus:** value.

7. DATIVE CASE

7.1. *CIL* VII 5 [*ILS* 4786; *RIB* 88]: Winchester (Britannia). Sandstone altar commemorating several groups of goddesses.

> Mātrib(us) Italis Germānīs Gal(līs) Brit(annīs) [A]ntōnius
> [Lu]crētiānus [b(ene)]f(iciārius) co(n)sulāris rest(ituit).

Notes: **māter, mātris,** f: mother; **Italus, -a, -um:** of Italy; **Germānus, -a, -um:** of Germany; **Gallus, -a, -um:** of Gaul; **Britannus, -a, -um:** of Britain; **Antōnius Lucrētiānus, Antōniī Lucrētiānī,** m: a man's name (the cognomen *Lucrētiānus* is derived from *lucrum, -ī,* n: profit); **beneficiārius consulāris, beneficiāriī consulāris,** m: an assistant to a senior officer; **restituō, -ere, restituī, restitūtus:** replace, restore; the direct object of *restituit* is *hoc,* whose antecedent is the temple to these Mother Goddesses.

7.2. *CIL* VII 33 [*RIB* 16]: London (Londinium, Britannia). Oolite sarcophagus found at the north side of Westminster Abbey. Two sons remember their father.

> Memoriae Valerī Amandīnī. Valerī (filiī) Superventor
> et Marcellus patrī fēcērunt.

Notes: **memoria, -ae,** f: memory, remembrance; **Valerius Amandīnus, Valeriī Amandīnī,** m: a man's name (*Amandīnus:* from the gerundive of *amō,* "belonging to someone who must be loved"); **filius, -ī,** m: son; **Superventor, -ōris,** m: a man's name, related to *superventus, -ūs,* m: arrival ("someone who has arrived"); **Marcellus, -ī,** m: a man's name; **pater, patris,** m: father; **faciō, -ere, fēcī, factus:** make, do; the direct object of *fēcērunt* is *hoc,* whose antecedent is the sarcophagus.

7.3.   *CIL* VII 74 [*RIB* 132]: Custom Scrubs (Britannia). Gabled relief in fine-grained oolite with Mars in panoply on the front. His crested helmet, side plumes, and cheek pieces are especially prominent. The left side of this relief shows an altar with offerings. The stone was built into a summer house at Watercombe House, Bisley. To Romulus.

Deō Rōm[u]lō Gulioepius dōnāvit. Iuventīnus fēcit.

Notes: **deus, -ī**, m: god; **Rōmulus, -ī**, m: Romulus, the legendary founder of the city of Rome; **Gulioepius, -iī**, m: a Celtic man's name; **dōnō, -āre, -āvī, -ātus**: give as a present; **Iuventīnus, -ī**, m: a Romanized Celtic man's name, from *iuvenis, -e*: young, youthful; **faciō, -ere, fēcī, factus**: make, do; the direct object of *fēcit* and *dōnāvit* is *hoc*, whose antecedent is the statue.

7.4.   *CIL* VII 509 [*RIB* 1333]: Benwell (Condercum), a Roman fort on Hadrian's Wall (Britannia). Plain-sided altar found in the north part of the fort. To Mars the victorious.

Deō Martī Victōr(ī) Vindex v(ōtum) s(olvit).

Notes: **deus, -ī**, m: god; **Mars, Martis**, m: Mars, the Roman god of war; **Victor, -ōris**, m: conquerer, victor; **Vindex, Vindicis**, m: a man's name, "champion, avenger"; **vōtum, -ī**, n: vow; **solvō, -ere, solvī, solūtus**: loosen, free, release, fulfill.

7.5.   *RIB* 1316: Newcastle-upon-Tyne (Pons Aelius, Britannia). Altar showing a jug in relief on the left, a patera on the right. To Jupiter.

I(ovī) O(ptimō) M(aximō) prō salūte et victōriā Aug(ustī).

Notes: **Iuppiter, Iovis**, m: Jupiter, the supreme Roman god; **optimus, -a, -um**: best; **maximus, -a, -um**: greatest; **prō** + ablative: for, on behalf of; **salūs, salūtis**, f: health, safety, welfare; **victōria, -ae**, f: victory; **Augustus, -ī**, m: Augustus, the emperor of Rome, see 6.1.

7.6.   Ovid, *Metamorphoses* 1.555–556: Apollo tries to embrace Daphne-the-tree. Meter: dactylic hexameter.

Complexusque suīs rāmōs, ut membra, lacertīs
oscula dat lignō; refugit tamen oscula lignum.

Notes: **complector, -ī, complexus sum:** embrace (*complexus:* perfect deponent participle); **suus, -a, -um:** his/her/its/their own; **rāmus, -ī, m:** branch, twig; **ut:** as; **membrum, -ī, n:** limb; **lacertus, -ī, m:** upper arm; **osculum, -ī, n:** mouth, kiss; **dō, dare, dedī, datus:** give; **lignum, -ī, n:** wood; **refugiō, -ere, refūgī:** recede from, shrink; **tamen:** nevertheless.

8. IMPERFECT TENSE

8.1. Ovid, *Metamorphoses* 1.10–11: Ovid describes the world before it was created. Meter: dactylic hexameter.

> Nullus adhūc mundō praebēbat lūmina Tītān,
> nec nova crescendō reparābat cornua Phoebē.

Notes: **nullus, -a, -um:** no, none, not any; **adhūc:** thus far, yet, still; **mundus, -ī, m:** universe, world; **praebeō, -ēre, -uī, -itus:** provide, supply; **lūmen, lūminis, n:** light; **Tītān, Tītānis/os, m:** one of the children of Sky and Earth (here, the sun god); **novus, -a, -um:** new; **crescō, -ere, crēvī, crētus:** grow (*crescendō:* ablative singular gerund, "by growing"); **reparō, -āre, -āvī, -ātus:** restore, renew; **cornū, -ūs, n:** horn, "moon"; **Phoebē, -ēs, f:** the moon goddess (for the name, see 6.2).

8.2. Ovid, *Metamorphoses* 1.91–93: Ovid describes the superior moral state of the early world. Meter: dactylic hexameter.

> Poena metusque aberant, nec verba minantia fixō
> aere ligābantur, nec supplex turba timēbat
> iūdicis ōra suī, sed erant sine vindice tūtī.

Notes: **poena, -ae, f:** punishment, penalty; **metus, -ūs, m:** fear, apprehension, dread; **absum, -esse, āfuī, āfutūrus:** be absent; **verbum, -ī, n:** word; **minor, -ārī, -ātus sum:** threaten (*minantia:* present deponent participle, "threatening"); **fixus, -a, -um:** firm, fixed; **aes, aeris, n:** copper, bronze; **ligō, -āre, -āvī, -ātus:** bind, connect; **supplex, supplicis:** suppliant; **turba, -ae, f:** uproar, disturbance, crowd; **timeō, -ēre, -uī:** be afraid, fear; **iūdex, iūdicis, m:** judge; **ōs, ōris, n:** face; **suus, -a, -um:** his/her/its/their own;

sine + ablative: without; **vindex, vindicis**, m/f: avenger, punisher; **tūtus, -a, -um**: safe.

8.3. Vergil, *Aeneid* 8.655–658: Vergil describes the beautiful shield that Venus has asked her husband Vulcan to create for her son Aeneas. On the shield, Vulcan depicts the major events of Rome's history. Here, when the Gauls attack Rome (390 BCE), sacred geese from Juno's temple precinct save the city by warning the citizens of the approaching enemy. Meter: dactylic hexameter.

> Atque hīc aurātīs volitans argenteus anser
> porticibus Gallōs in līmine adesse canēbat;
> Gallī per dūmōs aderant arcemque tenēbant
> dēfensī tenebrīs et dōnō noctis opācae.

Notes: **hīc**: here; **aurātus, -a, -um**: golden, glittering; **volitō, -āre, -āvī, -ātus**: flutter, fly (*volitans*: present active participle, "flying"); **argenteus, -a, -um**: silver; **anser, anseris**, m: goose; **porticus, -ūs**, f: portico, colonnade; **Gallōs...adesse**: indirect statement, "that the Gauls were present"; **līmen, līminis**, n: threshold, doorway; **canō, -ere, cecinī, cantus**: sing; **dūmus, -ī**, m: bramble, thicket; **adsum, -esse, affuī**: be at hand, be here; **arx, arcis**, f: citadel, fortress; **teneō, -ēre, -uī, tentus**: hold; **dēfendō, -ere, dēfendī, dēfensus**: defend, guard, protect (*dēfensī*: "having been protected"); **tenebrae, -ārum**, f (plural): darkness, shadows; **dōnum, -ī**, n: gift; **nox, noctis**, f: night; **opācus, -a, -um**: dark, shadowy.

9. COMPLEMENTARY INFINITIVES

9.1. Martial 1.32: Don't know why, but I just don't like you. Meter: elegiac couplets.

> Nōn amo tē, Sabidī, nec possum dīcere quārē:
> hoc tantum possum dīcere: nōn amo tē.

Notes: **amō, -āre, -āvī, -ātus**: like, love (although the last syllable of *amō* is usually long, here, and in the next line, the syllable must be short for the meter to work out correctly); **Sabidius, -ī, m:** a man's name; **nec:** and...not; **possum, posse, potuī:** be able, can; **dīcō, -ere, dixī, dictus:** say; **quārē:** why? by what means?; **tantum:** only.

9.2. Caesar, *de Bello Gallico* 1.4.1: Having discovered that a Helvetian noble, Orgetorix, has plotted rebellion against Caesar, the pro-Roman Helvetian government places him on trial according to their tribal custom. Orgetorix dies before the trial, probably from suicide.

> Mōribus suīs Orgetorigem ex vinclīs causam dīcere coēgerunt.

Notes: **mōs, mōris, m:** habit, custom; (in plural) character, morals; **suus, -a, -um:** "their own"; **Orgetorix, -igis, m:** a wealthy Helvetian aristocrat who instigated a Helvetian migration into southwest Gaul; **ex** + ablative: from; **vinc(u)lum, -ī, n:** chain; **causam dīcere:** plead a case; **cōgō, -ere, coēgī, coactus:** compel, force.

9.3. Cicero, *Philippica* 2.7: Just as vituperative as Cicero's speeches against Catiline were his fourteen speeches against Marc Antony, composed in 44 and 43 BCE. After Caesar's death, his lieutenant Antony quickly rose to power, and Cicero considered him a dire threat to the Republic. These damning speeches in part contributed to Antony's order for Cicero's execution in 43. The *Second Philippic* is a staunch defense of Cicero's career and a scathing attack on Antony's. Here, Cicero warns of the futility of using private correspondence as evidence.

> Quam multa ioca solent esse in epistulīs, quae prōlāta
> sī sint, inepta videantur, quam multa sēria neque tamen
> ullō modō dīvolganda!

Notes: **Quam multa:** how many (take *multa* with *ioca*); **iocus, -ī, m:** joke, jest (this noun can be neuter in the plural); **soleō, -ēre, solitus sum:** be accustomed (semi-deponent verb, with active forms and active meanings in the present system, and passive forms and active meanings in the perfect system); **epistula, -ae, f:** letter; **quae:** relative pronoun referring to *ioca*; **prōferō, -ferre, prōtulī, prōlātus:** bring forward, reveal in public; **sint:** construe with *prōlāta* (subjunctive verb in a future less vivid conditional, "which [*quae*], if they were revealed in public"); **ineptus, -a, -um**: foolish, silly; **videantur**: "they would seem"; **sērius, -a, -um**: weighty, important; **neque**: and...not; **tamen**: nonetheless; **ullus, -a, -um**: any; **modus, -ī**, m: method, way; **dīvolganda** (*sunt*): future passive periphrastic with *neque*, "ought not to be divulged/made public" (Cicero uses the archaic *dīvolganda* instead of the classical *dīvulganda*).

10. *VOLO, NOLO, MALO*

10.1. Martial 1.9: You may think you're great, but you're really insignificant. Meter: elegiac couplets.

> Bellus homō et magnus vīs īdem, Cotta, vidērī:
>   sed quī bellus homō est, Cotta, pusillus homō est.

Notes: **bellus, -a, -um**: handsome, beautiful; **homō, hominis**, m: man; **vīs**: "you wish" (from *volō, velle, voluī*); **īdem**: likewise; **Cotta, -ae**, m: a man's name; **vidērī**: to seem; **sed quī**: "but he who"; **pusillus, -a, -um**: petty, insignificant.

10.2. Martial 11.13: Martial describes the tomb of the actor Paris, who was born in Egypt. Paris had an affair with Domitian's wife and subsequently was executed by the emperor. Meter: hendecasyllabics.

> Quisquis Flāminiam teris, viātor,
> nōlī nōbile praeterīre marmor.
> Urbis dēliciae salēsque Nīlī,
> ars et grātia, lūsus et voluptās,
> Rōmānī decus et dolor theātrī
> atque omnēs Venerēs Cupīdinēsque
> hōc sunt condita, quō Paris, sepulchrō.

Notes: **quisquis**: whoever; **Flāminia, -ae**, f: Flaminian Way, a road in ancient Rome; **terō, -ere, trīvī, trītus**: wear away; **viātor, -ōris**, m: traveler (*viātor*: vocative singular); **nōlī**: be unwilling (to), don't; **nōbilis, -e**: well-known, famous; **praetereō, -īre, -iī, -itus**: pass by; **marmor, -oris**, n: marble; **urbs, urbis**, f: city; **dēliciae, -ārum**, f (plural): delight; **sāl, salis,** m: salt, cunning, wit; **Nīlus, -ī,** m: the river Nile; **ars, artis,** f: art, craft, skill; **grātia, -ae,** f: charm, beauty, grace; **lūsus, -ūs,** m: sport, game; **voluptās, -ātis,** f: pleasure; **decus, decoris,** n: honor, dignity; **dolor, -ōris,** m: pain, grief; **theātrum, -ī,** n: theater; **Venus, Veneris,** f: Venus, goddess of love; **Cupīdō, Cupīdinis,** m: Cupid, son of Venus; **hōc**...**sepulchrō:** ablative of place where; **condō, -ere, condidī, conditus:** bury (*condita sunt*: perfect passive); **quō:** where (Paris has been buried); **sepulchrum, -ī,** n: tomb.

10.3.   Cicero, *pro Milone* 9: Delivered in 52 BCE in defense of his friend Milo, who was accused of killing their mutual enemy Clodius Pulcher, the existing speech is a highly polished version of the original. Clodius's death created such turmoil in Rome – people were rioting, and the Senate House was burned down – that Pompey came into the city with his troops to restore order. Here, Cicero praises a brave but unnamed Roman soldier who avenged an insult to his family.

> Facere enim probus adulescens perīculōsē quam perpetī turpiter māluit.

Notes: **faciō, -ere, fēcī, factus:** do, make, act; **enim:** for; **probus, -a, -um:** excellent, upright, righteous; **adulescens, adulescentis,** m/f: youth, young person; **perīculōsē:** dangerously; **quam:** than; **perpetior, -ī, perpessus sum:** experience hardship, suffer (deponent verb, see 2.1); **turpiter:** shamefully, disgracefully; **mālō, malle, māluī:** prefer, be more willing.

11. FUTURE TENSE

11.1.   Cicero, *Philippica* 2.111: After a sustained verbal attack, Cicero imagines that he has left Marc Antony speechless.

> Respondēbisne ad haec, aut omnīnō hiscere audēbis?

Notes: **-ne:** an enclitic introducing a question; **respondeō, -ēre, respondī, responsus:** reply, answer; **ad** + accusative: to; **haec:** "these things" (accusative plural, neuter); **aut:** or; **omnīnō:** entirely, altogether; **hiscō, -ere** (no third or fourth principal parts): gape, open the mouth as if to speak; **audeō, -ēre, ausus sum**: dare (semi-deponent verb, see 9.3).

11.2. Livy, *ab Urbe Condita* 1.13.3: To supply his men with wives, Romulus has organized a mass kidnapping of women from the neighboring Sabines. The Sabines attack Rome to reclaim their sisters and daughters, but the women themselves plead for peace.

> "Nōs causa bellī, nōs volnerum ac caedium virīs ac parentibus sumus; melius perībimus quam sine alterīs vestrum viduae aut orbae vīvēmus."

Notes: **causa, -ae**, f: cause, reason; **bellum, -ī**, n: war; **volnerum**: archaic genitive from *vulnus, vulneris*, n: wound; **ac**: and; **caedēs, -is**, f: slaughter, killing; **vir, -ī**, m: husband (*virīs ac parentibus*: datives of disadvantage); **melius**: better (comparative adverb of *bonus, -a, -um*: good); **pereō, -īre, -iī, -itus**: die, pass away; **quam**: than; **sine** + ablative: without; **alter, altera, alterum**: another, either; **vestrum**: partitive genitive with *alterīs*; **viduus, -a, -um**: unmarried, widowed, bereft; **aut**: or; **orbus, -a, -um**: childless, orphaned, bereft; **vīvō, -ere, vixī, victus**: live.

11.3. Martial 5.81: Only the rich get richer. Meter: elegiac couplets.

> Semper pauper eris, sī pauper es, Aemiliāne:
> dantur opēs nullīs nunc nisi dīvitibus.

Notes: **pauper, pauperis**: poor; **Aemiliānus, -ī**, m: a man's name; **dō, dare, dedī, datus**: give (*dantur*: "[riches] are given"); **ops, opis**, f: wealth; (in plural) riches; **nullus, -a, -um**: no one; **nisi**: unless, except; **dīves, dīvitis**: rich, opulent.

12. SUBSTANTIVES

12.1. *CIL* IV 813: Pompeii. Painted wall graffito at the Via Mercurii. Don't be lazy.

> Ōtiōsīs locus hic nōn est. Discēde, morātor.

Notes: ōtiōsus, -a, -um: at leisure, without occupation; **discēdō, -ere, discessī**: depart, go away; **morātor, -ōris, m**: delayer.

12.2. Vergil, *Aeneid* 1.34–35: Aeneas and the Trojan survivors are sailing from Sicily on calm seas just before Juno sends a devastating storm that tosses the fleet to Carthage. Meter: dactylic hexameter.

> Vix ē conspectū Siculae tellūris in altum
> vēla dabant laetī et spūmās salis aere ruēbant.

Notes: **vix**: scarcely; **ē** + ablative: from, out of; **conspectus, -ūs, m**: sight; **Siculus, -a, -um**: Sicilian; **tellūs, -ūris, f**: land; **altum, -ī, n**: the deep (sea); **vēlum, -ī, n**: sail; **laetus, -a, -um**: happy; **spūma, -ae, f**: foam, spray; **sāl, salis, n**: salt (metonymy for the sea); **aes, aeris, n**: bronze (metonymy for the bronze prow of a ship); **ruō, -ere, ruī**: rush, hasten, "plow"

12.3. Martial 1.16: Martial is unpretentious about the literary merits of his epigrams. Meter: elegiac couplets.

> Sunt bona, sunt quaedam mediocria, sunt mala plūra
> quae legis hīc: aliter nōn fit, Avīte, liber.

Notes: **quīdam, quaedam, quoddam**: a certain, some; **mediocris, -e**: ordinary, mediocre; **plūs, plūris**: more, comparative of *multus, -a, -um*; **legō, -ere, lēgī, lectus**: read; **hīc**: here; **aliter**: otherwise; **fiō, fierī, factus sum**: become; **Avītus, -ī, m**: a man's name, "ancestral"; **liber, librī, m**: book.

13. BASIC ABLATIVE CONSTRUCTIONS

13.1. Catullus 43: Catullus unfavorably compares the girlfriend of the spendthrift Formianus (the subject also of poem 41) with the incomparable Lesbia. Meter: hendecasyllabics.

> Salvē, nec minimō puella nāsō
> nec bellō pede nec nigrīs ocellīs

nec longīs digitīs nec ōre siccō
nec sānē nimis ēlegante linguā,
dēcoctōris amīca Formiānī.
Tēn prōvincia narrat esse bellam?
Tēcum Lesbia nostra comparātur?
Ō saeclum insapiens et infacētum!

Notes: **salvē:** hello, greetings (see 5.2); **minimus, -a, -um:** smallest, very small, least; **nāsus, -ī,** m: nose; **bellus, -a, -um:** pretty, handsome; **pēs, pedis,** m: foot; **niger, nigra, nigrum:** dark, black; **ocellus, -ī,** n: eye; **longus, -a, -um:** long; **digitus, -ī,** m: finger; **ōs, ōris,** n: mouth; **siccus, -a, -um:** dry; **sānē:** sensibly, reasonably; **nimis:** too much; **ēlegans, ēlegantis:** refined, elegant; **lingua, -ae,** f: tongue; **dēcoctor, -ōris,** m: spendthrift, debtor; **amīca, -ae,** f: girlfriend; **Formiānus, -ī,** m: a man's name, referring to someone from Formiae, on the western coast of Italy between Rome and Naples; **tēn** = *tē* + *-ne*; **prōvincia, -ae,** f: province, the backwoods; **narrō, -āre, -āvī, -ātus:** tell, report, relate; **tēcum** = *cum tē*; **comparō, -āre, -āvī, -ātus:** compare; **saec(u)lum, -ī,** n: age, generation; **insapiens, insapientis:** unwise; **infacētus, -a, -um:** dull, stupid.

13.2. Caesar, *de Bello Gallico* 4.33.1: The British practice of fighting from chariots. See also 43.2.

Genus hoc est ex essedīs pugnae: prīmō per omnīs partīs perequitant et tēla cōiciunt, atque ipsō terrōre equōrum et strepitū rotārum ordinēs plērumque perturbant; et, cum sē inter equitum turmās insinuāvērunt, ex essedīs dēsiliunt et pedibus proeliantur.

Notes: **genus, generis,** n: type, kind; **essedum, -ī,** n: a Celtic war chariot; **pugna, -ae,** f: battle; **prīmō:** at first; **perequitō, -āre, -āvī, -ātus:** ride about; **tēlum, -ī,** n: weapon; **cōiciō, -ere, cōiēcī, cōiectus:** throw, cast, toss; **ipse, ipsa, ipsum:** very, itself; **terror, -ōris,** m: fright, dread; **equus, -ī,** m: horse (*equōrum:* subjective genitive); **strepitus, -ūs,** m: din, noise; **rota, -ae,** f: wheel; **ordō, ordinis,** m: line, row, order; **plērumque:** generally, for the most part; **perturbō, -āre, -āvī, -ātus:** disturb thoroughly, throw into complete confusion; **cum:** when; **eques, equitis,** m: horseman, cavalryman; (in plural) cavalry; **sē:** British fighters, "themselves" (reflexive pronoun); **turma, -ae, f**: squadron, troop; **insinuō, -āre, -āvī, -ātus**: work one's way into, penetrate; **dēsiliō, -īre, dēsiluī, dēsultus**: leap down; **proelior, -ārī, -ātus sum**: fight, join in battle (deponent verb).

13.3. Caesar, *de Bello Gallico* 6.28.1–2: The *ūrī*, one of the strange animals of the Hercynian Forest, east of the Rhine River in Germany.

> Tertium est genus eōrum, quī ūrī appellantur. Hī sunt magnitūdine paulō infrā elephantōs, speciē et colōre et figūrā taurī. Magna vīs eōrum est et magna vēlōcitās, neque hominī neque ferae, quam conspexērunt, parcunt.

Notes: **tertius, -a, -um**: third; **genus, generis, n**: kind, type; **eōrum**: referring to the strange animals of the Hercynian Forest; **ūrus, -ī, m**: wild cattle; **appellō, -āre, -āvī, -ātus**: call; **hī** (*ūrī*): these; **magnitūdō, magnitūdinis, f**: size; **paulō**: a little; **infrā** + accusative: below, lower than; **speciēs, -ēī, f**: appearance; **figūra, -ae, f**: image, shape, form; **vīs, vis, f** (irregular noun): power, strength; **vēlōcitās, -ātis, f**: speed; **conspiciō, -ere, conspexī, conspectus**: catch sight of, perceive; **fera, -ae, f**: wild beast; **parcō, -ere, pepercī** + dative: spare, refrain from injuring.

14. DATIVE WITH SPECIAL VERBS AND ADJECTIVES

14.1. Caesar, *de Bello Gallico* 6.13.8–9: The hierarchy of the Druids.

> Hīs autem omnibus druidibus praeest ūnus, quī summam inter eōs habet auctōritātem. Hōc mortuō, aut, sī quī ex reliquīs excellit dignitāte succēdit, aut, sī sunt plūrēs parēs, suffrāgiō druidum, nōn numquam etiam armīs dē principātū contendunt.

Notes: **autem**: moreover; **druidēs, -um, m** (plural): Druids; **praesum, -esse, praefuī** + dative: be in charge; **summus, -a, -um**: greatest;

auctōritās, -ātis, f: authority; **morior, -ī, mortuus sum**: die; **hōc mortuō**: ablative absolute; **aut…aut**: either…or; **sī quī**: "if there is anyone who"; **reliquus, -a, -um**: remaining, last; **excellō, -ere, excelluī**: stand out, excel; **dignitās, -ātis**, f: excellence, dignity, worth (construe with *parēs*); **succēdō, -ere, successī, successus**: succeed; **plūs, plūris**: several, many, more; **pār, paris**: equal; **suffrāgium, -iī**, n: vote; **nōn numquam**: sometimes; **etiam**: even, also; **arma, -ōrum**, n (plural): weapons; **dē** + ablative: about, concerning; **principātus, -ūs**, m: first rank, leadership; **contendō, -ere, contendī, contentus**: struggle.

14.2. Caesar, *de Bello Gallico* 6.21.1: How the Germans differ from the Celts.

> Germānī multum ab hāc consuētūdine differunt. Nam neque druidēs habent, quī rēbus dīvīnīs praesint neque sacrificiīs student.

Notes: **multum**: greatly, much; **consuētūdō, consuētūdinis**, f: custom; **differō, -ferre, distulī, dīlātus**: differ; **nam**: for, on the other hand; **neque…neque**: neither…nor; **praesum, -esse, praefuī** + dative: preside over, have charge over; **quī…praesint**: relative clause of purpose with a present subjunctive verb; **studeō, -ēre, -uī** + dative: strive for, be devoted to, pursue.

14.3. Caesar, *de Bello Gallico* 6.22.1–2: The nomadic lifestyle of the Germans.

> Agrī cultūrae nōn student, māiorque pars eōrum victūs in lacte, cāseō, carne consistit. Neque quisquam agrī modum certum aut fīnīs habet propriōs; sed magistrātūs ac principēs in annōs singulōs, gentibus cognātiōnibusque hominum, quī cum ūnā coiērunt, quantum et quō locō vīsum est agrī, attribuunt, atque annō post aliō transīre cōgunt.

Notes: **agrī cultūrae**: agriculture; **studeō, -ēre, -uī** + dative: pursue; **māior**: comparative adjective from *magnus, -a, -um*; **victus, -ūs**, m: food; **lac, lactis**, n: milk; **cāseus, -ī**, m: cheese; **carō,**

carnis, f: flesh, meat; **consistō, -ere, constitī:** consist of, be formed of; **neque:** nor; **ager, agrī, m:** field, land; **modum certum:** a fixed amount; **fīnis, -is, m:** boundary; (in plural) territory; **proprius, -a, -um:** one's own; **magistrātus, -ūs, m:** magistrate, state official; **princeps, principis, m:** leader, chieftain; **in annōs singulōs:** every year, each year; **gens, gentis, f:** clan (*gentibus:* indirect object of *attribunt*); **cognātiō, -ōnis, f:** blood-relations (*cognātiōnibus:* indirect object of *attribunt*); **cum ūnā:** together with; **coeō, -īre, -iī, -itus:** come together; **quantus, -a, -um:** how much; **quō locō:** in which place (ablative of place where); **vīsum est:** it seemed best; **agrī:** partitive genitive with *quantum*; **attribuō, -ere, attribuī, attribūtus:** assign; **annō post aliō:** the following year; **transeō, -īre, -iī, -itus:** cross over; **cōgō, -ere, coēgī, coactus:** compel, force.

14.4. Caesar, *de Bello Gallico* 6.27.1–2: The *alcēs*, one of the strange animals of the Hercynian Forest, east of the Rhine River in Germany.

> Sunt item quae appellantur alcēs. Hārum est consimilis caprīs figūra et varietās pellium, sed magnitūdine paulō antecēdunt, mutilaeque sunt cornibus, et crūra sine nōdīs articlīsque habent, neque quiētis causā prōcumbunt neque, sī quō adflictae cāsū concidērunt, ērigere sēsē aut sublevāre possunt.

Notes: **item:** likewise; **appellō, -āre, -āvī, -ātus:** call; **alcēs, alcis, f:** elk, moose; **consimilis, -e** + dative: exactly similar, alike in all respects; **caper, caprī, m:** he-goat; **figūra, -ae, f:** form, shape; **varietās, -ātis, f:** variety, diversity, mottled appearance; **pellis, -is, f:** skin, hide; **magnitūdō, magnitūdinis, f:** size; **paulō:** a little bit (ablative of degree of difference); **antecēdō, -ere, antecessī, antecessus:** surpass, precede; **mutilus, -a, -um:** mutilated, stunted; **cornū, -ūs, n:** horn (*cornibus:* ablative of respect); **crūs, crūris, n:** leg; **nōdus, -ī, m:** joint; **artic(u)lus, -ī, m:** knuckle, toe; **quiēs, quiētis, f:** rest; **causā** + genitive (postpositive preposition that follows its object): for the sake of, on account of; **prōcumbō, -ere, -uī, -itus:** lie down; **sī quō casū:** "if by some accident"; **adflīgō, -ere, adflixī, adflictus:** knock down, injure; **concidō, -ere, concidī:** fall; **cāsus, -ūs, m:** fall; **ērigō, -ere, ērexī, ērectus:** lift up; **sublevō, -āre, -āvī, -ātus:** raise, lift.

15. PERFECT TENSE

15.1. *CIL* VI 15346 [*ILS* 8403]: Rome. Tombstone inscription, second century BCE. A beloved wife.

> Hospes, quod deicō paullum est; astā ac pellege.
> Heic est sepulcrum hau pulcrum pulcrai fēminae.
> Nōmen parentēs nōminārunt Claudiam.
> Suom mareitum corde deilexit souō.
> Gnātōs duōs creāvit, hōrunc alterum
> in terrā linquit, alium sub terrā locat.
> Sermōne lepidō, tum autem incessū commodō.
> Domum servāvit, lānam fēcit. Dixī. Abei.

Notes: This inscription has a number of alternate spellings (*heic*, *pulcrai*) that may reflect local pronunciations; **hospes, -itis**, m: guest, stranger; **quod**: that which; **paullum, -ī**, n: trifle, a little thing; **deicō** = *dīcō, -ere, dixī, dictus*: say; **astō, -āre, astitī**: stand, wait (the tombstone directly addresses passers-by); **ac**: and also; **pellege**: a slip for *perlege* from *perlegō, -ere, perlēgī, perlectus*: read carefully; **heic** = *hīc*: here; **sepulc(h)rum, -ī**, n: grave; **hau**: not at all; **pulcrai** = *pulchrae* from *pulcher, pulchra, pulchrum*: pretty, noble; **nōmen, nōminis**, n: name; **nōminārunt** = *nōmināvērunt* from *nōminō, -āre, -āvī, -ātus*: call; **Claudiam**: in apposition to *nōmen* (the name derives unflatteringly from *claudus, -a, -um*: lame); **suom** = *suum* from *suus, -a, -um*: "her own"; **mareitum** = *marītum* from *marītus, -ī*, m: husband; **cor, cordis**, n: heart, mind, soul; **deilexit** = *dīlexit* from *dīligō, -ere, dīlexī, dīlectus*: love, esteem, value; **souō** = *suō*; **gnātus, -ī**, m: child; **creō, -āre, -āvī, -ātus**: produce, give birth to; **hōrunc** = *hōrum*; **alter...alius**: the one...the other; **linquō, -ere, līquī**: leave; **sub** + ablative: under; **terra, -ae**, f: earth (one child lives, the other has died); **sermō, -ōnis**, m: talk, conversation; **lepidus, -a, -um**: charming, agreeable, amusing; **tum**: then; **autem**: moreover; **incessus, -ūs**, m: walk, step, gait; **commodus, -a, -um**: desirable, agreeable; **domus, -ūs**, f: house, household; **servō, -āre, -āvī, -ātus**: preserve, watch over; **lāna, -ae**, f: wool; **faciō, -ere, fēcī, factus**: here, "spin"; **abei** = *abī*: imperative singular from *abeō, -īre, -iī, -itus*: go away.

15.2. Catullus 51.13–16: From Catullus's translation of a poem by the Greek poetess Sappho (ca. 600 BCE, from the island of Lesbos).

Catullus recognizes that too much free time can get a person into trouble. Meter: Sapphic strophe.

> Ōtium, Catulle, tibī molestum est:
> ōtiō exsultās nimiumque gestīs:
> ōtium et rēgēs prius et beātās
> perdidit urbēs.

Notes: ōtium, -iī, n: leisure; molestus, -a, -um: annoying, bothersome; exsultō, -āre, -āvī: exult, rejoice; nimium: too much; gestiō, -īre, -īvī: be eager, thirst, long; et...et: both...and; rex, rēgis, m: king; prius: before; beātus, -a, -um: blessed; perdō, -ere, perdidī, perditus: destroy, ruin; urbs, urbis, f: city.

15.3. Martial 5.9: The unexpected consequences of too much medical attention. Meter: elegiac couplets.

> Languēbam: sed tū comitātus prōtinus ad mē
> vēnistī centum, Symmache, discipulīs;
> centum mē tetigēre manūs aquilōne gelātae:
> nōn habuī febrem, Symmache, nunc habeō.

Notes: langueō, -ēre (no third or fourth principal parts): be fatigued; comitātus, -a, -um: accompanied, followed; prōtinus: at once, immediately; veniō, -īre, vēnī, ventus: come; centum (indeclinable): one hundred; Symmachus -ī, m: a Greek man's name, "an ally in battle"; discipulus, -ī, m: student, follower (*discipulīs*: ablative governed by an understood *cum*); tetigēre = *tetigērunt* from *tangō, -ere, tetigī, tactus*: touch; manus, -ūs, f: hand; aquilō, aquilōnis, m: north wind; gelō, -āre, -āvī, -ātus: chill; febris, -is, f: fever.

16. PLUPERFECT TENSE

16.1. Caesar, *de Bello Gallico* 4.21.3–4: The route for Caesar's first invasion of Britain in 55 BCE.

> Ipse cum omnibus cōpiīs in Morinōs proficiscitur, quod inde erat brevissimus in Britanniam trāiectus. Hūc nāvīs undique ex fīnitimīs regiōnibus et quam superiōre

aestāte ad Veneticum bellum effēcerat classem iubet
convenīre.

Notes: **ipse:** Caesar; **cōpiae, -ārum,** f (plural): supplies, provisions,
troops; **in Morinōs:** into the territory of the Morini, a Belgic tribe;
proficiscor, -ī, profectus sum: set out; **quod:** because; **inde:** from
that place; **brevissimus:** superlative of *brevis, -e:* short; **trāiectus, -ūs,**
m: passage; **hūc:** here, to this place; **nāvis, -is,** f: ship; **undique:** from
all sides; **fīnitimus, -a, -um:** neighboring, adjoining; **regiō, -ōnis,** f:
province, district; **superior, superius:** former, earlier; **quam:** construe with *classem;* **aestās, -ātis,** f: summer; **ad Veneticum bellum:**
fought in the summer of 56 BCE; **Veneticus, -a, -um:** referring to the
Veneti, a seafaring Celtic tribe who dwelled in the peninsula of Are-
morica (Brittany, near modern Vannes), whom Caesar defeated after
a persistent and ingeniously fought naval battle (*BG* 3.7.4–15.1); **classis, -is,** f: fleet (direct object of *convenīre*); **iubeō, iubēre, iussī, iussus:**
order; **conveniō, -īre, convēnī, conventus:** convene, assemble, meet.

16.2. Livy, *ab Urbe Condita* 1.2.1: Before Aeneas can marry Lavinia,
Latinus's daughter, and found Alba Longa, he must fight Turnus,
who was betrothed to Lavinia before Aeneas's arrival in Italy.

Turnus rex Rutulōrum, cui pacta Lavinia ante adven-
tum Aeneae fuerat, praelatum sibi advenam aegrē
patiens simul Aenēae Latinōque bellum intulerat.

Notes: **rex, rēgis,** m: king; **Rutulī, -ōrum,** m (plural): a race of Aeneas's
Italian enemies; **cui:** to whom; **pacta, -ae,** f: fiancée, bride; **Lavinia,
-ae,** f: the daughter of Latinus (king of the Latins and Aeneas's ally in
Italy); **ante** + accusative: before; **adventus, -ūs,** m: arrival; **praeferō,
-ferre, praetulī, praelātus:** prefer, give preference to; **sibi:** reflexive,
referring to Turnus; **advena, -ae,** m/f: immigrant, foreigner (direct
object of *patiens*); **aegrē:** with difficulty; **patior, -ī, passus sum:** suffer,
endure; **simul:** at the same time; **Aenēae Latinōque:** datives with the
compound *intulerat;* **bellum inferre:** wage war.

16.3. Martial 1.47: A physician or an undertaker? What is the difference? Meter: elegiac couplets.

Nūper erat medicus, nunc est vispillo Diaulus:
quod vispillo facit, fēcerat et medicus.

Notes: **nūper**: recently; **medicus, -ī, m**: physician, surgeon; **vispillō, -ōnis, m**: undertaker (final -o scans as short both times in this poem in order for the meter to work out correctly); **Diaulus, -ī, m**: Greek man's name, recalling either the double flute or a foot-race of two laps; **quod**: that which; **faciō, -ere, fēcī, factus**: make, do; **et**: also.

17. FUTURE PERFECT TENSE

17.1.   *ILS* 8731: Rome. Oval leaden plate affixed to an iron neck collar of a slave who has a history of runing away.

> Fūgī. Tenē mē. Cum revocuveris mē d(ominō) m(ihi) Zōnīnō, accipis solidum.

Notes: **fugiō, -ere, fūgī**: run away; **teneō, -ēre, -uī, tentus**: hold, detain; **cum**: when; **revocuveris** = *revocāveris* from *revocō, -āre, -āvī, -ātus*: recall, summon; **dominus, -ī, m**: master; **mihi**: dative of possession; **Zōnīnus, -ī, m**: a man's name, "belonging to the celestial zone"; **accipiō, -ere, accēpī, acceptus**: take, receive; **solidus, -ī, m**: a gold coin (first introduced by Diocletian ca. 301 CE).

17.2.   Cicero, *pro Milone* 93: Despite his love for the city, Milo would prefer not to live in a Rome lacking in moral fortitude.

> Ego cēdam atque abībō. Sī mihi bonā rē pūblicā fruī nōn licuerit, at carēbō malā, et quam prīmum tetigerō bene mōrātam et līberam cīvitātem, in eā conquiescam.

Notes: **cēdō, -ere, cessī, cessus**: depart, go away; **abeō, -īre, -iī, -itus**: go away; **mihi**: dative of reference with *licuerit*; **fruor, fruī, fructus sum** + ablative: enjoy; **licet, -ēre, -uī** + dative: it is allowed; **careō, -ēre, -uī** + ablative: abstain from; **malā** (*rē pūblicā*); **quam** (*cīvitātem*); **prīmum**: first; **tangō, -ere, tetigī, tactus**: touch, reach; **mōrātus, -a, -um**: civilized, endowed with good customs; **līber, lībera, līberum**: free, not slavish; **conquiescō, -ere, conquiēvī, conquiētus**: rest, find peace of mind.

17.3. Caesar, *de Bello Gallico* 4.25.3: When the Romans approach Britain in 55 BCE, the troops are afraid to jump from the ships and begin the attack. The standard-bearer shames his compatriots into action. See also 35.2.

> Atque nostrīs mīlitibus cunctantibus, maximē propter
> altitūdinem maris, quī decimae legiōnis aquilam ferēbat,
> contestātus deōs, ut ea rēs legiōnī fēlīciter ēvenīret,
> "Dēsilīte," inquit, "mīlitēs, nisi vultis aquilam hostibus
> prōdere; ego certē meum reī pūblicae atque imperātōrī
> officium praestiterō."

Notes: **mīles, -itis,** m: soldier; **cunctor, -ārī, -ātus sum:** delay, hesitate (*cunctantibus:* present deponent participle, "delaying"); **propter** + accusative: because of; **altitūdō, altitūdinis,** f: height, depth; **mare, -is,** n: sea; **quī:** he who; **decimus, -a, -um:** tenth; **legiō, -ōnis,** f: body of soldiers, legion; **aquila, -ae,** f: eagle, the legion's most important standard (see note at 22.1); **contestor, -ārī, -ātus sum:** call as a witness, entreat; **ut:** introduces an indirect command ("that this situation turn out successfully"); **legiōnī:** dative of reference; **fēlīciter:** favorably, successfully; **ēveniō, -īre, ēvēnī, ēventus:** turn out, result, happen; **dēsiliō, -īre, dēsiluī, dēsultus:** leap down; **inquit:** he says; **hostis, -is,** m: enemy; **prōdō, -ere, prōdidī, prōditus:** surrender, give up, abandon; **certē:** certainly, at least; **rēs pūblica, reī pūblicae,** f: the state; **imperātor, -ōris,** m: general; **officium, -iī,** n: duty; **praestō, -stāre, -stitī, -stitus:** discharge, perform, do.

18. NUMBERS AND INDEFINITE PRONOUNS

18.1. *CIL* IV 3884 [*ILS* 5145]: Pompeii. Father and son sponsor six days of gladitorial games, as advertised on the front of a private house.

> D(ecimī) Lucrētī Satrī Valentis, flāminis Nerōnis
> Caesaris Aug(ustī) fīlī perpetuī, gladiātōrum paria
> XX et D(ecimī) Lucretiō Valentis fīlī glad(iātōrum)

paria X pug(nābunt) Pompēīs VI V IV III pr(īdiē)
Īdūs Apr(īlēs). Vēnātiō lēgitima et vēla erunt. Scr(ipsit)
Aemilius Celer sing(ulāris) ad lūna(m).

Notes: **Decimus Lucrētius Satrius Valens, Decimī Lucrētiī
Satriī Valentis,** m: a man's name (*Decimus*: the tenth; *Lucrētius*:
from *lucrum, -ī,* n: profit; *Satrius*: comparative from *satur, -a, -um*:
well-fed; *Valens*: strong, vigorous); **flāmen, flāminis,** m: priest;
Nerō, Nerōnis, m: Nero reigned from 54 CE to 68 CE (his name
derives from a Sabine word meaning "bravery"); for the name Caesar, see 6.1; **Augustus, -ī,** m: the emperor of Rome; **fīlius, -iī,** m:
son (*fīlī*: in apposition to *Nerōnis Caesaris*); **perpetuus, -a, -um**:
continuous, lifetime (*perpetuī* modifies *flāminis*); **gladiātor, -ōris,**
m: gladiator; **pār, paris**: equal, pair (*paria*: neuter substantive,
"pairs"); **Decimus Lucretius Valens**: Satrius's son (*Lucretiō* is a slip
for *Lucretiī*); **pugnō, -āre, -āvī, -ātus**: fight; **Pompēiī, -ōrum,** m
(plural): the town of Pompeii, destroyed by the eruption of Vesuvius in 79 CE (*Pompēīs*: locative case); **prīdiē**: on the day before
(an accusative or genitive follows *pridiē*); **Īdūs, -uum,** f (plural):
the Ides, the day of the full moon (the 13th or 15th of the month);
Aprīlis, -e: belonging to the month of April (in April, the Ides fall
on the 13th); **VI...prīdiē**: the games are to be held on five consecu-
tive days: remember that the Romans counted inclusively (VI a.d.
Id. Apr. is April 8); **vēnātiō, -ōnis,** f: beast hunt; **lēgitimus, -a, -um**:
lawful, legitimate, suitable; **vēlum, -ī,** n: covering, awning; **scrībō,
-ere, scrīpsī, scriptus**: write (the direct object of *scripsit* is *hoc*,
whose antecedent is the placard); **Aemilius Celer, Aemiliī Celeris,**
m: perhaps the same Aemilius Celer of 1.2; **singulāris, -e**: alone; **ad**
+ accusative: here, "by the light of"; **lūna, -ae,** f: moon.

18.2. *CIL* VII 58 [*RIB* 164]: Bath (Aquae Sulis, Britannia). Tombstone,
built into the city wall west of the north gate. For a very dear child.

D(īs) (et) m(ānibus) Succ(essae) Petrōniae. Vix(it)
ann(ōs) III m(ensēs) IIII d(iēs) IX. Vet(tius) Rōmulus
et Vict(ōria) Sabīna fīl(iae) kār(issimae) fēc(ērunt).

Notes: **deus, -ī,** m: god; **mānēs, -ium,** m (plural): spirits of the dead;
Successa Petrōnia, Successae Petrōniae, f: a girl's name (*Successa*:
from *successus, -ūs,* m: success; *Petrōnia*: from *petrō, -ōnis,* m: a rustic);
vīvō, -ere, vixī, victus: live; **annus, -ī,** m: year; **mensis, -is,** m: month;

diēs, -ēī, m: day; **Vettius Rōmulus, Vettiī Rōmulī**, m: a man's name (*Rōmulus* recalls the founder of Rome); **Victōria Sabīna, Victōriae Sabīnae**, f: a woman's name (see 19.1 for a note on the empress *Sabīnia Furia Tranquillīna*; *Sabīna* recalls the ancient Italian tribe of the Sabines); **fīlia, -ae**, f: daughter; **kārissimae** = *cārissimae*, the superlative from *cārus, -a, -um*: cherished; the direct object of *fēcērunt* is *hoc*, whose antecedent is the monument.

18.3. Martial 6.8: Should she have married the poor aristocrat or the wealthy low-life? Meter: hendecasyllabics.

> Praetōrēs duo, quattuor tribūnī,
> septem causidicī, decem poētae
> cuiusdam modo nuptiās petēbant
> ā quōdam sene. Nōn morātus ille
> praecōnī dedit Eulogō puellam.
> Dīc, numquid fatuē, Sevēre, fēcit?

Notes: **praetor, -ōris**, m: an elected Roman magistrate; **tribūnus, -ī**, m: tribune, representative; **causidicus, -ī**, m: advocate; **cuiusdam**: an objective genitive, referring to the unnamed woman whom everyone wants to marry; **modo**: just now; **nuptiae, -ārum**, f (plural): marriage, wedding; **quōdam**: construe with *sene*, the guardian of our unnamed *cuiusdam*; **petō, -ere, -īvī, -ītus**: seek; **moror, -ārī, -ātus sum**: delay (*morātus*: perfect deponent participle, "having delayed"); **praecō, -ōnis**, m: crier, herald, auctioneer (a lucrative but socially low profession); **Eulogus, -ī**, m: a Greek man's name, "Mr. Smooth-Talker"; **numquid fatuē**: very foolishly (*numquid* is an intensifier); **Sevērus, -ī**, m: a Roman man's name, "Mr. Serious."

19. DEMONSTRATIVE PRONOUNS

19.1. *CIL* VII 344 [*ILS* 502; *RIB* 897]: Old Carlisle (Britannia). Monumental altar in honor of Gordian III and his family.

> I(ovī) O(ptimō) M(aximō), prō salū[te] imperātōris
> M(arcī) Antōnī Gordiānī P(iī) [F(ēlīcis)] Invictī

Aug(ustī)   et   Sab[īn]iae   Furiae   Tranquil(līn)ae
coniugī(s) eius tōtāque domū dīvīn(ā) eōrum, āla
Aug(usta) Gordiā(na) ob virtūtem appellāta posuit, cui
pra(e)est Aemilius Crispīnus pr(a)ef(ectus) eq(uitum)
nātus in prō(vinciā) Āfricā dē Tusdrō sub cūr(ā) Nōniī
Philippī lēg(ātī) Aug(ustī) prō pr(a)e[tō(re)], [At]ticō et
Praetextātō co(n)s(ulibus).

Notes: **Iuppiter, Iovis,** m: Jupiter, the supreme Roman god; **optimus, -a, -um:** best; **maximus, -a, -um:** greatest; **prō** + ablative: for, on behalf of; **salūs, salūtis,** f: health, safety, welfare; **imperātor, -ōris,** m: emperor, victorious Roman general; **Marcus Antōnius Gordiānius Pius Fēlix Invictus Augustus, Marcī Antōniī Gordiāniī Piī Fēlīcis Augustī,** m: Roman emperor, commonly known as Gordian III (*Pius*: from *pius, -a, -um*: good, patriotic, devoted, honest, upright; *Fēlix*: from *fēlix, fēlīcis*: bringing good luck, lucky; *Invictus*: from *invictus, -a, -um*: unconquered, invincible; *Augustus, -ī,* m: a title for the emperor of Rome, see 6.1); **Sabīnia Furia Tranquillīna, Sabīniae Furiae Tranquillīnae,** f: a Roman empress, born in 225 CE, died after 244 CE, wife of Gordian III (for *Sabīna* see 18.2; ironically, *Furia* and *Tranquillīna* are antonyms, "frenzy" and "calm"); **coniunx, coniugis,** m/f: spouse; **tōtus, -a, -um:** whole, entire; **domus, -ūs,** f: house, household (*domū:* object of the preposition *prō* at the beginning of the inscription); **dīvīnus, -a, -um:** divine, noble; **āla, -ae,** f: wing, squadron; **ob** + accusative: on account of, because of; **virtūs, virtūtis,** f: excellence, manliness, moral excellence, courage, virtue; **appellātus, -a, -um:** called; **pōnō, -ere, posuī, positus:** place, put (the direct object of *posuit* is *hoc*, whose antecedent is the altar); **praesum, -esse, praefuī** + dative: preside over; **Aemilius Crispīnus, Aemiliī Crispīnī,** m: a man's name (*Crispīnus:* "belonging to something curled, wrinkled, or twisted"); **praefectus equitum, praefectī equitum,** m: cavalry commander; **nātus, -a, -um:** born; **prōvincia, -ae,** f: province; **Āfrica, -ae,** f: the Roman province of Northern Africa; **dē** + ablative: from; **Tusdrus, -ī,** m: the city of Thysdrus in Tunisia; **sub** + ablative: under; **cūra, -ae,** f: care, concern, attention; **Nōnius Philippus, Nōniī Phillipī,** m: a man's name (*Nōnius:* "the ninth"; *Philippus:* "horse-lover"); **lēgātus, -ī,** m: lieutenant, envoy; **praetor, -ōris,** m: magistrate; **Atticus, -ī,** m: a man's name referring to someone who loves all things Greek (Attica); **Praetextātus, -ī,** m: a man's name, recalling the magisterial purple-bordered *toga praetexta*

worn by Roman boys before they reached adulthood; **consul, -ulis,**
m: a high political office in Rome, by imperial appointment in the
third century CE; **Atticō et Praetextātō consulibus:** an ablative
absolute, lacking a participle, which establishes the inscription's
date according to the consuls (243 CE).

19.2. Martial 5.43: Dentures or real teeth? Which is better? Meter:
elegiac couplets.

> Thāis habet nigrōs, niveōs Laecānia dentēs.
> Quae ratiō est? Emptōs haec habet, illa suōs.

Notes: **Thāis, Thāidis/os,** f: a famous courtesan, her name is Greek
for a type of bandage; **niger, nigra, nigrum:** black; **niveus, -a, -um:**
snowy white; **Laecānia, -ae,** f: a woman's name, Greek for a deceiver
or prostitute; **dens, dentis,** m: tooth; **quae:** interrogative adjective;
ratiō, -ōnis, f: reason; **emptus, -a, -um:** bought, purchased; **haec:**
the latter (Laecānia); **illa:** the former (Thāis); **suus, -a, -um:** "her
own"; **emptōs haec illa suōs:** chiasmus.

19.3. Caesar, *de Bello Gallico* 6.13.3–4: The Druids, one of the two
important social classes in Gaul.

> Sed dē hīs duōbus generibus alterum est druidum,
> alterum equitum. Illī rēbus dīvīnīs intersunt, sacrificia
> pūblica ac prīvāta prōcūrant, religiōnēs interpretantur:
> ad hōs magnus adulescentium numerus disciplīnae
> causā concurrit, magnōque hī sunt apud eōs honōre.

Notes: **genus, generis,** n: type, kind; **alterum...alterum:** the
one...the other; **eques, equitis,** m: knight, of equestrian rank; **Illī:**
Druids; **intersum, -esse, interfuī** + dative: be present, take part;
sacrificium, -iī, n: sacrifice; **prōcūrō, -āre, -āvī, -ātus:** attend to,
take care of; **religiō, -ōnis,** f: observance of a religious ceremony;
interpretor, -ārī, -ātus sum: explain; **adulescens, adulescentis,** m: young man (*adulescentium:* partitive genitive with *magnus numerus*); **disciplīna, -ae,** f: instruction, training; **causā** +
genitive: for the sake of, on account of; **concurrō, -ere, concurrī,**

concursus: run together; hī: Druids; apud + accusative: among; eōs: the Gauls; honor, honōris, m: honor, glory.

19.4. Caesar, *de Bello Gallico* 6.17.1–2: The gods particularly worshipped by the Gauls.

Deum maximē Mercuriam colunt. Huius sunt plūrima simulācra: hunc omnium inventōrem artium ferunt, hunc viārum atque itinerum ducem, hunc ad quaestūs pecūniae mercātūrāsque habēre vim maximam arbitrantur. Post hunc, Apollinem et Martem et Iovem et Minervam.

Notes: **deum** = *deōrum* from *deus, -ī*, m: god (*deōrum*: partitive genitive); **colō, -ere, coluī, cultus**: cultivate, honor, worship; **huius** and **hunc**: Mercury (the god's name derives from *merx, mercis*, f: profit); **simulācrum, -ī**, n: image; **inventor, -ōris**, m: originator, inventor; **ars, artis**, f: skill, craft; **ferunt**: they say (triggers the indirect statements: *hunc…* [*esse*] *inventōrem* and *hunc…* [*esse*] *ducem*); **via, -ae**, f: road; **iter, itineris**, n: journey; **dux, ducis**, m: leader; **quaestus, -ūs**, m: gain; **pecūnia, -ae**, f: money; **mercātūra, -ae**, f: trade, commercial transactions; **vīs, vis**, f (irregular noun): strength, power; **arbitror, -ārī, -ātus sum**: think; **Apollinem…Minervam**: direct objects of an implied *colunt*.

19.5. Cicero, *in Catilinam* 1.2: Cicero expresses his righteous indignation that Catiline has gotten away with his political depravities for too long.

Ō tempora! Ō mōrēs! Senātus haec intellegit, consul videt; hic tamen vīvit. Vīvit? Immō vērō etiam in senātum venit, fit pūblicī consilī particeps, nōtat et dēsignat oculīs ad caedem ūnum quemque nostrum.

Notes: **mōs, mōris**, m: habit, custom; (in plural) character, morals; **haec**: these things; **intellegō, -ere, intellexī, intellectus**: understand; **hic**: Catiline; **vīvō, -ere, vixī, victus**: live; **immō**: rather, on the contrary, more precisely; **vērō**: indeed; **fīō, fierī, factus sum**: become; **consilium, -iī**, n: plan; **particeps, participis** + genitive: participant in; **dēsignō, -āre, -āvī, -ātus**: point out; **oculus, -ī**, m: eye; **caedēs, -is**, f: slaughter; **quisque, quidque**: each one.

20. REFLEXIVE PRONOUNS

20.1. *CIL* VII 93a, addit. 306 [*ILS* 4558; *RIB* 213]: Martlesham, Suffolk (Britannia). Bronze shield-shaped base for an equestrian statuette. Extant are the stump of a right hoof and a headless foe, lying on his back. To a Celtic Mars.

> Deō Martī Corotiācō Simplicia prō sē v(ōtum) p(osuit)
> l(ibens) m(eritō). Glaucus fēcit.

Notes: **deus, -ī, m:** god; **Mars, Martis, m:** Mars, the Roman god of war; **Corotiācus, -ī, m:** a Celtic name for Mars; **Simplicia, -ae, f:** a woman's name, from *simplex, simplicis:* pure, simple; **prō** + ablative: for, on behalf of; **sē:** herself (Simplicia); **vōtum, -ī, n:** vow; **pōnō, -ere, posuī, positus:** place, put; **libens, libentis:** willing, joyful; **meritō:** deservedly, rightly; **Glaucus, -ī, m:** a Greek man's name, "gray-eyed, blue-eyed" (often used to describe the Greek goddess Athena); the direct object of *fēcit* is *hoc,* whose antecedent is the statue base.

20.2. Catullus 58: The Lesbia loved by both Catullus and his friend Caelius proves unfaithful. Meter: hendecasyllabics.

> Caelī, Lesbia nostra, Lesbia illa,
> illa Lesbia, quam Catullus ūnam
> plūs quam sē atque suōs amāvit omnēs,
> nunc in quadriviīs et angiportīs
> glūbit magnanimī Remī nepōtēs.

Notes: **Caelius, -iī, m:** a Roman man's name; **noster, nostra, nostrum:** our; **quam:** whom (Lesbia); **ūnus, -a, -um:** alone; **plūs quam:** more than; **suōs omnēs:** all his comrades; **quadrivium, -iī, n:** crossroads; **angiportum, -ī, n:** alley; **glūbō, -ere** (no third or fourth principal parts): peel, "defile"; **magnanimus, -a, -um:** high-minded, great-spirited; **Remus, -ī, m:** twin brother of Romulus, the legendary founder of Rome; **nepōs, -ōtis, m:** grandson, descendant.

20.3. Caesar, *de Bello Gallico* 6.27.3–5: The preposterous ways in which the German *alcēs* are hunted.

> Hīs sunt arborēs prō cubīlibus: ad eās sē applicant atque
> ita paulum modo reclīnātae quiētem capiunt. Quārum

ex vestīgiīs cum est animadversum ā vēnātōribus quō sē
recipere consuērint, omnīs eō locō aut ab rādīcibus sub-
ruunt aut accīdunt arborēs, tantum ut summa speciēs
eārum stantium relinquātur. Hūc cum sē consuētūdine
reclīnāvērunt, infirmās arborēs pondere adflīgunt atque
ūnā ipsae concidunt.

Notes: **hīs**: dative of reference; **arbor, -oris**, f: tree; **prō** + ablative: for, in place of; **cubīle, -is**, n: bed, couch; **ad eās** (*arborēs*);
applicō, -āre, -āvī, -ātus: place near, attach, "support"; **paulum
modo reclīnātae**: "having leaned over slightly"; **quiēs, quiētis**, f:
rest; **quārum**: "these" (correlative use of the relative pronoun);
vestīgium, -iī, n: track, footstep; **est animaversum** (impersonal):
it has been noticed ("when hunters have noticed"); **vēnātor, -ōris**,
m: hunter; **quō**: where; **recipiō, -ere, recēpī, receptus**: withdraw, retreat; **consuērint** = *consuēverint* from *consuescō, -ere,
consuēvī, consuētus*: be accustomed; **omnīs** (*arborēs*); **aut... aut**:
either... or; **rādix, rādīcis**, f: root, foundation; **subruō, -ere,
subruī, subrutus**: undermine, tear from below; **accīdō, -ere,
accīdī, accīsus**: cut, weaken; **tantum... relinquātur**: "so far
that the complete appearance of them standing is left" (result
clause); **speciēs, -ēī**, f: appearance; **stō, stāre, stetī, status**: stand;
consuētūdō, consuētūdinis, f: custom, habit; **reclīnō, -āre, -āvī,
-ātus**: lean back; **infirmus, -a, -um**: weak; **pondus, ponderis**, n:
weight; **adflīgō, -ere, adflixī, adflictus**: knock down; **ūnā**: at the
same time, together; **concidō, -ere, concidī**: fall down, tumble to
the ground; **ipsae** (*alcēs*).

21. PASSIVE VERBS

21.1. Catullus 8.12–19: Catullus is tired of Lesbia's philandering and
decides to break off his relationship with her once and for all
(until the next time, that is!). Meter: limping iambics.

> Valē, puella! Iam Catullus obdūrat,
> nec tē requīret, nec rogābit invītam.
> At tū dolēbis, cum rogāberis nulla.
> Scelesta, vae tē! Quae tibī manet vīta?
> Quis nunc tē adībit? Cui vidēberis bella?

Quem nunc amābis? Cuius esse dīcēris?
Quem bāsiābis? Cui labella mordēbis?
At tū, Catulle, destinātus obdūrā.

Notes: **obdūrō, -āre, -āvī, -ātus:** be hard, hold out, endure;
requīrō, -ere, requīsīvī, requīsītus: seek again, search for; **rogō,
-āre, -āvī, -ātus:** ask for; **invītus, -a, -um:** unwilling; **at:** but; **doleō,
-ēre, -uī:** feel pain; **cum:** when; **nulla:** used colloquially, "not at
all"; **scelestus, -a, -um:** wicked, accursed; **vae tē:** alas for you!; **quī,
quae, quod:** what, which?; **maneō, -ēre, mansī, mansus:** remain,
stay; **vīta, -ae, f:** life; **quis, quid:** who, what?; **adeō, -īre, -iī, -itus:**
approach; **videor, -ērī, vīsus sum:** seem; **bellus, -a, -um:** pretty,
handsome; **bāsiō, -āre, -āvī, -ātus:** kiss; **cui:** "whose?" (dative of
possession); **labellum, -ī, n:** a little lip; **mordeō, -ēre, momordī,
morsus:** bite; **destinātus, -a, -um:** determined, destined.

21.2.   Martial 3.12: A fine dinner party, but where was the dinner?
Martial echoes Catullus 13, also adressed to a Fabullus (see
38.3). Meter: hendecasyllabics.

Unguentum, fateor, bonum dedistī
convīvīs here, sed nihil scidistī.
Rēs salsa est bene olēre et ēsurīre:
quī nōn cēnat et unguitur, Fabulle,
hic vērē mihi mortuus vidētur.

Notes: **unguentum, -ī, n:** ointment, perfume; **fateor, -ērī, fassus
sum:** confess, acknowledge; **convīva, -ae, m/f:** banquet guest; **here**
= *herī:* yesterday; **nihil, n** (indeclinable): nothing; **scindō, -ere,
scidī, scissus:** carve; **salsus, -a, -um:** witty, facetious; **oleō, -ēre,
-ui:** smell; **ēsuriō, -īre,** (no third principal part), **-ītus:** be hungry;
unguō, -ere, unxī, unctus: anoint, smear with perfume; **mortuus,
-a, -um:** dead.

21.3.   Martial 5.13.1–4: I may be poor, but at least I'm famous! Meter:
elegiac couplets.

Sum, fateor, semperque fuī, Callistrate, pauper,
    sed nōn obscūrus nec male nōtus eques,
sed tōtō legor orbe frequens et dīcitur "Hīc est,"
    quodque cinis paucīs, hoc mihi vīta dedit.

Notes: **Callistratus, -ī, m:** a man's name, "glorious in war" (also the name of a Greek orator of the fourth century BCE); **pauper, pauperis:** poor; **obscūrus, -a, -um:** obscure, indistinct; **male nōtus:** unknown (literally, "known badly"); **eques, equitis, m:** knight, man of the equestrian rank; **legō, -ere, lēgī, lectus:** gather, collect, read; **frequens, frequentis:** often, constant, repeated; **quodque:** explaining *hoc* (i.e., fame); understand *dedit* in the *quodque* clause; **cinis, cineris, m:** death; **paucus, -a, -um:** few, little.

21.4. Caesar, *de Bello Gallico* 6.14.1–2: The social privileges of the Druids in Gaul.

> Druidēs ā bellō abesse consuērunt, neque tribūta ūnā
> cum reliquīs pendunt; mīlitiae vacātiōnem omniumque
> rērum habent immūnitātem. Tantīs excitātī praemiīs et
> suā sponte multī in disciplīnam conveniunt et ā parenti-
> bus propinquīsque mittuntur.

Notes: **ā bellō abesse:** take no part in war; **consuērunt** = *consuēvērunt* from *consuescō, -ere, consuēvī, consuētus:* be accustomed; **tribūtum, -ī, n:** tax, tribute; **ūnā cum** + ablative: together with, at the same rate as; **reliquus, -a, -um:** remaining, rest; **pendō, -ere, pependī, pensus:** pay, weigh out; **mīlitia, -ae, f:** military service (*mīlitiae:* objective genitive with *vacātiōnem*); **vacātiō, -ōnis, f:** freedom, exemption; **omnium rērum:** objective genitive with *immūnitātem*; **immūnitās, -ātis, f:** immunity, exemption; **excitō, -āre, -āvī, -ātus:** arouse, attract; **tantīs praemiīs:** ablative of means; **praemium, -iī, n:** reward; **suā sponte:** by their own will (ablative of means); **disciplīna, -ae, f:** instruction, teaching; **conveniō, -īre, convēnī, conventus:** assemble; **parens, parentis, m/f:** parent; **propinquus, -ī, m:** relative; **mittō, -ere, mīsī, missus:** send.

22. IMPERSONAL VERBS

22.1. Caesar, *de Bello Gallico* 4.26.1–3: The Roman troops are at a disadvantage in fighting the Britons during Caesar's first British campaign (55 BCE).

> Pugnātum est ab utrīsque ācriter. Nostrī tamen, quod
> neque ordinēs servāre neque firmiter insistere neque

signa subsequī poterant, atque alius aliā ex nāvī, qui-
buscumque signīs occurrerat, sē aggregābat, magnopere perturbābantur; hostēs vērō, nōtīs omnibus vadīs,
ubi ex lītore aliquōs singulārīs ex nāvī ēgredientīs
conspexerant, incitātīs equīs impedītōs adoriēbantur,
plūrēs paucōs circumsistēbant, aliī ab latere apertō in
ūniversōs tēla cōiciēbant.

Notes: **pugnō, -āre, -āvī, -ātus:** fight (*pugnātum est:* "it was
fought"); **uterque, utraque, utrumque:** each (of two), both; **ācriter:**
bitterly, fiercely; **nostrī:** nominative plural ("our men"); **quod:**
because; **neque...neque:** neither...nor; **ordinēs servāre:** keep
rank; **firmiter:** steadily, firmly; **insistō, -ere, institī:** keep one's foot-
ing; **signum, -ī, n:** military standard (tall poles topped with military insignia and symbols that were often used as rallying points
in battle); **subsequor, -ī, -secūtus sum:** follow after; **alius aliā ex
nāvī:** one soldier from this ship, another from that; **nāvis, -is, f:**
ship; **quīcumque, quaecumque, quodcumque:** whoever, whichever, whatever; **occurrō, -ere, occurrī, occursus** + dative: meet
with, encounter; **sē aggregāre:** join oneself to; **magnopere:** very
much; **perturbō, -āre, -āvī, -ātus:** confuse, disorder; **hostis, -is, m:**
enemy; **nōtīs...vadīs:** ablative absolute; **noscō, -ere, nōvī, nōtus:**
know, be familiar with; **vadum, -ī, n:** shoal, shallow; **lītus, lītoris,
n:** seashore, beach; **singulārīs:** one by one; **ēgredior, -ī, ēgressus
sum:** step out; **conspiciō, -ere, conspexī, conspectus:** catch sight of;
incitātīs equīs: ablative absolute; **incitātus, -a, -um:** spurred on, set
in rapid motion; **equus, -ī, m:** horse; **impediō, -īre, -īvī, -ītus:** hin-
der, obstruct; **adorior, -īrī, adortus sum:** attack, assail; **plūs, plūris:**
several, many, more; **paucus, -a, -um:** few, little; **circumsistō, -ere,
circumstetī:** surround; **latus, lateris, n:** side, flank; **apertus, -a,
-um:** open, exposed; **in** + accusative: against; **ūniversus, -a, -um:**
the entire group (in contrast with *singulārīs*); **tēlum, -ī, n:** weapon,
missile, javelin, spear; **cōiciō, -ere, cōiēcī, cōiectus:** throw together,
hurl, toss, cast.

22.2.   Catullus 70: On the fickleness of a lover. Meter: elegiac couplets.

Nullī sē dīcit mulier mea nūbere malle
quam mihi, nōn sī sē Iuppiter ipse petat.

Dīcit: sed mulier cupidō quod dīcit amantī,
in ventō et rapidā scrībere oportet aquā.

Notes: **Nullī sē…nūbere malle**: indirect statement; **nullī**: dative
singular; **mulier, mulieris**, f: woman; **nūbō, -ere, nupsī, nuptus**
+ dative: marry, wed; **quam**: than; **petō, -ere, -īvī, -ītus**: seek,
demand, ask, beg (*petat*: present subjunctive in a future less vivid
conditional, "should seek"); **cupidus, -a, -um**: desirous, eager;
quod: what, that which; **amans, amantis**, m/f: lover; **ventus, -ī**, m:
wind; **scrībere oportet**: "one ought to write".

22.3. Cicero, *ad Atticum* 4.2.4: Cicero describes the senatorial debate
(occuring on the Kalends of October 57 BCE) regarding the restoration of his property that had been confiscated during his exile.
Although other senators spoke in favor of restoration, Clodius,
responsible for Cicero's exile, filibustered against it.

Tum ad Clōdium ventum est; cupiit diem consūmere
neque eī fīnis est factus, sed tamen cum hōrās trīs ferē
dixisset, odiō et strepitū senātūs coactus est aliquandō
perōrāre.

Notes: **tum**: then, next; **ventum est**: "it came to", i.e., it was Clodius's
turn to speak; **cupiō, -ere, -īvī/-iī, -ītus**: desire, wish for; **consūmō,
-ere, consumpsī, consumptus**: consume, expend, squander; **eī**: dative
of agent; **fīnis, -is**, m: end; **tamen**: nonetheless; **cum**: circumstantial;
hōra, -ae, f: hour; **trīs**: three; **ferē**: nearly; **odium, -iī**, n: hatred, hos-
tility; **senātūs**: subjective genitive; **strepitus, -ūs**, m: racket, uproar;
cōgō, -ere, coēgī, coactus: compel; **aliquandō**: finally; **perōrō, -āre,
-āvī, -ātus**: conclude, deliver the final part of the speech.

22.4. Cicero, *Philippica* 2.68: Cicero attacks Marc Antony for pur-
chasing the property of Caesar's enemy, Pompey, whom Cicero
supported as a defender of the Republic.

Ō audāciam immānem! Tū etiam ingredī illam domum
ausus es, tū illud sanctissimum līmen intrāre, tū
illārum aedium dīs penātibus ōs impūrissimum ostendere? Quam domum aliquamdiū nēmō aspicere pot-
erat, nēmō sine lacrimīs praeterīre, hāc tē in domō tam

diū dēversārī nōn pudet? In quā, quamvīs nihil sapiās,
tamen nihil tibi potest esse iūcundum.

Notes: **audācia, -ae,** f: audacity, recklessness; **immānis, -e:** vast,
monstrous, savage; **etiam:** even; **ingredior, -ī, ingressus sum:**
advance, enter; **domus, -ūs,** f: house; **audeō, -ēre, ausus sum:** dare
(semi-deponent verb); **sanctus, -a, -um:** holy, sacred, pure; **līmen,
līminis,** n: threshold, entrance; **intrō, -āre, -āvī, -ātus:** enter, go
into; **aedēs, -is,** f: shrine, temple; **dīs:** dative plural from *deus, -ī,*
m: god; **penātēs, -ium,** m (plural): the gods of the home, hearth,
or family line; **ōs, ōris,** n: mouth, face, expression; **impūrus,
-a, -um:** filthy, foul, disgusting; **ostendō, -ere, ostendī, ostensus:** show, display; **quam:** "this" (correlative usage of the relative
adjective); **aliquamdiū:** for some time; **nēmō, nēminis,** m/f: no
one; **aspiciō, -ere, aspexī, aspectus:** gaze on, face, contemplate;
sine + ablative: without; **lacrima, -ae,** f: tear; **praetereō, -īre, -iī,
-itus:** pass by, disregard; **hāc:** with *domō;* **tē:** direct object of *pudet;*
tam diū: for so long a time; **dēversor, -ārī, -ātus sum:** lodge, live,
dwell; **pudet:** it shames, makes ashamed; **in quā** *(domō);* **quamvīs:**
although; **nihil:** nothing; **sapiō, -ere, -īvī:** understand *(sapiās:*
present subjunctive); **tamen:** nonetheless; **iūcundus, -a, -um:**
pleasant, agreeable.

22.5. Vergil, *Aeneid* 4.450–451: Distraught at Aeneas's departure, Dido
decides that she cannot continue living. Meter: dactylic hexameter.

> Tum vērō infēlix fātīs exterrita Dīdō
> mortem ōrat; taedet caelī convexa tuērī.

Notes: **infēlix, infēlīcis:** unhappy, unlucky; **fātum, -ī,** n: fate, destiny; **exterreō, -ēre, -terruī, -territus:** frighten, terrify; **mors, mortis,** f: death; **ōrō, -āre, -āvī, -ātus:** beg for; **taedet:** it wearies (her);
caelum, -ī, n: sky, heaven; **convexum, -ī,** n: hollow, vault; **tueor,
-ērī, tuitus sum:** look at.

22.6. Ovid, *Metamorphoses* 1.137–140: Ovid describes how humans
in the Iron Age overused and misused the earth. Meter: dactylic
hexameter.

> Nec tantum segetēs alimentaque dēbita dīves
> poscēbātur humus, sed itum est in viscera terrae,

quāsque recondiderat Stygiīsque admōverat umbrīs,
effodiuntur opēs, inrītāmenta malōrum.

Notes: **tantum:** only; **seges, -etis,** f: crop (*segetēs:* accusative of respect); **alimentum, -ī,** n: food, nourishment (*alimenta:* accusative of respect); **dēbeō, -ēre, -uī, -itus:** owe; **dīves, dīvitis:** rich (modifies *humus*); **poscō, -ere, poposcī:** ask, demand; **humus, -ī,** f: ground, earth (*humus:* subject of *poscēbātur*); **itum est:** an impersonal usage of *eō;* literally, "there was a going" or "they went"; **viscus, visceris,** n: entrails, inner parts; **quāsque:** refers to *opēs;* **recondō, -ere, recondidī, reconditus:** hide, conceal (take *terra* as the subject of both *recondiderat* and *admōverat*); **Stygius, -a, -um:** of the river Styx (the border between the worlds of the living and the dead), of the underworld; **admoveō, -ēre, admōvī, admōtus:** move toward; **umbra, -ae,** f: shadow, shade (the underworld was viewed as dark and gloomy); **effodiō, -ere, effodī, effossus:** dig out; **ops, opis,** f: wealth, riches; **inrītāmentum, -ī,** n: incentive, incitement; **malum, -ī,** n: evil (*malōrum:* substantive, "evils"; take *inrītāmentum malōrum* in apposition to *opēs*); Ovid goes on to explain that greed and war result from *opēs terrae.*

22.7. Tacitus *Annales* 13.21.1: Nero had tried to murder his mother, Agripinna, by drowning, but the attempt failed. Afterward, the emperor's advisor Burrus visits Agrippina and reveals Nero's charges against her (see Dio 62.12–13). Tacitus impersonally reports that there was a visit ("there is a going") but omits the messenger's name.

Sīc lēnitō principis metū et lūce ortā itur ad Agrippīnam,
ut nosceret obiecta dissolveretque vel poenās lueret.

Notes: **sīc:** thus; **lēnitō ... ortā:** ablatives absolute; **lēniō, -īre, -īvī, -ītus:** mitigate, alleviate, assuage; **princeps, principis,** m: emperor; **metus, -ūs,** m: fear, apprehension, dread; **lux, lūcis,** f: light; **orior, -īrī, ortus sum:** rise, begin; **itur:** an impersonal usage of *eō* ("there is a going to" or "someone goes"); **ut:** so that (introducing a purpose clause); **noscō, -ere, nōvī, nōtus:** know; **obiciō, -ere, obiēcī, obiectus:** cast, oppose, throw before (*obiecta:* substantive, "charges"); **dissolvō, -ere, dissolvī, dissolūtus:** refute; **vel:** or; **poena, -ae,** f: penalty; **luō, -ere, luī:** pay.

23. COMPARATIVES

23.1.   Caesar, *de Bello Gallico* 4.25.1: As Caesar tries to launch his first attack on Britain from his ships in 55 BCE, his men hesitate. The aquaphobic soldiers are unwilling to begin their assault from the surf while the Britons posture on familiar ground. Caesar uses his warships to intimidate the enemy.

Quod ubi Caesar animadvertit, nāvīs longās, quārum et speciēs erat barbarīs inusitātior et mōtus ad ūsum expedītior, paulum removērī ab onerāriīs nāvibus et rēmīs incitārī et ad latus apertum hostium constituī, atque inde fundīs, sagittīs, tormentīs hostīs prōpellī ac summovērī iussit; quae rēs magnō ūsuī nostrīs fuit.

Notes: **quod**: "this," referring to the hesitation of Caesar's troops and the British homefield advantage; **animadvertō, -ere, animadvertī, animadversus**: notice; **nāvis, -is, f**: ship; **nāvīs longās**: subject of *removērī, incitārī, constituī*; **et . . . et**: both . . . and; **speciēs, -ēī, f**: appearance; **inusitātus, -a, -um**: unfamiliar; **mōtus, -ūs, m**: motion, movement; **ūsus, -ūs, m**: use, practice, advantage; **expedītus, -a, -um**: unencumbered, convenient; **paulum**: a little; **removeō, -ēre, remōvī, remōtus**: move back, withdraw; **nāvis onerāria, nāvis onerāriae, f**: transport ship; **rēmus, -ī, m**: oar; **incitō, -āre, -āvī, -ātus**: urge on, hasten; **ad latus apertum**: against the exposed flank; **hostis, -is, m**: enemy; **constituō, -ere, constituī, constitūtus**: position, establish; **inde**: from that place; **funda, -ae, f**: sling; **sagitta, -ae, f**: arrow; **tormentum, -ī, n**: artillery, missiles; **prōpellō, -ere, prōpulī, prōpulsus**: drive back; **summoveō, -ēre, summōvī, summōtus**: force back; **quae rēs**: referring to Caesar's repositioning of the fleet; **magnō ūsuī nostrīs**: double dative.

23.2.   Caesar, *de Bello Gallico* 5.14.3: The British practice of using warpaint.

Omnēs vērō sē Britannī vitrō inficiunt, quod caeruleum efficit colōrem, atque hōc horridiōrēs sunt in pugnā

aspectū; capillōque sunt prōmissō atque omnī parte
corporis rāsā, praeter caput et labrum superius.

Notes: **vitrum, -ī,** n: woad; **inficiō, -ere, infēcī, infectus:** tinge,
dye, stain; **caeruleus, -a, -um:** dark blue; **efficiō, -ere, effēcī, effec-**
tus: produce, make, effect; **hōc:** ablative of cause; **horridus, -a, -um:**
wild, frightful; **pugna, -ae,** f: battle; **aspectus, -ūs,** m: appearance,
sight *(aspectū:* ablative of description); **capillus, -ī,** m: hair *(capillō:*
ablative of description); **prōmissus, -a, -um:** flowing down, hang-
ing down; **corpus, corporis,** n: body; **rādō, -ere, rāsī, rāsus:** shave,
scrape (clean); **praeter** + accusative: except for; **caput, capitis,** n:
head; **labrum, -ī,** n: lip; **superius:** comparative of *superus, -a, -um:*
high (here, "upper").

23.3. Caesar, *de Bello Gallico* 5.17.1: The British seem less enthusias-
tic for battle than they had been.

Posterō diē procul ā castrīs hostēs in collibus
constitērunt, rārīque sē ostendere et lēnius quam prīdiē
nostrōs equitēs proeliō lacessere coepērunt.

Notes: **posterus, -a, -um:** subsequent, next; **procul:** at a distance;
castra, -ōrum, n (plural): camp; **collis, -is,** m: hill; **constō, -āre,**
constitī: take a stand; **rārus, -a, -um:** scattered, far apart; **ostendō,**
-ere, ostendī, ostensus: show, display; **lēnis, -e:** gentle; **prīdiē:** the
day before; **eques, equitis,** m: horseman, cavalryman; **proelium,**
-iī, n: battle; **lacessō, -ere, -īvī, -ītus:** harass, assail, attack; **coepī,**
coepisse, coeptus: begin.

23.4. Vergil, *Aeneid* 1.142–143: Neptune has just quelled the storm
against the Trojans which had been raised by Aeolus, king of the
winds, and ordered by Juno. Meter: dactylic hexameter.

Sīc ait et dictō citius tumida aequora plācat
collectāsque fugat nūbēs sōlemque redūcit.

Notes: **sīc:** thus; **ait:** he (Neptune) spoke; **dictum, -ī,** n: word, command; **cito:** quickly; **tumidus, -a, -um:** swelling; **aequor, -oris,** n:
sea; **plācō, -āre, -āvī, -ātus:** calm, quiet; **colligō, -ere, collēgī, col-**
lectus: collect, gather; **fugō, -āre, -āvī, -ātus:** put to flight, rout;

nūbēs, -is, f: cloud; sōl, sōlis, m: sun; redūcō, -ere, reduxī, reductus: bring back.

23.5.   Martial 1.10: She's not pretty, but her consumptive cough (and her fortune) are very attractive. Meter: limping iambics.

> Petit Gemellus nuptiās Marōnillae
> et cupit et instat et precātur et dōnat.
> Adeōne pulchra est? Immō foedius nīl est.
> Quid ergō in illā petitur et placet? Tussit.

Notes: **petō, -ere, -īvī, -ītus:** seek; **Gemellus, -ī,** m: the suitor of our poem ("Twin"); **nuptiae, -ārum,** f (plural): marriage, wedding, nuptials; **Marōnilla, -ae,** f: a diminitutive feminine name, referring to a variety of Greek wine (*Marōn*); **instō, instāre, institī:** press upon, pursue, harass, solicit; **precor, -ārī, -ātus sum:** ask, beg, beseech; **adeō:** so, very; **-ne:** enclitic introducing a question; **immō:** no, indeed, by no means; **foedus, -a, -um:** loathsome, ugly, detestable; **placeō, -ēre, -uī, -itus:** be pleasing, please, be agreeable (to); **tussiō, -īre** (no third or fourth principal parts): cough.

24. ABLATIVE OF COMPARISON

24.1.   Catullus 82: Catullus may be accusing Quintius of having an affair with Lesbia. He mentions Quintius again in poem 100. Meter: elegiac couplets.

> Quintī, sī tibi vīs oculōs dēbēre Catullum
> aut aliud sī quid cārius est oculīs,
> ēripere eī nōlī multō quod cārius illī
> est oculīs seu quid cārius est oculīs.

Notes: **Quintius, -ī,** m: a Roman man's name, "fifth"; **tibi:** dative of possession; **volō, velle, voluī:** want, wish, be willing; **oculus, -ī,** m: eye; **dēbeō, -ēre, -uī, -itus:** owe; **aliud...quid:** anything else; **cārus, -a, -um** + dative: dear, precious; **nōlī...ēripere:** do not take away; **eī:**

dative of disadvantage (referring to Catullus); **multō**: by far (ablative of degree of difference); **illī**: dative (Catullus); **seu**: or if.

24.2. Vergil, *Aeneid* 1.544–545: Achates describes Aeneas's character to Dido, queen of Carthage. Meter: dactylic hexameter.

> Rex erat Aenēās nōbīs, quō iustior alter
> nec pietāte fuit, nec bellō māior et armīs.

Notes: **rex, rēgis**, m: king; **quō**: ablative of comparison (refers to Aeneas); **iustus, -a, -um**: just, fair, righteous; **alter, altera, alterum**: another; **pietās, -ātis**, f: loyalty, devotion, duty (*pietāte*: ablative of respect); **bellum, -ī**, n: warfare (*bellō*: ablative of respect); **magnus, -a, -um**: illustrious (*māior*: comparative); **arma, -ōrum**, n (plural): arms, equipment.

24.3. Martial 1.109.1–5: Martial spoofs Catullus 2, comparing Publius's lapdog to Lesbia's pet sparrow. Meter: hendecasyllabics.

> Issa est passere nēquior Catullī,
> Issa est pūrior osculō columbae,
> Issa est blandior omnibus puellīs,
> Issa est cārior Indicīs lapillīs,
> Issa est dēliciae catella Pūblī.

Notes: **Issa, -ae**, f: the name of a beloved pet, recalling an island in the Adriatic; **passer, passeris**, m: sparrow; **nēquam**: naughty (*nēquior*: comparative); **pūrus, -a, -um**: clean, chaste, blameless; **osculum, -ī**, n: kiss; **columba, -ae**, f: dove; **blandus, -a, -um**: charming; **cārus, -a, -um** + dative: dear, precious; **Indicus, -a, -um**: from India; **lapillus, -ī**, m: little stone, pebble; **dēliciae, -ārum**, f (plural): delight, darling; **catella, -ae**, f: puppy, lapdog; **Pūblī** = *Pūbliī* from *Pūblius, -ī*, m: a man's name.

24.4. Caesar, *de Bello Gallico* 6.26.1–2: An ungulate, one of the strange animals of the Hercynian Forest, east of the Rhine River in Germany. Had Caesar seen the animal? Or were the locals pulling his leg?

> Est bōs cervī figūrā, cuius ā mediā fronte inter aurīs
> ūnum cornū exsistit excelsius magisque dīrectum

eīs, quae nōbīs nōta sunt, cornibus. Ab eius summō
sīcut palmae rāmīque lātē diffunduntur. Eadem est
fēminae marisque nātūra, eadem forma magnitūdōque
cornuum.

Notes: **bōs, bovis**, m/f: ox, bull, cow (the Romans called any large
animal, including elephants, *bōs*); **cervus, -ī**, m: deer; **figūra, -ae**, f:
shape (*figurā*: ablative of description); **cuius ā mediā fronte**: "from
the middle of whose forehead"; **auris, -is**, f: ear; **cornū, -ūs**, n: horn
(Reindeer and caribou shed their antlers yearly. Caesar's informant
had possibly seen an animal who had shed one antler but not the
other); **exsistō, -ere, exstitī**: appear, stand; **excelsus, -a, -um**: high;
dīrectus, -a, -um: straight up; **eīs...cornibus**: ablative of comparison; **nōscō, -ere, nōvī, nōtus**: know; **summum, -ī**, n: top; **sīcut**: just
as; **palma, -ae**, f: hand, palm branch; **rāmus, -ī**, m: branch; **lātē**:
widely; **diffundō, -ere, diffūdī, diffūsus**: spread out; **īdem, eadem,
idem**: the same; **mās, maris**, m: male; **magnitūdō, magnitūdinis**,
f: size.

25. SUPERLATIVES

25.1. Catullus 49: Catullus fulsomely thanks the great orator Marcus
Tullius Cicero for some unknown favor, perhaps in ironic imita-
tion. Meter: hendecasyllabics.

Disertissime Rōmulī nepōtum
quot sunt quotque fuēre, Marce Tullī,
quotque post aliīs erunt in annīs,
grātiās tibi maximās Catullus
agit pessimus omnium poēta,
tantō pessimus omnium poēta,
quantō tū optimus omnium patrōnus.

Notes: **disertus, -a, -um**: clever, eloquent; **Rōmulus, -ī**, m: legendary founder of Rome; **nepōs, -ōtis**, m: grandson, descendant; **quot**:
how many; **fuēre** = *fuērunt*; **post**: afterward, later; **alius, alia, aliud**:
other; **grātiās agere**: give thanks, thank; **tantō...quantō**: by as
much...as; **pessimus** (*sum*); **tū** (*es*); **patrōnus, -ī**, m: patron.

25.2.   Cicero, *in Catilinam* 1.9: Cicero is astonished and outraged that Catiline could get away with plotting the murder of a consul in a city as distinguished as Rome, with a governing body as august as the Roman Senate.

> Ō dī immortālēs! Ubīnam gentium sumus? Quam rem pūblicam habēmus? In quā urbe vīvimus? Hīc, hīc sunt in nostrō numerō, patrēs conscriptī, in hōc orbis terrae sanctissimō gravissimōque consiliō, quī dē nostrō omnium interitū, quī dē huius urbis atque adeō dē orbis terrārum exitiō cōgitent.

Notes: **dī:** from *deus*, *-ī*, m: god; **ubīnam gentium:** where in the world; **patrēs conscriptī:** senators; **orbis, orbis**, m: circle, ring (*orbis terrae:* world); **sanctus, -a, -um:** holy, sacred, pure; **gravis, -e:** dignified; **consilium, -iī,** n: assembly, council; **interitus, -ūs,** m: ruin, death, destruction; **dē nostrō** (*et*) **omnium interitū:** Cicero is talking about his own death (*nostrō*) as well as the deaths of all the law-abiding members of the Senate (*omnium*); **adeō:** even; **exitium, -iī,** n: ruin, destruction; **cōgitō, -āre, -āvī, -ātus:** think, intend, plan (*cōgitent:* present subjunctive in a relative clause of characteristic).

25.3.   Caesar, *de Bello Gallico* 1.2.1: Caesar introduces his first Gallic foe.

> Apud Helvētiōs longē nōbilissimus fuit et dītissimus Orgetorix.

Notes: **Helvētiī, -ōrum,** m (plural): a tribe in Gaul (Switzerland); **longē:** by far; **nōbilis, -e:** well-known, famous; **dīvēs, dīvitis:** rich (the stem changes to *dīt-* in the superlative); **Orgetorix, -igis,** m: see 9.2.

26. RELATIVE CLAUSES

26.1.   Caesar, *de Bello Gallico* 1.1.1: The opening words of Caesar's *de Bello Gallico* describe the geography of the three provinces of Gaul.

> Gallia est omnis dīvīsa in partīs trīs, quārum ūnam incolunt Belgae, aliam Aquītānī, tertiam quī ipsōrum linguā Celtae, nostrā Gallī appellantur.

Notes: **dīvīsa:** perfect passive participle used as predicate adjective; understand *partem* with *ūnam, aliam, tertiam*; **incolō, -ere, -uī:** live in, inhabit, dwell; **Belgae, -ārum,** m (plural): a group of Celtic tribes inhabiting the west bank of the Rhine River and giving their name to the Roman province Gallia Belgica; **Aquītānī, -ōrum,** m (plural): the peoples in southern Gaul dwelling between the Atlantic, the Pyranees, and the Garonne River, giving their name to the Roman province Gallia Aquitania; **ipsōrum linguā:** in their own language; **nostrā** (*linguā*); **appellō, -āre, -āvī, -ātus:** call.

26.2. Caesar, *de Bello Gallico* 1.2.3: Continuing his verbal map of Gaul, Caesar explains the political ramification of geography.

> Id hōc facilius eīs persuāsit, quod undique locī nātūrā Helvētiī continentur: ūnā ex parte flūmine Rhēnō lātissimō atque altissimō, quī agrum Helvētium ā Germānīs dīvidit; alterā ex parte monte Iūrā altissimō, quī est inter Sēquanōs et Helvētiōs; tertiā lacū Lemannō et flūmine Rhodanō, quī prōvinciam nostram ab Helvētiīs dīvidit.

Notes: **id:** subject of *persuāsit*, explained by the *quod* clause; **hōc:** ablative of cause; **facilis, -e:** easy (*facilius:* comparative adverb); **persuādeō, -ēre, persuāsī, persuāsus** + dative: persuade, convince; **quod:** the fact that; **undique:** from all sides; **locus, -ī,** m: place, region, area; **contineō, -ēre, continuī, contentus:** hold in; **ūnā ex parte:** on one side; **flūmen, flūminis,** n: stream, river; **Rhēnus, -ī,** m: the Rhine; **lātus, -a, -um:** broad, wide; **altus, -a, -um:** high, deep; **dīvidō, -ere, dīvīsī, dīvīsus:** divide; **alter, altera, alterum:** the other (of two); **mons, montis,** m: mountain; **Iūra, -ae,** m: the Jura Mountains, north of the Alps; **inter** + accusative: between; **Sēquanī, -ōrum,** m (plural): a tribe of Gallia Lugdunensis west of the Jura Mountains; **tertiā** (*ex parte*); **lacus Lemannus, lacūs Lemannī,** m: modern Lake Geneva, in western Switzerland; **flūmen Rhodanum, flūminis Rhodanī,** m: the Rhone River, flowing from Switzerland into southeastern France; **prōvinciam nostram:** Cisalpine Gaul.

26.3. Caesar, *de Bello Gallico* 4.21.7: Caesar's orders to Commius, his British ally and the chieftain of the Atrebates.

> Et cum eīs ūnā Commium, quem ipse, Atrebatibus superātīs, rēgem ibi cōnstituerat, cuius et virtūtem

et consilium probābat et quem sibi fidēlem esse
arbitrābātur, cuiusque auctōritās in hīs regiōnibus
magnī habēbātur, mittit.

Notes: understand Caesar as the subject of *mittit*; **ūnā:** together;
Commium: direct object of *mittit*; **ipse:** Caesar; **Atrebatibus**
superātīs: ablative absolute; **Atrebatēs, -ium,** m (plural): a tribe of
northwestern Gallia Belgica; **superō, -āre, -āvī, -ātus:** overcome,
conquer; **rex, rēgis,** m: king (*rēgem:* object complement of *con-
stituerat*); **constituō, -ere, constituī, constitūtus:** place, appoint;
virtūs, virtūtis, f: courage, bravery; **consilium, -iī,** n: counsel,
good judgment; **probō, -āre, -āvī, -ātus:** approve; **fidēlis, -e:** faithful, trustworthy; **arbitror, -ārī, -ātus sum:** think; **auctōritās, -ātis,**
f: influence, authority; **magnī habēbātur:** "was considered great"
(*magnī:* genitive of value).

26.4. **Caesar, *de Bello Gallico* 6.13.1–2:** The plight of the lower classes
in Gaul.

In omnī Galliā eōrum hominum, quī aliquō sunt
numerō atque honōre, genera sunt duo. Nam plēbēs
paene servōrum habētur locō, quae nihil audet per sē,
nūllō adhibētur consiliō. Plērīque, cum aut aere aliēnō
aut magnitūdine tribūtōrum aut iniūriā potentiōrum
premuntur, sēsē in servitūtem dicant nōbilibus, quibus
in hōs eadem omnia sunt iūra, quae dominīs in servōs.

Notes: **eōrum hominum:** construe with *genera duo*; **aliquī, aliqua, aliquod:** some, any; **numerus, -ī,** m: account, estimation,
esteem; **honor, -ōris,** m: respect, distinction (*numerō atque honōre:*
ablatives of description); **plēbēs, -ēī,** f: common people; **paene:**
nearly, almost; **quae:** modifies *plēbēs*; **nullō** = *nullī*; **adhibeō, -ēre,**
-uī, -itus + dative: bring forward, summon, admit; **consilium,**
-ī, n: deliberation, council; **plērīque, plēraeque, plēraque** (plural): the most, the majority; **aut...aut...aut:** either...or...or; **aes,**
aeris, n: copper, money (*aes aliēnum:* debt; used here as an ablative of means); **magnitūdō, magnitūdinis,** f: size; **tribūtum, -ī,** n:
tax, tribute; **potens, potentis:** powerful (man); **premō, -ere, pressī,**
pressus: press; **dicō, -āre, -āvī, -ātus:** dedicate, devote, offer; **qui-**
bus, dominīs: datives of possession; **in hōs:** over them; **iūs, iūris,**
n: right, justice, law; **quae** (*iūra*) **dominīs** (*sunt*) **in servōs.**

26.5. Caesar, *de Bello Gallico* 6.21.2: The gods particularly worshipped by the Germans.

> Deōrum numerō eōs sōlōs dūcunt, quōs cernunt et
> quōrum apertē opibus iuvantur, Sōlem et Vulcānum et
> Lūnam; reliquōs nē fāmā quidem accēpērunt.

Notes: **deus, -ī,** m: god; **sōlus, -a, -um:** only, alone; **dūcō, -ere, duxī, ductus:** consider; **cernō, -ere, crēvī, crētus:** discern, distinguish; **quōrum:** whose (referring to the gods, take as possessive with *opibus*); **apertē:** openly; **ops, opis,** f: power, wealth; **iuvō, iuvāre, iūvī, iūtus:** help, assist; **Sōl, Sōlis,** m: sun, the sun god; **Vulcānus, -ī,** m: the god of fire; **Lūna, -ae,** f: Moon; **reliquus, -a, -um:** remaining; **nē... quidem:** not even; **fāma, -ae,** f: rumor, reputation.

27. CORRELATIVES

27.1. Catullus 87: Catullus declares that he has loved Lesbia as much as any man has ever loved a woman. Meter: elegiac couplets.

> Nulla potest mulier tantum sē dīcere amātam
> vērē, quantum ā mē Lesbia amāta mea est.
> Nulla fidēs ullō fuit umquam foedere tanta,
> quanta in amōre tuō ex parte reperta meā est.

Notes: **mulier, mulieris,** f: woman; **tantum... quantum:** as much as; **amātam** (*esse*): perfect passive infinitive in indirect statement; **vērē:** truly; **fidēs, -ēī,** f: faith, trust; **ullus, -a, -um:** any; **umquam:** ever; **foedus, foederis,** n: treaty, alliance; **in amōre tuō:** "in your love" (i.e., in love of you); **ex parte... meā:** "on my part"; **re(p)periō, -īre, re(p)perī, re(p)pertus:** find, discover.

27.2. Ovid, *Metamorphoses* 3.381–384: Echo, the chattering nymph whom Juno punished by reducing her merely to a voice, has fallen in love with the handsome youth Narcissus. Echo's voice calls out to Narcissus; he hears the voice, but sees no one. Meter: dactylic hexameter.

> Hic stupet, utque aciem partēs dīmittit in omnēs,
> vōce "Venī!" magnā clāmat: vocat illa vocantem.

Respicit et rursus nullō veniente "Quid" inquit
"mē fugis?" Et totidem, quot dixit, verba recēpit.

Notes: **hic:** Narcissus; **stupeō, -ēre, stupuī:** be amazed, **utque** = *ut* + *-que* (here, *ut* is temporal); **aciēs, -ēī,** f: edge, piercing look, glance; **dīmittō, -ere, dīmīsī, dīmissus:** send forth, cast; **vox, vōcis,** f: voice; **clāmō, -āre, -āvī, -ātus:** shout (Narcissus is the subject of *clāmat*); **vocō, -āre, -āvī, -ātus:** summon; **illa:** Echo; **vocantem** (*Narcissum*); **respiciō, -ere, respexī, respectus:** look back (Narcissus is the subject of *respicit* as well as *inquit* and *recēpit*); **rursus:** again; **nullō veniente:** ablative absolute; **quid:** why?; **totidem…quot:** as many as (understand with *verba*); Echo is the subject of *dixit*; **verbum, -ī,** n: word; **recipiō, -ere, recēpī, receptus:** receive, take back.

27.3.   Livy, *ab Urbe Condita* 1.42.1–2: The fifth king of Rome, Lucius Tarquinius Priscus, has just died, and Tanaquil, his queen, has chosen her son-in-law Servius Tullius as her husband's successor. Fearing an uprising led by Tarquinius's sons, Servius takes steps to strengthen his position. Ruling 578–535 BCE, Servius was known as the "Law-Giver."

Nec iam pūblicīs magis consiliīs Servius quam prīvātīs mūnīre opēs, et nē, quālis Ancī līberum animus adversus Tarquinium fuerat, tālis adversus sē Tarquinī līberum esset, duās fīliās iuvenibus rēgiīs, Luciō atque Arruntī Tarquiniīs, iungit; nec rūpit tamen fātī necessitātem hūmānīs consiliīs quīn invidia regnī etiam inter domesticōs infīda omnia atque infesta faceret.

Notes: **magis…quam:** more than; **consilium, -iī,** n: consultation, deliberation; **mūniō, -īre, -īvī, -ītus:** fortify, protect (*mūnīre:* historical infinitive; translate as a regular finite verb with Servius as the subject); **ops, opis,** f: power, strength; **nē:** triggers a negative purpose clause *tālis…esset*; **quālis…fuerat:** correlative clause depending on *nē tālis…esset*; **quālis…tālis:** as much as; **Ancus, -ī,** m: Ancus Marcius, the fourth king of Rome (reigned 640–616 BCE); **līberum** = *līberōrum* from *līberī, -ōrum*, m (plural): children; **animus, -ī,** m: mind, spirit, heart; **adversus** + accusative: against; **Tarquinius, -ī,** m: Lucius Tarquinius Priscus, the fifth king of Rome; **tālis** (*animus*); **sē:** Servius Tullius; **līberum:** depends on an understood *animus*; **fīlia, -ae**, f: daughter; **iuvenis, -is**, m: young man; **rēgius, -a, -um**: royal; **Luciō atque Arruntī Tarquiniīs**: the sons of Lucius Tarquinius Priscus (take in apposition to *iuvenibus rēgiīs*); **iungō, -ere, iunxī, iunctus**: join, "marry"; **rumpō, -ere, rūpī, ruptus**: break (Servius is the subject); **fātum, -ī**, n: fate, destiny; **necessitās, -ātis**, f: inevitability; **quīn**: but that; **invidia, -ae**, f: envy, ill will, jealousy; **regnum, -ī**, n: kingdom; **inter** + accusative: between, among, within; **domesticī, -ōrum**, m (plural): members of the household; **infīdus, -a, -um**: faithless, treacherous; **infestus, -a, -um**: dangerous, hostile.

28. DEPONENT VERBS

28.1. *ILS* 6037: Lyon (Lugdunum, Gallia Lugdunensis). Painted above a gate. Not all bed-and-breakfasts are as nice as mine.

> Mercurius hīc lucrum prōmit[t]it, Apollō salūtem.
> Septumānus hospitium cum prandiō. Quī vēnerit,
> melius ūtētur post; hospes, ubi maneās, prospice.

Notes: **Mercurius, -ī**, m: Mercury, the Roman god of commerce; **hīc**: here; **lucrum, -ī**, n: profit; **prōmittō, -ere, prōmīsī, prōmissus**: promise; **Apollō, Apollinis**, m: Apollo, the Greek god of poetry and healing; **salūs, salūtis**, f: health, safety, welfare; **Septumānus, -ī**, m: a man's name (an archaic spelling of *septimānus, -a, -um*: seventh, soldier of the seventh legion); **hospitium, -iī**, n: hospitality; **prandium, -iī**, n: a late breakfast, lunch; **veniō, -īre, vēnī, ventus**: come, arrive, reach; **melius**: better; **ūtor, -ī, ūsus sum** + ablative: use, "fare"; **post**: afterward, next; **hospes, hospitis**, m: guest, host; **ubi**: where; **maneō, -ēre, mansī, mansus**: stay, remain; **proscipiō, -ere, prospexī, prospectus**: look out, take care, exercise forethought.

28.2. Martial 3.43: You can try to look younger, but you can't cheat death. Meter: elegiac couplets.

> Mentīris iuvenem tinctīs, Laetīne, capillīs,
>   tam subitō corvus, quī modo cycnus erās.
> Nōn omnēs fallis; scit tē Prōserpina cānum:
>   persōnam capitī dētrahet illa tuō.

Notes: **mentior, -īrī, -ītus sum**: assert falsely, lie (introduces an indirect statement without an infinitive, understand *esse*); **iuvenis, -is**, m: young man; **tinctus, -a, -um**: colored, dyed; **Laetīnus, -ī**, m: a man's name, "Mr. Cheerful"; **capillus, -ī**, m: hair; **tam**: so; **subitō**: suddenly; **corvus, -ī**, m: raven (a black-feathered bird); **modo**: just now, a moment ago; **cycnus, -ī**, m: swan (a white-feathered bird); **fallō, -ere, fefellī, falsus**: deceive, trick; **sciō, -īre, scīvī, scītus**: know (introduces an indirect statement without an infinitive); **cānus, -a, -um**: gray-haired, white-haired; **persōna, -ae**, f: actor's mask; **caput, capitis**, n: head; **dētrahō, -ere, dētraxī, dētractus**: pull down (something in the accusative case) from (someone in the dative case); **illa**: Proserpina, the queen of the Underworld.

28.3. Caesar, *de Bello Gallico* 6.16.1–3: Gallic superstitions.

Nātiō est omnium Gallōrum admodum dēdita religiōnibus, atque ob eam causam quī sunt adfectī graviōribus morbīs quīque in proeliīs perīculīsque versantur, aut prō victimīs hominēs immolant aut sē immolātūrōs vovent, administrīsque ad ea sacrificia druidibus ūtuntur; quod, prō vītā hominis nisi hominis vīta reddātur, nōn posse deōrum immortālium nūmen plācārī arbitrantur, pūblicēque eiusdem generis habent instītūta sacrificia.

Notes: **nātiō, -ōnis**, f: tribe, race, people; **admodum**: completely; **dēdō, -ere, dēdidī, dēditus**: devote; **religiō, -ōnis**, f: rite, worship, religious scruple; **ob** + accusative: on account of, because of; **adficiō, -ere, adfēcī, adfectus**: influence, affect; **gravis, -e**: severe; **morbus, -ī**, m: disease; **proelium, -iī**, n: battle; **perīculum, -ī**, n: danger; **versō, -āre, -āvī, -ātus**: be involved in (here with a reflexive, or middle sense, as in Greek); **aut...aut**: either...or; **prō victimīs**: "as victims"; **immolō, -āre, -āvī, -ātus**: sacrifice; **voveō, -ēre, vōvī, vōtus**: promise solemnly (triggers an indirect statement: *immolātūrōs* [*esse*]); **administer, administrī**, m: attendant; **ad** + accusative: for the purpose of; **sacrificium, -iī**, n: sacrifice; **ūtor, -ī, ūsus sum** + ablative: use; **quod**: because; **reddō, -ere, reddidī, redditus**: give back, exchange (*reddātur*: subjunctive verb in indirect statement); **nūmen, nūminis**, n: divine spirit; **plācō, -āre, -āvī, -ātus**: appease, calm; **arbitror, -ārī, -ātus sum**: think; **genus,**

generis, n: type, kind; **instituō, -ere, instituī, institūtus**: put in place, establish.

28.4. Cicero, *in Catilinam* 1.1: The opening words of Cicero's first vituperative speech against Catiline. Cicero chides Catiline for his arrogance.

> Quō usque tandem abūtēre, Catilīna, patientiā nostrā?
> Quam diū etiam furor iste tuus nōs ēlūdet? Quem ad
> fīnem sēsē effrēnāta iactābit audācia?

Notes: **quō**: to what purpose?; **usque**: continuously, all the way; **tandem**: at length (used to emphasize urgency or exasperation); **abūtor, -ī, -ūsus sum** + ablative: abuse; **quam diū**: how long?; **ēlūdō, -ere, ēlūsī, ēlūsus**: mock; **effrēnātus, -a, -um**: unbridled, unchecked (with *audācia*); **iactō, -āre, -āvī, -ātus**: throw, shake, disturb; **audācia, -ae**, f: recklessness, confidence.

28.5. Vergil, *Aeneid* 1.198–207: Aeneas and his Trojans have just survived the Juno-sent storm, and Aeneas gives them encouragement on the shores of Carthage. Meter: dactylic hexameter.

> "Ō sociī (neque enim ignārī sumus ante malōrum),
> ō passī graviōra, dabit deus hīs quoque fīnem.
> Vōs et Scyllaeam rabiem penitusque sonantīs
> accestis scopulōs, vōs et Cyclōpia saxa
> expertī: revocāte animōs maestumque timōrem
> mittite; forsan et haec ōlim meminisse iuvābit.
> Per variōs cāsūs, per tot discrīmina rērum
> tendimus in Latium, sēdēs ubi fāta quiētās
> ostendunt; illīc fās regna resurgere Trōiae.
> Dūrāte, et vōsmet rēbus servāte secundīs."

Notes: **socius, -iī**, m: ally, follower; **ignārus, -a, -um** + genitive: ignorant of; **ante**: previously, in the past; **malum, -ī**, n: evil, misfortune; **patior, -ī, passus sum**: suffer, endure; **gravis, -e**: serious; **quoque**: also; **fīnis, -is**, m: end; **Scyllaeus, -a, -um**: of Scylla, a sea monster who tried to eat sailors; **rabiēs, -ēī**, f: rage, madness, fury; **penitus**: deeply; **sonō, -āre, -āvī, -ātus**: resound, roar; **accestis** = *accessistis* from *accēdō, -ere, accessī*: approach; **scopulus, -ī**, m: rock, cliff; **Cyclōpius, -a, -um**: of the Cyclopes, the one-eyed giants who live in Sicily; **saxum, -ī,** n: rock, cliff, crag; **experior, -īrī, expertus sum:** try, experience; **revocō, -āre, -āvī, -ātus:** recall, restore; **animus, -ī,** m: soul, spirit; **maestus, -a, -um:** sad, mournful, gloomy; **timor, -ōris,** m: fear, dread; **forsan** = *forsitan:* perhaps; **ōlim:** at some time; **meminī, meminisse:** remember (see note on 5.8); **iuvō, -āre, iūvī, iūtus:** please; **varius, -a, -um:** varied, different; **cāsus, -ūs,** m: misfortune; **tot:** so many; **discrīmen, discrīminis,** n: crisis, danger; **tendō, -ere, tetendī, tentus:** hasten; **Latium, -iī,** n: Latium, the central area of Italy, the district around Rome; **sēdēs, sēdis,** f: seat, habitation, region; **fātum, -ī,** n: fate; **quiētus, -a, -um:** calm, peaceful; **ostendō, -ere, ostendī, ostensus:** show, promise; **illīc:** there; **fās** (indeclinable): divine will; **regnum, -ī,** n: kingdom; **resurgō, -ere, resurrexī, resurrectus:** rise again; **Trōia, Trōiae,** f: the city of Troy; **dūrō, -āre, -āvī, -ātus:** endure; **-met:** intensive enclitic (*vōsmet:* "you, your very selves"); **servō, -āre, -āvī, -ātus:** preserve, save, rescue; **secundus, -a, -um:** favorable.

28.6. Vergil, *Aeneid* 1.335–337: In Carthage Aeneas unknowingly meets his mother, Venus, and flatters her by comparing her to one of Diana's attendants. Venus rejects the compliment. Meter: dactylic hexameter.

Tum Venus: "Haud equidem tālī mē dignor honōre;
virginibus Tyriīs mōs est gestāre pharetram
purpureōque altē sūrās vincīre coturnō."

Notes: **tum:** then; **Venus, Veneris,** f: goddess of love (understand *dixit*); **haud:** by no means; **equidem:** indeed; **tālis, -e:** such; **dignor, -ārī, -ātus sum:** deem worthy; **honor, -ōris,** m: honor, glory, reward; **virgō, virginis,** f: girl, maiden; **Tyrius, -a, -um:** Tyrian, Carthaginian; **mōs, mōris,** m: custom, law; **gestō, -āre, -āvī, -ātus:** wear, carry; **pharetra, -ae,** f: quiver; **purpureus, -a, -um:** purple; **altē:** high up; **sūra, -ae,** f: calf of the leg; **vinciō, -īre, vinxī, vinctus:** bind, tie; **coturnus, -ī,** m: high boot.

28.7. Vergil, *Aeneid* 1.144–147: Cymothoe, a sea nymph, and Triton, the sea god and son of Neptune, help Neptune calm the storm that Juno ordered against the Trojans. Meter: dactylic hexameter.

Cȳmothoē simul et Trītōn adnixus acūtō
dētrūdunt nāvīs scopulō; levat ipse tridentī

> et vastās aperit Syrtīs et temperat aequor
> atque rotīs summās levibus perlābitur undās.

Notes: **Cȳmothoē, -ēs,** f: Cymothoe, a sea nymph, "swift as a wave"; **simul:** at the same time; **Trītōn, -ōnis,** m: Triton, a sea god; **adnītor, -ī, -nixus sum:** lean against; **acūtus, -a, -um:** sharp, pointed; **dētrūdō, -ere, dētrūsī, dētrūsus:** push off, dislodge; **nāvis, -is,** f: ship; **scopulus, -ī,** m: rock, cliff; **levō, -āre, -āvī, -ātus:** lift, raise; **ipse:** Neptune; **tridens, tridentis,** m: trident; **vastus, -a, -um:** desolate, vast, enormous; **aperiō, -īre, aperuī, apertus:** open; **syrtis, -is,** f: sandbar, reef, here likely referring to either Syrtis Major (Gulf of Sidra) on the northern coast of Libya or Syrtis Minor (Gulf of Gabès) on the eastern coast of Tunisia; **temperō, -āre, -āvī, -ātus:** calm, control; **aequor, -oris,** n: level surface, sea; **rota, -ae,** f: wheel, chariot; **summus, -a, -um:** highest (superlative of *superus, -a, -um*); **levis, -e:** light, swift; **perlābor, -ī, -lapsus sum:** glide over; **unda, -ae,** f: wave, sea.

29. INFINITIVES IN COMPLEX SENTENCES

29.1. Caesar, *de Bello Gallico* 6.21.3–5: The German culture of war and hunting.

> Vīta omnis in vēnātiōnibus atque in studiīs reī mīlitāris consistit: ab parvulīs labōrī ac dūritiae student. Quī diūtissimē impūberēs permansērunt, maximam inter suōs ferunt laudem: hōc aliī statūram, aliī vīrēs nervōsque confirmārī putant. Intrā annum vērō vīcēsimum fēminae nōtitiam habuisse in turpissimīs habent rēbus; cuius reī nulla est occultātiō, quod et prōmiscuē in flūminibus perluuntur et pellibus aut parvīs rēnōnum tegimentīs ūtuntur, magnā corporis parte nūdā.

Notes: **vēnātiō, -ōnis,** f: hunting; **studium, -iī,** n: pursuit, eagerness; **rēs mīlitāris, reī mīlitāris,** f: warfare; **consistō, -ere,**

constitī: be occupied, be taken up with; **parvulus, -a, -um**: very young (*parvulīs*: substantive, "childhood"); **labor, -ōris**, m: work, labor; **dūritia, -ae**, f: hardship, austerity; **studeō, -ēre, -uī** + dative: strive for, be devoted to, pursue; **diū**: for a long time (*diūtissimē*: superlative adverb); **impūbēs, impūberis**: celibate, youthful; **permaneō, -ēre, permansī, permansus**: remain; **inter** + accusative: between, among, within; **suōs** (*hominēs*); **laus, laudis**, f: praise; **hōc**: ablative of cause; **aliī...aliī**: some...others; **statūra, -ae**, f: size; **statūram** (*confirmārī*); **vīs, vis**, f (irregular noun): strength; **nervus, -ī**, m: muscle; **confirmō, -āre, -āvī, -ātus**: strengthen, assure; **putō, -āre, -āvī, -ātus**: think; **intrā** + accusative: before; **vīcēsimus, -a, -um**: twentieth; **fēminae**: objective genitive; **nōtitia, -ae**, f: knowledge ("sex"); **turpis, -e**: disgraceful, shameful; **habent**: they consider; **cuius rēī**: "in this matter (of sex)"; **occultātiō, -ōnis**, f: hiding; **prōmiscuē**: together, in common; **flūmen, flūminis**, n: stream; **perluō, -ere, perluī, perlūtus**: bathe, wash; **pellis, -is**, f: skin, hide; **rēnō, -ōnis**, m: fur; **tegimentum, -ī**, n: covering; **ūtor, -ī, ūsus sum** + ablative: use; **magnā...nūdā**: ablative absolute.

29.2. Cicero, *Philippica* 2.30: Cicero charges that Marc Antony hypocritically condemns Cicero's involvement in Caesar's murder, while praising Brutus, who wielded the dagger.

> Ergō ego scelerātus appellor ā tē, quem tū suspicātum aliquid suspicāris; ille, quī stillantem prae sē pūgiōnem tulit, is ā tē honōris causā nōminātur? Estō; sit in verbīs tuīs hic stupor; quantō in rēbus sententiīsque māior?

Notes: **ergō**: therefore; **ego**: Cicero; **scelerātus, -ī**, m: criminal; **appellō, -āre, -āvī, -ātus**: call; **tē**: Antony; **suspicātum** (*esse*); **suspicor, -ārī, -ātus sum**: suspect; **aliquis, aliquid**: someone, something; **ille**: Brutus; **stillō, -āre, -āvī, -ātus**: drip; **prae** + ablative: in front of; **pūgiō, pūgiōnis**, m: dagger; **ferō, ferre, tulī, lātus**: hold; **is**: Brutus; **honor, -ōris**, m: honor, glory; **causā** + genitive: for the sake of; **nōminō, -āre, -āvī, -ātus**: call; **estō**: "so be it" (third person singular imperative of *esse*); **sit**: hortatory subjunctive of *esse*; **verbum, -ī**, n: word; **stupor, -ōris**, m: stupidity; **quantō** (*stupor est*); **quantō**: how much (construe with *māior*); **rēs, rēī**, f: action; **sententia, -ae**, f: opinion, intention.

29.3. Vergil, *Aeneid* 1.94–101: In the midst of the storm that Juno ordered against the Trojans, Aeneas cries out in despair. Meter: dactylic hexameter.

> "Ō terque quaterque beātī,
> quīs ante ōra patrum Trōiae sub moenibus altīs
> contigit oppetere! Ō Danaum fortissime gentis
> Tȳdīdē! Mēne Īliacīs occumbere campīs
> nōn potuisse tuāque animam hanc effundere dextrā
> saevus ubi Aeacidae tēlō iacet Hector, ubi ingens
> Sarpēdōn, ubi tot Simoīs correpta sub undīs
> scūta virum galeāsque et fortia corpora volvit?"

Notes: **ter:** three times; **quater:** four times; **beātus, -a, -um:** blessed; **quīs** = *quibus*; **ōs, ōris,** n: mouth, face, expression; **pater, patris,** m: father; **moenia, -ium,** n (plural): walls; **contingō, -ere, contigī, contactus:** happen; **oppetō, -ere, -īvī, -ītus:** meet (death); **Danaum** = *Danaōrum* from *Danaus, -a, -um:* Greek; **fortis, -e:** strong, courageous; **gens, gentis,** f: nation, race; **Tȳdīdēs, -ae,** m: Diomedes, son of Tydeus; **-ne:** introduces a question; **Īliacus, -a, -um:** Trojan; **occumbō, -ere, occubuī, occubitus:** fall (in death); **campus, -ī,** m: plain, field, battlefield; **nōn potuisse:** infinitive used as main verb in an exclamation; **anima, -ae,** f: breath, life, soul; **effundō, -ere, effūdī, effūsus:** pour out; **dexter, dextra, dextrum:** right (hand); **saevus, -a, -um:** fierce, cruel; **Aeacidēs, -ae,** m: Achilles, descendant of Aeacus; **tēlum, -ī,** n: weapon; **iaceō, -ēre, iacuī, iacitus:** lie; **Hector, -oris,** m: Hector, a Trojan warrior and the best son of Priam; **ingens, ingentis:** huge; **Sarpēdōn, -onis,** m: Sarpedon, a Lycian king and Trojan ally; **tot:** so many; **Simoīs, Simoentis,** m: Simois, a river near Troy; **corripiō, -ere, corripuī, correptus:** snatch up; **unda, -ae,** f: wave; **scūtum, -ī,** n: shield; **virum** = *virōrum*; **galea, -ae,** f: helmet; **corpus, corporis,** n: body; **volvō, -ere, volvī, volūtus:** roll, revolve.

30. INDIRECT STATEMENT

30.1.   *CIL* IV 1904: Pompeii. The burden of graffiti.

> Admīror, ō pariens, tē nōn cecidisse ruīnīs quī tot scrīptōrum taedia sustineās.

Notes: **admīror, -ārī, -ātus sum:** wonder; **pariens:** a slip for *pariēs, parietis,* m: wall; **cadō, -ere, cecidī, cāsus:** fall; **ruīna, -ae,** f: ruin; **tot:** so many; **scriptor, -ōris,** m: writer, scribbler; **taedium, -iī,** n: nuisance, weariness; **sustineō, -ēre, sustinuī, sustentus:** support, sustain.

30.2. Martial 3.61: If you don't ask for anything, I won't refuse you anything. Meter: elegiac couplets.

> Esse nihil dīcis quidquid petis, improbe Cinna:
> sī nīl, Cinna, petis, nīl tibi, Cinna, negō.

Notes: **quidquid petis:** subject of *esse;* **petō, -ere, -īvī, -ītus:** ask; **improbus, -a, -um:** bad, wicked, shameless; **Cinna, -ae,** m: a Roman cognomen from *cinnus, -ī,* m: grimace; **nīl** = *nihil;* **negō, -āre, -āvī, -ātus:** deny, refuse.

30.3. Martial 5.47: Philo never eats at home. Meter: elegiac couplets.

> Numquam sē cēnāsse domī Philo iūrat, et hoc est:
> nōn cēnat, quotiens nēmo vocāvit eum.

Notes: **numquam:** never; **cēnāsse** = *cēnāvisse* from *cēnō, -āre, -āvī, -ātus:* dine; **domī:** at home (locative case); **Philō, -ōnis,** m: a Greek man's name, "lover" (final -o scans as short in this poem in order for the meter to work out correctly); **iūrō, -āre, -āvī, -ātus:** swear, take an oath; **et hoc est:** "and this is true"; **quotiens:** as many times as, as often as; **nēmō, nēminis,** m/f: no one (final -o scans as short here, as above); **vocō, -āre, -āvī, -ātus:** summon, invite.

30.4. Cicero, *in Catilinam* 1.2: Cicero suggests Catiline's punishment. (Use this passage to contrast how the accusative/infinitive construction functions with impersonal verbs such as *oportet.*)

> Ad mortem tē, Catilīna, dūcī iussū consulis iam prīdem oportēbat, in tē conferrī pestem quam tū in nōs omnīs iam diū māchināris.

Notes: **iussus, -ūs,** m: order, decree (this noun is used only in the ablative singular); **iam:** already; **prīdem:** for a long time; **oportet,** oportēre, oportuit: it is fitting; in + accusative: against; conferō, -ferre, contulī, collātus: bring together; pestis, -is, f: plague, destruction; māchinor, -ārī, -ātus sum: devise, plan.

30.5. Caesar, *de Bello Gallico* 6.17.2: How Roman and Gallic ideas about the gods are similar.

> Dē hīs eandem ferē, quam reliquae gentēs, habent
> ōpiniōnem: Apollinem morbōs dēpellere, Minervam
> operum atque artificiōrum initia trādere, Iovem impe-
> rium caelestium tenēre, Martem bella regere.

Notes: īdem, eadem, idem: the same; ferē: nearly; reliquus, -a, -um: remaining; gens, gentis, f: nation, people; (*Gallī*) habent; ōpiniō, -ōnis, f: idea, notion, expectation; Apollinem...regere: four indirect statements; morbus, -ī, m: disease; dēpellō, -ere, dēpulī, dēpulsus: drive away, ward off; opus, operis, n: work, labor; artificium, -iī, n: trade, skill; initium, -iī, n: beginning, element, first principles; trādō, -ere, tradidī, traditus: hand down; impe-rium, -iī, n: command, control, dominion; caelestis, -e: heavenly (*caelestium*: substantive, objective genitive, "heavens"); bellum, -ī, n: war; regō, -ere, rexī, rectus: guide, direct.

30.6. Catullus 72: Catullus, disillusioned but sober, explores the emo-tional roller coaster of his affair with Lesbia. Meter: elegiac couplets.

> Dīcēbās quondam sōlum tē nōsse Catullum,
> Lesbia, nec prae mē velle tenēre Iovem.
> Dīlexī tum tē nōn tantum ut vulgus amīcam,
> sed pater ut gnātōs dīligit et generōs.
> Nunc tē cognōvī: quārē etsī impensius ūror,
> multō mī tamen es vīlior et lēvior.
> Quī potis est, inquis? Quod amantem iniūria tālis
> cōgit amāre magis, sed bene velle minus.

Notes: quondam: once; nōsse = *nōvisse* from *noscō, -ere, nōvī, nōtus*: know; prae + ablative: before, in comparison with; dīligō, -ere, dīlexī, dīlectus: love, esteem, value; tum: then, next, at that time; **nōn tantum...sed**: not only...but (also); **ut** + indicative: as, like; **vulgus, -ī**, n: crowd, mob, rabble; **vulgus** (*dīligit*); **gnātus, -ī**, m: son; **gener, generī**, m: son-in-law; **cognōscō, -ere, cognōvī, cognitus**: know; **quārē**: wherefore; **etsī**: even if; **impensus, -a, -um**: strong, considerate (*impensius*: comparative adverb); **ūrō, -ere, ussī, ustus**: burn; **multō**: ablative of degree of difference; **mī** = *mihi*; **vīlis, -e**: of little value, cheap; **lēvis, -e**: smooth, delicate; **quī potis est**: "how can it be?"; **quod**: because; **amans, amantis**, m/f: lover; **tālis, -e**: such, of such a kind; **cōgō, -ere, coēgī, coactus**: compel; **magis**: more; **bene velle**: wish well; **minus**: less.

30.7. Vergil, *Aeneid* 1.124–129: Noticing the storm raised against the Trojans, Neptune is angry that Juno and Aeolus are interfering in his divine realm. Meter: dactylic hexameter.

> Intereā magnō miscērī murmure pontum
> ēmissamque hiemem sensit Neptūnus et īmīs
> stāgna refūsa vadīs, graviter commōtus; et altō
> prospiciens summā placidum caput extulit undā.
> Disiectam Aenēae tōtō videt aequore classem,
> fluctibus oppressōs Trōas caelīque ruīnā.

Notes: **intereā**: meanwhile; **misceō, -ēre, -uī, mixtus**: confuse; **murmur, murmuris**, n: murmur, rumble; **pontus, -ī**, m: sea; **ēmittō, -ere, ēmīsī, ēmissus**: send forth; **hiems, hiemis**, f: winter, storm; **sentiō, -īre, sensī, sensus**: perceive; **Neptūnus, -ī**, m: Neptune, the god of the sea; **īmus, -a, -um**: lowest (superlative of *inferus -a, -um*); **stāgnum, -ī**, n: deep water, still water; **refundō, -ere, refūdī, refūsus**: pour back; **vadum, -ī**, n: shallow, shoal; **graviter**: severely; **commoveō, -ēre, commōvī, commōtus**: disturb; **altum, -ī**, n: the deep (sea); **prospiciō, -ere, prospexī, prospectus**: see, look out over; **summus, -a, -um**: highest (superlative of *superus, -a, -um*); **placidus, -a, -um**: calm, peaceful; **caput, capitis**, n: head; **efferō, -ferre, extulī, ēlātus**: raise up; **unda, -ae**, f: wave, sea; **disiciō, -ere, disiēcī, disiectus**: scatter, disperse; **Aenēās, -ae**, m: Aeneas, the Trojan leader; **tōtus, -a, -um**: all, every; **aequor, -oris**, n: sea, waves; **classis, -is**, f: fleet; **fluctus, -ūs**, m: wave, flood, sea; **opprimō, -ere, oppressī, oppressus**: overwhelm, crush; **Trōs, Trōis**, m: Trojan; **caelum, -ī**, n: sky; **ruīna, -ae**, f: downfall.

31. PARTICIPLES

31.1. Martial 3.14: To starve in Rome or at home? Meter: iambic strophe.

> Rōmam petēbat ēsurītor Tuccius
> profectus ex Hispāniā;
> occurrit illī sportulārum fābula:
> ā ponte rediit Mulviō.

Notes: **petō, -ere, -īvī, -ītus:** seek; **ēsurītor, -ōris,** m: hungry person; **Tuccius, -ī,** m: a Roman cognomen (the most famous member of this family was a Vestal who, accused of unchastity, vindicated herself by carrying water in a sieve [ca. 240 BCE, Livy, *Periochae* 20]); **proficiscor, -ī, profectus sum:** depart; **occurrō, -ere, occurrī, occursus** + dative: meet; **sportula, -ae,** f: little basket, distribution of the dole; **fābula, -ae,** f: rumor, story, tale; **pons, pontis,** m: bridge (the Mulvian Bridge was just outside the *Porta Flaminia,* the north gate of Rome; Tuccius never even entered Rome!); **redeō, -īre, -iī, -itus:** return.

31.2. Martial 5.66: An ungracious acquaintance. Meter: elegiac couplets.

> Saepe salūtātus numquam prior ipse salūtās:
> sīc eris aeternum, Pontiliāne, valē.

Notes: **salūtō, -āre, -āvī, -ātus:** greet; **numquam:** never; **prior, prius:** first; **aeternum valē:** a common way of addressing the deceased; **Pontiliānus, -ī,** m: a Roman name from *pons, pontis,* m: bridge.

31.3. Caesar, *de Bello Gallico* 5.8.2: At the beginning of his second invasion of Britain in 54 BCE, Caesar is driven off course.

> Et lēnī Āfricō prōvectus, mediā circiter nocte ventō
> intermissō, cursum nōn tenuit et, longius dēlātus aestū,
> ortā lūce, sub sinistrā Britanniam relictam conspexit.

Notes: understand Caesar as the subject of the passage; **lēnis, -e:** smooth, gentle; **Āfricus, -ī,** m: southwest wind; **prōvehō, -ere,**

prōvexī, prōvectus: carry forward; **circiter**: approximately; **nox, noctis,** f: night; **ventō**...**intermissō**: ablative absolute; **ventus, -ī,** m: wind; **intermittō, -ere, intermīsī, intermissus**: break, discontinue; **cursus, -ūs,** m: course; **longius**: comparative adverb; **dēferō, -ferre, dētulī, dēlātus**: carry away, confer upon; **aestus, -ūs,** m: tide; **orior, -īrī, ortus sum**: rise, begin; **lux, lūcis,** f: light; **sub sinistrā**: on the left; **relinquō, -ere, relīquī, relictus**: leave behind; **conspiciō, -ere, conspexī, conspectus**: catch sight of.

31.4. Cicero, *in Catilinam* 1.5: While Catiline plots destruction from within Rome, his associates lie in wait outside the city walls, gathering forces against the lawful Republic.

> Castra sunt in Ītaliā contrā populum Rōmānum in Etrūriae faucibus conlocāta, crescit in diēs singulōs hostium numerus; eōrum autem castrōrum imperātōrem ducemque hostium intrā moenia atque adeō in senātū vidētis intestīnam aliquam cōtīdiē perniciem reī pūblicae mōlientem.

Notes: **castra, -ōrum,** n (plural): camp; **contrā** + accusative: against; **faucēs, -ium,** f (plural): mountain pass; **conlocō, -āre, -āvī, -ātus**: place; **crescō, -ere, crēvī, crētus**: grow, increase; **in diēs singulōs**: "each successive day"; **imperātor, -ōris,** m: general; **dux, ducis,** m: leader; **intrā** + accusative: within; **moenia, -ium,** n (plural): walls; **adeō**: indeed, truly; **intestīnus, -a, -um**: internal; **aliquī, aliqua, aliquod**: some, any; **cōtīdiē**: every day; **perniciēs, -ēī,** f: destruction, threat; **mōlior, -īrī, -ītus sum**: try, attempt (participle modifying *imperātōrem ducemque*).

31.5. Vergil, *Aeneid* 1.52–54: Aeolus keeps the winds imprisoned when they are not working. Meter: dactylic hexameter.

> Hīc vastō rex Aeolus antrō
> luctantīs ventōs tempestātēsque sonōrās
> imperiō premit ac vinclīs et carcere frēnat.

Notes: **vastus, -a, -um**: vast, desolate; **rex, rēgis,** m: king (Aeolus was the king of the winds); **antrum, -ī,** n: cave; **luctor, -ārī, -ātus sum**: wrestle, struggle; **ventus, -ī,** m: breeze, wind; **tempestās,**

-ātis, f: storm; **sonōrus, -a, -um**: roaring; **imperium, -iī**, n: power; **premō, -ere, pressī, pressus**: control; **vinc(u)lum, -ī**, n: chain; **carcer, carceris**, m: prison; **frēnō, -āre, -āvī, -ātus**: curb, restrain.

31.6.   Vergil, *Aeneid* 1.102–105: Aeneas, dismayed at the ill fortune of the Trojans, has just cried out in despair when Juno's storm against the Trojans begins. Meter: dactylic hexameter.

> Tālia iactantī strīdens Aquilōne procella
> vēlum adversa ferit, fluctūsque ad sīdera tollit.
> Franguntur rēmī, tum prōra āvertit et undīs
> dat latus, insequitur cumulō praeruptus aquae mons.

Notes: **tālia iactantī** (*eī*): "to him (Aeneas) tossing about/shouting such things" (dative of reference); **tālis, -e**: such, of such sort; **iactō, -āre, -āvī, -ātus**: throw away, cast, hurl, shout; **strīdeō, -ēre, -ī**: creak, roar; **Aquilō, -ōnis**, m: north wind; **procella, -ae**, f: blast, gale; **vēlum, -ī**, n: sail; **adversus, -a, -um**: in front, opposite, hostile, unfavorable; **feriō, -īre** (no third or fourth principal parts): strike, beat; **fluctus, -ūs**, m: tide, flood, sea; **sīdus, sīderis**, n: star, sky; **tollō, -ere, sustulī, sublātus**: lift, raise; **frangō, -ere, frēgī, fractus**: break, shatter; **rēmus, -ī**, m: oar; **tum**: then; **prōra, -ae**, f: prow; **āvertō, -ere, āvertī, āversus**: turn; **unda, -ae**, f: wave, sea; **latus, lateris**, n: side; **insequor, -ī, -secūtus sum**: follow, pursue; **cumulus, -ī**, m: heap, mass; **praeruptus, -a, -um**: towering, steep; **mons, montis**, m: mountain.

31.7.   Vergil, *Aeneid* 1.340–342: Dido became queen of Carthage because of family intrigue at Tyre. Meter: dactylic hexameter.

> Imperium Dīdō Tyriā regit urbe profecta,
> germānum fugiens. Longa est iniūria, longae
> ambāgēs.

Notes: **imperium, -iī**, n: power; **Dīdō, -ūs**, f: queen of Carthage; **Tyrius, -a, -um**: Tyrian, Phoenician; **regō, -ere, rexī, rectus**: rule; **proficiscor, -ī, profectus sum**: set out, depart; **germānus, -ī**, m: brother; **fugiō, -ere, fūgī**: flee; **iniūria, -ae**, f: insult, injustice; **ambāgēs, -is**, f: devious tale, double talk, evasion.

32. ABLATIVES ABSOLUTE

32.1. *CIL* VII 451, addit. 309 [*ILS* 3562; *RIB* 1041]: Bollihope Common, Stanhope, County Durham (Britannia). An altar commemorating a successful hunt.

Silvānō Invictō sacr(um). G(aius) Tetius Veturius Miciānus pr[(a)e]f(ectus) ālae Sebōsiannae ob aprum eximiae formae captum, quem multī antecessōrēs eius praedārī nōn potuērunt, v(ōtō) s(usceptō) l(ibens) p(osuit).

Notes: **Silvānus, -ī,** m: Silvanus, a Roman god of the greenwood, or *silva;* **invictus, -a, -um:** unconquered, invincible; **sacrum, -ī,** n: a holy thing or place; **Gaius Tetius Veturius Miciānus, Gaiī Tetiī Veturiī Miciānī,** m: a man's name; **praefectus, -ī,** m: prefect, an officer in the Roman army; **āla, -ae,** f: wing, cavalry squadron; **Sebōsiannus, -a, -um:** this squadron was originally raised from the Sebusiani of Gaul (Loire Valley); **ob** + accusative: on account of, because of; **aper, aprī,** m: wild boar; **eximius, -a, -um:** exceptional, distinguished; **forma, -ae,** f: form, shape, beauty; **capiō, -ere, cēpī, captus:** take, seize, capture; **quem:** the boar; **multī, -ae, -a:** many; **antecessor, -ōris,** m: forerunner; **eius:** Gaius Tetius; **praedor, -ārī, -ātus sum:** plunder, carry off; **vōtum, -ī,** n: vow; **suscipiō, -ere, suscēpī, susceptus:** undertake; **libens, libentis,** willing, joyful; **pōnō, -ere, posuī, positus:** place, put (understand *sacrum* as direct object).

32.2. Caesar, *de Bello Gallico* 4.21.5: The Britons learn of Caesar's planned invasion in 55 BCE, and Caesar takes steps to secure allies.

Interim, consiliō eius cognitō et per mercātōrēs perlātō ad Britannōs, ā complūribus insulae cīvitātibus ad eum lēgātī veniunt, quī polliceantur obsidēs dare atque imperiō populī Rōmānī obtemperāre.

Notes: **interim:** meanwhile; **consilium, -iī,** n: plan; **eius:** Caesar; **cognoscō, -ere, cognōvī, cognitus:** learn, know; **mercātor, -ōris,** m: merchant; **perferō, -ferre, pertulī, perlātus:** carry through; **complūrēs, -a:** several, many; **insula, -ae,** f: island; **cīvitās, -ātis,** f: state, tribe; **lēgātus, -ī**, m: envoy; **polliceor, -ērī, pollicitus sum**: promise; **obses, obsidis**, m/f: hostage; **imperium, -iī**, n: command; **obtemperō, -āre, -āvī, -ātus** + dative: submit to, obey.

32.3. Caesar, *de Bello Gallico* 5.9.6: The Seventh Legion deploys into a formation to flush out hostile Britons from the woods in 54 BCE. In the *testūdō*, soldiers held their shields defensively: the front line held their shields in front, the men on the sides held their shields out to the side, soldiers within the formation held their shields overhead – this was, essentially, an ancient "tank."

At mīlitēs legiōnis septimae, testūdine factā et aggere ad mūnītiōnēs adiectō, locum cēpērunt eōsque ex silvīs expulērunt, paucīs vulneribus acceptīs.

Notes: **mīles, -itis**, m: soldier; **legiō, -ōnis**, f: legion; **septimus, -a, -um**: seventh; **testūdō, testūdinis**, f: turtle, tortoise; **agger, aggeris**, m: mound, earth; **mūnītiō, -ōnis**, f: fortification; **adiciō, -ere, adiēcī, adiectus**: join, add to; **eōs**: the Britons; **expellō, -ere, expulī, expulsus**: drive out, expel; **paucus, -a, -um**: few, little; **vulnus, vulneris**, n: wound; **accipiō, -ere, accēpī, acceptus**: receive.

33. INDEPENDENT USES OF THE SUBJUNCTIVE

33.1. *CIL* VII 140, addit. 306 [*ILS* 4730; *RIB* 306]: Lydney Park, Gloucestershire (Britannia). Lead plate. Cursing a thief.

Devō Nōdentī Silviānus ānilum perdedit; dēmediam partem dōnāvit Nōdentī. Inter quibus nōmen Seniciānī, nollis petmittās sānitātem, dōnec perfera(t) usque templum [Nō]dentis.

Notes: **Devō** = *deō* from *deus, -ī*, m: god; **Nōdens, Nōdentis**, m: a Celtic god of vengeance and healing; **Silviānus, -ī**, m: a man's name, "belonging to the woods" (see 32.1); **ānilum**: a slip for *ānulum* from *ānulus, -ī*, m: ring; **perdedit** = *perdidit* from *perdō*,

-ere, perdidī, perditus: lose; **dēmediam** = *dīmidiam* from *dīmidius, -a, -um*: half (Silvianus means to give half the ring's value to Nodens, should it be recovered); **dōnō, -āre, -āvī, -ātus**: give as a present, offer; **inter** + accusative: among; **quibus**: ablative with *inter*, instead of the accusative that we expect; **nōmen, nōminis, n**: name (understand *est*); **Seniciānus, -ī, m**: a man's name, "old man" (Silvanus names a suspect); **nollis** = *nōlis* from *nōlō, nolle, nōluī*: be unwilling, refuse (hortatory subjunctive introducing an indirect command); **petmittās** = *permittās* from *permittō, -ere, permīsī, permissus*: allow, permit (understand *ut* before *petmittās*, indirect command); **sānitās, -ātis, f**: health; **dōnec**: until; **perferō, -ferre, pertulī, perlātus**: bring, carry through, "return"; **usque**: all the way up to; **templum, -ī, n**: temple.

33.2. Martial 3.99: Don't take it personally! The addressee of this poem may have funded gladiatorial games. Meter: elegiac couplets.

> Īrascī nostrō nōn dēbēs, Cerdo, libellō:
> ars tua, nōn vīta, est carmine laesa meō.
> Innocuōs permitte salēs. Cur lūdere nōbīs
> nōn liceat, licuit sī iugulāre tibi?

Notes: **īrascor, -ī, īrātus sum**: be angry; **Cerdō, -ōnis, m**: a Roman name referring to a rather lowly craftsman (final -o scans as short here in order for the meter to work out correctly); **libellus, -ī, m**: little book; **ars, artis, f**: skill; **carmen, carminis, n**: song, poem; **laedō, -ere, laesī, laesus**: hurt, wound, injure; **innocuus, -a, -um**: harmless, innocent; **sāl, salis, m**: salt, cunning; (in plural) wit; **lūdō, -ere, lūsī, lūsus**: play; **licet, -ēre, licuit**: it is permitted (*liceat*: present subjunctive in a mixed conditional clause); **iugulō, -āre, -āvī, -ātus**: kill.

33.3. Cicero, *Philippica* 2.40: Cicero is answering Marc Antony's trumped-up charges of Cicero's unpopularity. At Rome, the wealthy classes frequently made bequests to friends and political allies as a sign of respect, esteem, and even flattery.

> Hērēditātēs mihi negāstī venīre. Utinam hoc tuum vērum crīmen esset! Plūrēs amīcī meī et necessāriī vīverent.

Notes: **hērēditās, -ātis,** f: inheritance; **negāstī** = *negāvistī* from *negō, -āre, -āvī, -ātus:* deny, refuse; **utinam:** if only, would that (introducing an optative subjunctive); **vērus, -a, -um:** true (*vērum:* subject complement); **crīmen, crīminis,** n: accusation, charge; **plūs, plūris:** more; **necessārius, -iī,** m: relative.

33.4. Vergil, *Aeneid* 4.659–662: Dido's final words before her suicide. Meter: dactylic hexameter.

> "Moriēmur inultae,
> sed moriāmur" ait. "Sīc, sīc iuvat īre sub umbrās.
> Hauriat hunc oculīs ignem crūdēlis ab altō
> Dardanus, et nostrae sēcum ferat ōmina mortis."

Notes: **morior, -ī, mortuus sum:** die (translate first plural as "I" not "we"); **inultus, -a, -um:** unavenged; **ait:** she said; **sīc:** thus; **iuvō, -āre, iūvī, iūtus:** please, help; **umbra, -ae,** f: shade, shadow; **hauriō, -īre, hausī, haustus:** drink; **ignis, -is,** m: fire, flame; **crūdēlis, -e:** cruel, harsh; **ab altō:** from the deep (sea); **Dardanus, -a, -um:** Trojan (Aeneas); **ferō, ferre, tulī, lātus:** carry, bear; **ōmen, ōminis,** n: omen, sign; **mors, mortis,** f: death.

33.5. Ovid, *Tristia,* 3.3.73–76: Ovid suggests these verses be used for his epitaph. Meter: elegiac couplets.

> Hīc ego quī iaceō tenerōrum lūsor amōrum
> ingeniō periī Nāso poēta meō;
> at tibi quī transīs nē sit grave quisquis amāstī
> dīcere "Nāsōnis molliter ossa cubent."

Notes: **iaceō, -ēre, -uī, -itus:** lie, lie dead; **tener, tenera, tenerum:** tender, delicate; **lūsor, -ōris,** m: player, humorous writer; **ingenium, -ī,** n: talent; **pereō, -īre, -iī, -itus:** die; **Nāsō, -ōnis,** m: (P. Ovidius) Naso (his cognomen means "nose"; final -o scans as short here in order for the meter to work out correctly); **transeō, -īre, -iī, -itus:** go across, pass by (*transīs:* subjunctive in relative clause of characteristic); **nē sit grave:** "let it not be difficult"; **quisquis:** whoever; **amāstī** = *amāvistī*; **os, ossis,** n: bone; **molliter:** gently, peacefully; **cubō, -āre, cubuī, cubitus:** lie.

34. CUM CLAUSES

34.1. Martial 1.38: Don't botch my poetry. Meter: elegiac couplets.

> Quem recitās meus est, ō Fīdentīne, libellus,
> sed, male cum recitās, incipit esse tuus.

Notes: **recitō, -āre, -āvī, -ātus:** recite; **Fīdentīnus, -ī,** m: a Roman name, "self-confident" or "cocky"; **libellus, -ī,** m: little book; **male:** badly; **incipiō, -ere, incēpī, inceptus:** begin.

34.2. Martial 3.15: Poor, naïve Cordus. Meter: elegiac couplets.

> Plūs crēdit nēmō tōtā quam Cordus in urbe.
> "Cum sit tam pauper, quōmodo?" Caecus amat.

Notes: **plūs, plūris:** more; **crēdō, -ere, crēdidī, crēditus:** believe, trust; **nēmō, nēminis,** m/f: no one; **Cordus, -ī,** m: a man's name from *cordus, -a, -um,* referring to late-season crops and lambs born out of season (our Cordus is, likewise, "out of season"); **tam:** so; **pauper, pauperis:** poor; **quōmodo:** how?; **caecus, -a, -um:** blind.

34.3. CIL X 846: Pompeii, temple of Isis, inscribed above the entrance to the temple precinct. The dedication commemorates the generosity of a very young philanthropist who restored the temple after the earthquake of 65 CE.

> N(umerius) Popidius N(umerī) f(īlius) Celsīnus aedem
> Īsidis terrae mōtū conlapsam ā fundāmentō p(ecūniā)
> s(uā) restituit. Hunc decuriōnēs ob līberālitātem cum
> esset annōrum sexs ōrdinī suō grātīs adlēgērunt.

Notes: **Numerius Popidius Celsīnus, Numeriī Popidiī Celsīnī,** m: a man's name (*Celsīnus:* belonging to something lofty or high); **fīlius, -iī,** m: son; **aedēs, -is,** f: temple, shrine; **Īsis, Īsidis,** f: the Egyptian goddess Isis; **mōtus, -ūs,** m: movement (*terrae mōtū:* earthquake); **conlābor, -ī, -lapsus sum:** collapse, fall down in ruin; **fundāmentum, -ī,** n: foundation; **pecūnia, -ae,** f: money; **restituō, -ere, restituī, restitūtus:** replace, restore; **hunc:** Numerius Popidius

Celsinus; **decuriō, -ōnis**, m: a member of a municipal Senate who governed and advised; **ob** + accusative: on account of; **līberālitās, -ātis**, f: generosity, kindness; **cum**: introduces a *cum* concessive clause ("although he was only six years old"); **annus, -ī**, m: year (*annōrum*: partitive genitive); **sexs** = *sex*: six (indeclinable); **ordō, ordinis**, m: rank, order; **grātīs**: without payment; **adlegō, -ere, adlēgī, adlectus**: admit, appoint, elect.

34.4. *CIL* VIII 152: Tombstone found near Thelepte (Africa), late second or early third century CE. Lucius praises his wife's companionship and frugality. The inscription forms an acrostic, with the first letter of each line spelling out the name of the deceased, rendered in crude hexameters.

> Urbānilla mihi coniunx verēcundiā plēna hīc sita est
> Rōmae comes negōtiōrum socia parsimōniō fulta.
> Bene gestīs omnibus, cum in patriā mēcum redīret,
> Au miseram Carthāgō mihi ēripuit sociam.
> Nūlla spēs vīvendī mihi sine coniuge tālī.
> Illa domum servāre meam, illa et consiliō iuvāre.
> Lūce prīvāta misera quescit in marmore clūsa.
> Lūcius ego coniunx hīc tē marmore texī
> Anc nōbīs sorte dedit fātu(m), cum lūcī darēmur.

Notes: **Urbānilla, -ae**, f: a woman's name (diminutive from *urbānus, -a, -um*: citified, elegant, sophisticated); **coniunx, coniugis**, m/f: spouse; **verēcundia, -ae**, f: modesty, respect; **plēnus, -a, -um** + ablative: rich in, full of; **sinō, -ere, sīvī, situs**: place, set down; **Rōmae**: locative case; **comes, comitis**, m/f: comrade, companion; **negōtium, -iī**, n: business; **socia, -ae**, f: companion, partner; **parsimōniō** = *parsimōniā* from *parsimōnia, -ae*, f: thrift (Lucius has erred in his declension); **fulciō, -īre, fulsī, fultus**: prop up, support; **gerō, -ere, gessī, gestus**: manage (*gestīs omnibus*: ablative absolute); **patria, -ae**, f: native land, homeland; **mēcum** = *cum mē*; **redeō, -īre, -iī, -itus**: return; **au**: goodness gracious! an interjection of consternation, used usually by women; **miser, misera, miserum**: wretched, pitiable (*miseram*: construe with *sociam*, a hyperbaton); **Carthāgō, Carthāginis**, f: an ancient city near modern Tunis, founded by the Phoenicians (and ruled by

Dido in Vergil's *Aeneid*), famously defeated by the Romans in 202 BCE, and utterly destroyed in 146 BCE. Refounded by the Romans, the city became important in the Empire; **mihi**: dative of disadvantage; **ēripiō, -ere, ēripuī, ēreptus**: snatch, take away by force; **spēs, speī**, f: hope; **vīvendī**: "of living" (gerund); **mihi**: dative of disadvatage; **sine** + ablative: without; **tālis, -e**: such, so great; **domus, -ūs**, f: house, home; **servō, -āre, -āvī, -ātus**: keep, preserve (*servāre*: historical infinitive; translate as a regular verb with *illa* as the subject); **consilium, -iī**, n: discussion, advice, council; **iuvō, -āre, iūvī, iūtus**: aid, support (*iuvāre*: historical infinitive, understand *mē* as the direct object); **lux, lūcis**, f: light (*lūce*: ablative of separation); **prīvō, -āre, -āvī, -ātus**: rob, deprive (Urbanilla is the subject of *prīvāta* and *quescit*); **quescit** = *quiescit* from *quiescō, -ere, quiēvī, quiētus*: rest, sleep; **marmor, -oris**, n: marble; **clūdō, -ere, clūdī, clūsus**: close, shut, block up (Urbanilla's husband uses the variant more common in compounds – i.e., *conclūdō*. Without a prefix, the verb is usually *claudō, -ere, clausī, clausus*); **Lūcius, -ī**, m: Urbanilla's devoted husband (for the name, see 6.1); **tegō, -ere, texī, tectus**: cover, hide; **anc** = *hanc*, referring to Urbanilla; **sors, sortis**, f: lot, chance; **fātum, -ī**, n: fate, destiny; **cum lūcī darēmur**: "for as long as we are given to the light".

35. PURPOSE CLAUSES

35.1. Martial 2.80: Fannius will do anything to avoid being punished! Meter: elegiac couplets.

> Hostem cum fugeret, sē Fannius ipse perēmit:
> hic, rogo, nōn furor est, nē moriāre, morī?

Notes: **hostis, -is**, m: enemy; **fugiō, -ere, fūgī**: flee; **Fannius, -ī**, m: perhaps Fannius Caepio, who led a conspiracy against Augustus in 23 or 22 BCE. Dio 54.3 tells us that Fannius was killed while trying to escape (the cognomen *Fannius* may refer to a type of paper); **perimō, -ere, perēmī, peremptus**: annihilate, destroy; **rogō, -āre, -āvī, -ātus**: ask (final -o scans as short here in order for the meter to work out correctly); **furor, -ōris**, m: fury, passion; **moriāre** = *moriāris* from *morior, -ī, mortuus sum*: die.

35.2. Caesar, *de Bello Gallico* 4.25.4–6: Upon reaching Britain, Caesar's standard-bearer has shamed his reluctant and aquaphobic compatriots into action. See also 17.3.

Hoc cum vōce magnā dixisset, sē ex nāvī prōiēcit atque in hostīs aquilam ferre coepit. Tum nostrī, cohortātī inter sē, nē tantum dēdecus admitterētur, ūniversī ex nāvī dēsiluērunt. Hōs item ex proximīs prīmīs nāvibus cum conspexissent, subsecūtī hostibus appropinquārent.

Notes: **nāvis, -is,** f: ship; **prōiciō, -ere, prōiēcī, prōiectus:** leap down; **in** + accusative: against; **hostis, -is,** m: enemy; **aquila, -ae,** f: eagle (see notes at 17.3 and 22.1); **coepī, coepisse, coeptus:** begin; **cohortor, -ārī, -ātus sum:** encourage (here with a reflexive, or middle sense as in Greek, "encourage each other"); **dēdecus, -oris,** n: disgrace, dishonor; **admittō, -ere, admīsī, admissus:** commit; **ūniversus, -a, -um:** all together; **dēsiliō, -īre, dēsiluī, dēsultus:** leap down; **hōs:** the men from the first ship who followed their standard-bearer; **item:** likewise; **proximus, -a, -um** (superlative of *prope*): closest, next; **conspiciō, -ere, conspexī, conspectus:** catch sight of; **subsequor, -ī, subsecūtus sum:** follow after; **appropinquō, -āre, -āvī, -ātus** + dative: approach.

35.3. Caesar, *de Bello Gallico* 6.22.3–4: The German lifestyle keeps the people hardy and preserves their image as "noble savages" in contrast with the opulence of city life at Rome.

Eius reī multās adferunt causās: nē, assiduā consuētūdine captī, studium bellī gerendī agrī cultūrā commūtent; nē lātōs fīnīs parāre studeant, potentiōrēsque humiliōrēs possessiōnibus expellant; nē accūrātius ad frīgora atque aestūs vītandōs aedificent; nē qua oriātur pecūniae cupiditās, quā ex rē factiōnēs dissensiōnēsque nascuntur; ut animī aequitāte plēbem contineant, cum suās quisque opēs cum potentissimīs aequārī videat.

Notes: **eius reī:** "for doing that" (moving every year), the reasons are explained by the following *nē* and *ut* purpose clauses; **adferō,**

-ferre, attulī, allātus: convey, allege; assiduus, -a, -um: continuous; consuētūdō, consuētūdinis, f: custom, habit; bellī gerendī: "of waging war" (gerundive construction); agrī cultūrā: ablative with the verb commūtō, -āre, -āvī, -ātus: exchange; lātus, -a, -um: wide; fīnis, -is, m: border; nē...parāre studeant: "lest they be eager to obtain"; potens, potentis: powerful; humilis, -e: humble, poor; accūrātius: comparative adverb of accūrātus, -a, -um: exact, meticulous, with care; frīgus, frīgoris, n: cold; aestus, -ūs, m: heat; vītō, -āre, -āvī, -ātus: avoid (ad...vītandōs: gerundive construction expressing purpose); aedificō, -āre, -āvī, -ātus: build; qua: any (nominative with cupiditās); orior, -īrī, ortus sum: arise; pecūnia, -ae, f: money; cupiditās, -ātis, f: desire; factiō, -ōnis, f: political party, faction; dissensiō, -ōnis, f: disagreement; nascor, -ī, nātus sum: be born, arise; aequitās, -ātis, f: uniformity, evenness (animī aequitāte: contentment); contineō, -ēre, continuī, contentus: hold back, detain, keep in hand; quisque, quaeque, quodque: each one, everybody; ops, opis, f: wealth; aequō, -āre, -āvī, -ātus: make equal.

35.4. Vergil, Aeneid 1.657–660: Venus schemes to make Dido fall in love with Aeneas. Meter: dactylic hexameter.

At Cytherēa novās artīs, nova pectore versat
consilia, ut faciem mūtātus et ōra Cupīdō
prō dulcī Ascaniō veniat, dōnīsque furentem
incendat rēgīnam atque ossibus implicet ignem.

Notes: at: but; Cytherēa, -ae, f: the Cytherean, Venus, whose sacred islands included Cythera, south of the Peloponnese; ars, artis, f: skill; pectus, pectoris, n: heart, soul; versō, -āre, -āvī, -ātus: keep turning; consilium, -iī, n: plan; faciēs, -ēī, f: face, appearance (faciem: accusative of respect); mūtō, -āre, -āvī, -ātus: transform, alter; ōs, ōris, n: face (ōra: accusative of respect); Cupīdō, Cupīdinis, m: Cupid; prō + ablative: for, in place of; dulcis, -e: sweet; Ascanius, -iī, m: Ascanius, the son of Aeneas; veniō, -īre, vēnī, ventus: come; dōnum, -ī, n: gift; furō, -ere (no third or fourth principal parts): rage; incendō, -ere, incendī, incensus: inflame, fire; rēgīna, -ae, f: queen; os, ossis, n: bone; implicō, -āre, -āvī, -ātus: enfold.

36. RESULT CLAUSES

36.1. Catullus 75: Catullus is losing his mind from loving Lesbia. Meter: elegiac couplets.

> Hūc est mens dēducta tuā mea, Lesbia, culpā
> atque ita sē officiō perdidit ipsa suō,
> ut iam nec bene velle queat tibi, sī optima fīās,
> nec dēsistere amāre, omnia sī faciās.

Notes: **hūc**: to this place; **mens, mentis,** f: mind; **dēdūco, -ere, dēduxī, dēductus**: lead down, bring down; **tuā...culpā**: "by your fault" (the entire clause could be translated idiomatically as "It's your fault that..."); **ita**: to such an extent...; **officium, -iī,** n: devotion; **perdō, -ere, perdidī, perditus**: destroy; **ipsa**: nominative with *mens*; **bene velle**: to wish well; **queō, -īre, -iī**: be able; **optimus, -a, -um**: best (superlative of *bonus, -a, -um*); **fīō, fierī, factus sum**: become (**sī...fīās**: "if you should become"); **dēsistō, -ere, dēstitī**: cease, stop.

36.2. Martial 1.89: Cinna, the coward, never raises his voice above a whisper. Meter: limping iambics.

> Garrīs in aurem semper omnibus, Cinna,
> garrīre et illud teste quod licet turbā,
> rīdēs in aurem, quereris, arguis, plōrās,
> cantās in aurem, iūdicās, tacēs, clāmās,
> adeōque penitus sēdit hic tibī morbus,
> ut saepe in aurem, Cinna, Caesarem laudēs.

Notes: **garriō, -īre, -īvī**: chatter; **auris, -is,** f: ear; **omnibus**: dative of possession; **Cinna, -ae,** m: for the name, see 30.2; **teste...turbā**: ablative absolute; **testis, -is,** m: witness; **licet, licēre, licuit**: it is allowed; **turba, -ae,** f: crowd; **rīdeō, -ēre, rīsī, rīsus**: laugh at, ridicule; **queror, -ī, questus sum**: complain, lament; **arguō, -ere, arguī, argūtus**: complain, allege; **plōrō, -āre, -āvī, -ātus**: cry aloud, wail; **cantō, -āre, -āvī, -ātus**: sing; **iūdicō, -āre, -āvī, -ātus**: conclude, declare; **taceō, -ēre, -uī, -itus**: be quiet; **adeō**: so, very; **penitus**: deeply; **sedeō, -ēre, sēdī, sessus**: sit, settle; **morbus, -ī,** m: disease; **tibi**: dative of reference; **Caesarem**: Julius Caesar (for the name, see 6.1).

36.3. Livy, *ab Urbe Condita* 1.4.6: Exposed by their evil great-uncle, King Amulius (of Alba Longa), the infant twins Romulus and Remus are found and suckled by a she-wolf.

> Tenet fāma cum fluitantem alveum, quō expositī erant
> puerī, tenuis in siccō aqua destituisset, lupam sitientem
> ex montibus quī circā sunt ad puerīlem vāgītum cursum
> flexisse; eam submissās infantibus adeō mītem prae-
> buisse mammās ut linguā lambentem puerōs magister
> rēgiī pecoris invēnerit.

Notes: **teneō, -ēre, -uī, tentus:** hold, maintain; **fāma, -ae,** f: rumor, reputation (triggers the indirect statements *lupam...flēxisse* [governing the temporal clause *cum...destituisset*] and *eam...mammās* [governing the result clause *ut...invēnerit*]); **fluitō, -āre, -āvī:** flow; **alveus, -ī,** m: riverbed; **quō:** where; **expōnō, -ere, exposuī, expositus:** abandon, expose; **puerī:** Romulus and Remus; **tenuis, -e:** thin, fine, slight; **siccum, -ī,** n: dry land; **destituō, -ere, destituī, destitūtus:** forsake, leave off; **lupa, -ae,** f: she-wolf; **sitiō, -īre** (no third or fourth principal parts): be thirsty; **mons, montis,** m: mountain; **quī circā sunt:** explains the location of the mountains; **puerīlis, -e:** youthful, babyish; **vāgītus, -ūs,** m: crying, bleating; **cursus, -ūs,** m: direction, course; **flectō, -ere, flexī, flexus:** bend, change; **submittō, -ere, submīsī, submissus:** lower; **infans, infantis,** m/f: child, infant; **adeō:** so, very; **mītis, -e:** mild, gentle (here, the force is adverbial); **praebeō, -ēre, -uī -itus:** provide, offer; **mamma, -ae,** f: teat; **lingua, -ae,** f: tongue; **lambō, -ere, lambī:** lick; **magister, magistrī,** m: master, chief, keeper; **rēgius, -a, -um:** royal, regal; **pecus, pecoris,** n: flock; **inveniō, -īre, invēnī, inventus:** find, come upon.

37. NOUN RESULT CLAUSES

37.1. Caesar, *de Bello Gallico* 4.29.1: The high tides in the English Channel.

> Eādem nocte accidit ut esset lūna plēna, quī diēs
> maritimōs aestūs maximōs in Ōceanō efficere consuēvit,
> nostrīsque id erat incognitum.

Notes: **eādem nocte:** August 30, 54 BCE; **accidit, -ere, accidit:** it happens; **plēnus, -a, -um:** full; **quī diēs:** explaining *eādem nocte,* "which time of day"; **maritimus, -a, -um:** of the sea, maritime; **aestus, -ūs, m:** storm, tide; **efficiō, -ere, effēcī, effectus:** produce, make, effect; **consuescō, -ere, consuēvī, consuētus:** be accustomed; **incognitus, -a, -um:** unrecognized, unknown (the tides in the Mediterranean are barely perceptible).

37.2. Cicero, *in Catilinam* 1.4: On the consul's obligations to ensure the Republic's security.

> Dēcrēvit quondam senātus utī L. Opīmius consul vidēret nē quid rēs pūblica dētrīmentī caperet: nox nulla intercessit: interfectus est propter quāsdam sēditiōnum suspīciōnēs C. Gracchus, clārissimō patre, avō, māiōribus, occīsus est cum līberīs M. Fulvius consulāris.

Notes: **dēcernō, -ere, dēcrēvī, dēcrētus:** vote, decree; **quondam:** formerly, once; **utī** = *ut*; **Lucius Opīmius, Luciī Opīmiī, m:** consul in 121 BCE, when the Senate passed for the first time a *senātus consultum ultimum,* a decree granting the consul temporary but extraordinary powers against private citizens in response to the crisis of Gaius Gracchus. Opimius, who ordered the deaths of 3,000 Gracchi supporters, was later charged with murdering Roman citizens, despite the fact that he was acting under a *senātus consultum ultimum.* He was acquitted. Cicero rightly fears that he himself might be brought up on similar charges; **dētrīmentum capere:** receive harm (here, *dētrīmentum* appears as partitive genitive with *quid*); **intercēdō, -ere, intercessī:** pass; **interficiō, -ere, interfēcī, interfectus:** kill; **propter** + accusative: because of; **sēditiō, -ōnis, f:** insurrection, rebellion; **suspīciō, -ōnis, f:** suspicion, mistrust; **Caius Gracchus, Caiī Gracchī, m:** Caius (Gaius) Gracchus (154–121 BCE) sought to reform the Roman judicial and economic systems and to extend Roman citizenship to Italian allies; **avus, -ī, m:** grandfather; **māiōres, -ium, m (plural):** ancestors (*patre, avō, māiōribus*: ablatives of source); **occīdō, -ere, occīdī, occīsus:** strike down, kill (note the asyndeton, or lack of connectives, between *interfectus est* and *occīsus est*); **līberī, -ōrum, m (plural):** children; **Marcus Fulvius Flaccus, Marcī Fulviī Flaccī, m:** consul in 125 BCE and tribune of the plebs in 122 BCE, Fulvius was Gracchus's ally who organized a protest when Opimius defeated Gracchus in a consular election. Under the authority of the *senātus consultum ultimum*, Opimius gathered an armed force and confronted the protestors. The protest quickly turned into a pitched battle within the walls of Rome; **consulāris, -e**: of consular rank.

37.3. Catullus 109: Catullus hopes that Lesbia's promises of eternal love are sincere. Meter: elegiac couplets.

> Iūcundum, mea vīta, mihī prōpōnis amōrem
> hunc nostrum inter nōs perpetuumque fore.
> Dī magnī, facite ut vērē prōmittere possit,
> atque id sincērē dīcat et ex animō,
> ut liceat nōbīs tōtā perdūcere vītā
> aeternum hoc sanctae foedus amīcitiae.

Notes: **iūcundus, -a, -um**: pleasant; **prōpōnō, -ere, prōposuī, prōpositus**: propose, offer (triggers an indirect statement); **perpetuus, -a, -um**: continual, everlasting; **fore** = *futūrum esse*; **facite**: imperative plural; **vērē**: truly; **prōmittō, -ere, prōmīsī, prōmissus**: promise; **sincērē**: truly, without dishonesty; **licet, -ēre, licuit**: it is permitted; **perdūcō, -ere, perduxī, perductus**: lead, conduct; **aeternus, -a, -um**: eternal, everlasting; **sanctus, -a, -um**: holy, sacred; **foedus, foederis, n**: treaty; **amīcitia, -ae, f**: friendship.

38. INDIRECT COMMANDS

38.1. *ILS* 8753: Hadrumetum, North Africa. Lead plate. A charioteer curses his rivals.

> Adiūrō tē, demōn, quīcunque es, et dēmandō tibi ex ānc
> ōrā ex ānc diē ex ōc mōmentō, ut equōs Prasinī et Albī
> cruciēs oc(c)īdās, et agitātorē(s) Clārum et Fēlīce(m)
> et Prīmulum et Rōmānum oc(c)īdās, collīdā(s), neque
> spīritum illīs lerinquās; adiūrō tē per eum quī tē resolvit
> temporibus deum pelagicum āerium. Ιαω Ιασδαω οοριω
> αηια Noctivagus, Tiberis, Ōceanus.

Notes: **adiūrō, -āre, -āvī, -ātus:** swear; **demōn** = *daemōn* from *daemōn, -ōnis,* m: spirit, devil; **quīcunque** = *quīcumque* from *quīcumque, quaecumque, quodcumque:* whoever, whichever, whatever; **dēmandō, -āre, -āvī, -ātus:** entrust; **ānc** = *hāc;* **ōra** = *hōra* from *hōra -ae,* f: hour; **diēs, -ēī,** m/f: day; **ōc** = *hōc;* **mōmentum, -ī,** n: turning point, minute, moment; **equus, -ī,** m: horse; **Prasinus, -a, -um:** green (here used as a substantive to refer to a racing club – a "Green faction" or "Green stable" – at Rome); **Albus, -a, -um:** white (another racing club at Rome); **cruciō, -āre, -āvī, -ātus:** torture; **occīdō, -ere, occīdī, occīsus:** kill, smite, beat to the ground; **agitātor, -ōris,** m: driver; **Clārus, -ī,** m: a man's name, "Famous"; **Fēlix, Fēlīcis,** m: a man's name, "Lucky"; **Prīmulus, -ī,** m: a man's name, "First"; **Rōmānus, -ī,** m: a man's name, "the Roman"; **collīdō, -ere, collīsī, collīsus:** strike together; **spīritus, -ūs,** m: breath; **lerinquās:** probably *relinquās* from *relinquō, -ere, relīquī, relictus:* leave behind (the transposition of the letters may reflect a magical practice to enhance the power of the curse); **resolvō, -ere, resolvī, resolūtus:** weaken; **deum** in apposition to *tē;* **pelagicus, -a, -um:** of the sea (Neptune, the Roman god of the sea, was also a god of horses); **āerius, -ia, -ium:** airborne, lofty, heavenly (implying swiftness); **Ιαω Ιασδαω οοριω αηια:** a nonsensical, magical incantation in Greek; **Noctivagus, -ī,** m: night-wanderer; **Tiberis, Tiberis,** m: the Tiber River; **Ōceanus, -ī,** m: Ocean; these three names may refer to the horses.

38.2. Caesar, *de Bello Gallico* 4.21.6: Caesar secures promises of an alliance from British envoys.

> Quibus audītīs, līberāliter pollicitus hortātusque, ut in
> eā sententiā permanērent, eōs domum remittit.

Notes: **quibus audītīs:** Caesar has just given an audience to envoys from Britain (see 32.2); **līberāliter:** generously, kindly; **polliceor, -ērī, pollicitus sum:** promise; **hortor, -ārī, -ātus sum:** urge, encourage; **sententia, -ae,** f: opinion, view, judgment; **permaneō, -ēre, permansī, permansus:** continue, remain; **eōs:** the British envoys; **remittō, -ere, remīsī, remissus:** send back.

38.3. Catullus 13.11–14: Having invited his friend Fabullus to a party at his house, Catullus describes the perfume that Fabullus will

experience there. See 21.2 for Martial's allusion to this poem.
Meter: hendecasyllabics.

> Nam unguentum dabo, quod meae puellae
> dōnārunt Venerēs Cupīdinēsque,
> quod tū cum olfaciēs, deōs rogābis,
> tōtum ut tē faciant, Fabulle, nāsum.

Notes: **unguentum, -ī,** n: perfume, ointment; **dabo:** final -o scans as short here in order for the meter to work out correctly; **dōnārunt** = *dōnāvērunt* from *dōnō, -āre, -āvī, -ātus:* give; **Venus, Veneris,** f: Venus, goddess of love; **Cupīdō, Cupīdinis,** m: Cupid, son of Venus; **olfaciō, -ere, olfēcī, olfactus:** smell; **rogō, -āre, -āvī, -ātus:** ask; **nāsus, -ī,** m: nose.

39. INDIRECT QUESTIONS

39.1. Vergil, *Aeneid* 1.305–309: After washing up on the shores of Carthage, Aeneas decides to find out about the place. Meter: dactylic hexameter.

> At pius Aenēās per noctem plūrima volvens,
> ut prīmum lux alma data est, exīre locōsque
> explōrāre novōs, quās ventō accesserit ōrās,
> quī teneant (nam inculta videt), hominēsne feraene,
> quaerere constituit sociīsque exacta referre.

Notes: **at:** but; **pius, -a, -um:** devoted, righteous; **Aenēās, -ae,** m: Aeneas, the Trojan leader; **nox, noctis,** f: night; **plūrimus:** superlative of *multus*; **volvō, -ere, volvī, volūtus:** roll, revolve, consider; **ut prīmum:** as soon as; **lux, lūcis,** f: light, dawn; **almus, -a, -um:** kind, nurturing; **exeō, -īre, -iī, -itus:** go out; **locus, -ī,** m: place; **explōrō, -āre, -āvī, -ātus:** explore, search out; **ventus, -ī,** m: breeze, wind; **accēdō, -ere, accessī:** approach, reach; **ōra, -ae,** f: shore; **incultus, -a, -um:** untilled, wild (*inculta:* substantive, "wilderness"); **-ne...-ne:** whether...or; **fera, -ae,** f: wild beast; **quaerō, -ere, quaesīvī, quaesītus:** inquire, ask; **constituō, -ere, constituī, constitūtus:** establish, resolve, decide; **socius, -iī,** m: ally; **exigō, -ere, exēgī,**

exactus: discover (*exacta*: substantive, "things learned"); **referō, -ferre, rettulī, relātus**: relate.

39.2.   Catullus 85: Catullus is emotionally torn regarding his tumultuous love affair with Lesbia. Meter: elegiac couplets.

> Ōdī et amō. Quārē id faciam, fortasse requīris.
> Nescio, sed fierī sentiō et excrucior.

Notes: **ōdī, odisse, ōsus** (no first or second principal parts): hate, detest; **quārē**: why; **fortasse**: perhaps; **requīrō, -ere, requīsīvī, requīsītus**: ask, inquire; **nesciō, -īre, -īvī, -ītus**: not know (final -o scans as short in this poem in order for the meter to work out correctly); **sentiō, -īre, sensī, sensus**: perceive, feel (triggers an indirect statement); **excruciō, -āre, -āvī, -ātus**: torment, torture.

39.3.   Catullus 93: Catullus proclaims that he is completely ignorant of the very famous and powerful Julius Caesar. Meter: elegiac couplets.

> Nīl nimium studeō, Caesar, tibi velle placēre,
> nec scīre utrum sīs albus an āter homō.

Notes: **nīl nimium studeō**: "I am not too eager"; **placeō, -ēre, -uī, -itus** + dative: please, be agreeable (to); **utrum... an**: whether... or; **albus, -a, -um**: white; **āter, ātra, ātrum**: black; the expression *utrum sīs albus an āter* is a Latin colloquialism for complete ignorance of a person.

39.4.   Martial 2.7: You do everything beautifully, you big fussbudget. Meter: elegiac couplets.

> Dēclāmās bellē, causās agis, Attice, bellē
> historiās bellās, carmina bella facis,
> compōnis bellē mīmōs, epigrammata bellē,
> bellus grammaticus, bellus es astrologus,
> et bellē cantās et saltās, Attice, bellē,
> bellus es arte lyrae, bellus es arte pilae.
> Nīl bene cum faciās, faciās tamen omnia bellē,
> vīs dīcam quid sīs? Magnus es ardaliō.

Notes: **dēclāmō, -āre, -āvī, -ātus**: declaim, give oratorical speeches; **bellus, -a, -um**: pretty, fine; **causās agere**: plead cases in court;

Atticus, -ī, m: a man's name (see 19.1); **historia, -ae, f:** history, story; **compōnō, -ere, composuī, compositus:** put together, compose; **mīmus, -ī, m:** mime play, farce; **epigramma, -atos/atis, n:** short poem, inscription; **grammaticus, -ī, n:** philologist; **astrologus, -ī, m:** astronomer; **cantō, -āre, -āvī, -ātus:** sing; **saltō, -āre, -āvī, -ātus:** dance; **lyra, -ae, f:** lyre; **pila, -ae, f:** ball, ball game; **vīs dīcam** = *vīs ut dīcam*; **ardaliō, -ōnis, m:** busybody, fusser.

39.5. Martial 2.38: Not to see you is the greatest gift. Meter: elegiac couplets.

> Quid mihi reddat ager quaeris, Line, Nōmentānus?
> Hoc mihi reddit ager: tē, Line, nōn videō.

Notes: **reddō, -ere, reddidī, redditus:** give back, return; **ager, agrī, m:** land, farm; **quaerō, -ere, quaesīvī, quaesītus:** ask, inquire, seek; **Linus, -ī, m:** a Greek name given to several mythological figures who died young (The most famous Linus was Apollo's son, who taught music to Hercules but was killed by the hero. Hercules was tried for murder but acquitted on the grounds of self-defense!); **Nōmentānus, -a, -um:** referring to the town of Nōmentum, near Rome on the Sabine border.

39.6. Caesar, *de Bello Gallico* 4.20.4–5: In preparation for his first invasion of Britain in 55 BCE, Caesar tries to secure intelligence from merchants (see 44.2).

> Itaque vocātīs ad sē undique mercātōribus, neque quanta esset insulae magnitūdō, neque quae aut quantae nātiōnēs incolerent, neque quem ūsum bellī habērent aut quibus institūtīs ūterentur, neque quī essent ad māiōrem nāvium multitūdinem idōneī portūs, reperīre poterat.

Notes: **itaque:** and thus, and so; **vocō, -āre, -āvī, -ātus:** call; **ad sē:** "to Caesar"; **undique:** from all sides; **mercātor, -ōris, m:** merchant; **quantus, -a, -um:** how great, how much; **magnitūdō, magnitūdinis, f:** size; **nātiō, -ōnis, f:** tribe, race, people; **incolō, -ere, -uī:** live, dwell, inhabit; **ūsus, -ūs, m:** use, practice, advantage; **bellum, -ī, n:** war; **institūtum, -ī, n:** undertaking, arrangement, institution; **ūtor, -ī, ūsus sum** + ablative: use; **quī:** interrogative adjective modifying *portūs*; **ad** + accusative: for; **nāvis, -is**, f: ship; **idōneus, -a, -um**: suitable, proper; **portus, -ūs**, m: harbor; **re(p)periō, -īre, re(p)perī, re(p)pertus**: find out, discover.

40. FEAR CLAUSES

40.1.   Caesar, *de Bello Gallico* 1.19.2: Caesar hesitates to wage war against Dumnorix because his brother Diviciacus is friendly to Roman interests.

> Hīs omnibus rēbus ūnum repugnābat, quod Dīviciācī
> frātris summum in populum Rōmānum studium, sum-
> mam in sē voluntātem, ēgregiam fidem, iustitiam, tem-
> perantiam cognōverat; nam nē eius suppliciō Dīviciācī
> animum offenderet verēbātur.

Notes: **Hīs omnibus rēbus:** referring to Dumnorix's hostile activi-
ties; **ūnum:** accusative of respect, explained by the *quod* clause;
repugnō, -āre, -āvī, -ātus + dative: oppose; **quod:** the fact that;
Dīviciācus, -ī, m: Dumnorix's brother; **summus, -a, -um:** highest
(superlative of *superus, -a, -um*); **in** + accusative: toward; **studium,
-iī**, n: enthusiasm, devotion; **sē:** Caesar; **voluntās, -ātis**, f: goodwill;
ēgregius, -a, -um: exceptional, extraordinary; **fidēs, -ēī**, f: loyalty,
honesty; **iustitia, -ae**, f: righteousness; **temperantia, -ae**, f: moderation, self-control; **cognoscō, -ere, cognōvī, cognitus:** recognize;
nē: introduces a positive fear clause (which Caesar fears *will* happen, but hopes *won't*); **eius:** Dumnorix; **supplicium, -iī**, n: punishment; **offendō, -ere, offendī, offensus:** displease, offend; **vereor,
-ērī, veritus sum:** fear, be anxious.

40.2.   Cicero, *in Catilinam* 4.14: Although his life is in mortal danger, Cicero assures the Senate that he has taken every precaution against Catiline's threats of assassination, describing both his private and public precautions. The *Fourth Oration* was deliv-ered in the Senate on 5 December 63 BCE.

> Sed ea, quae exaudiō, patrēs conscriptī, dissimulāre
> nōn possum. Iaciuntur enim vōcēs, quae perveniunt

ad aurīs meās, eōrum quī verērī videntur, ut habeam
satis praesidī ad ea, quae vōs statueritis hodiernō diē
transigenda.

Notes: **quae**: explaining *ea;* **exaudiō, -īre, -īvī, -ītus**: hear plainly;
patrēs conscriptī, patrium conscriptōrum, m (plural): senators;
dissimulō, -āre, -āvī, -ātus: conceal, disguise; **iaciō, -ere, iēcī,
iactus**: cast, declare, utter; **enim**: for, in fact; **vox, vōcis**, f: voice;
perveniō, -īre, pervēnī, perventus: arrive; **auris, -is**, f: ear; **vereor,
-ērī, veritus sum**: fear, fear to, be anxious; **videor, -ērī, vīsus sum**:
seem; **ut**: triggers a negative fear clause; **satis**: enough; **praesidium,
-iī**, n: protection, defense (*praesidī*: partitive gentitive with *satis*
– Cicero fears for his life); **statuō, -ere, statuī, statūtus**: decide;
hodiernus, -a, -um: of today; **transigenda** (*esse*): "must be accomplished" (future passive periphrastic in indirect statement), from
transigō, -ere, transēgī, transactus.

40.3. Livy, *ab Urbe Condita* 1.17.4: Romulus has just died, and, afraid
for Rome's future, the senators debate how to select a new leader.

Timor deinde patrēs incessit nē cīvitātem sine imperiō,
exercitum sine duce, multārum circā cīvitātium inrītātīs
animīs, vīs aliqua externa adorīrētur.

Notes: **timor, -ōris**, m: fear; **deinde**: then, next; **pater, patris**,
m: referring to the senators of Rome, the king's advisory council; **incēdō, -ere, incessī**: come over; **nē**: triggers a positive fear
clause; **cīvitās, -ātis**, f: state; **sine** + ablative: without; **imperium,
-iī**, n: power, sovereignty; **exercitus, -ūs**, m: army; **dux, ducis**, m:
leader; **circā**: around, nearby; **inrītātīs … animīs**: ablative absolute;
inrītō, -āre, -āvī, -ātus: stir up, agitate; **vīs, vis**, f (irregular noun):
strength; **aliquī, aliqua, aliquod**: some, any; **externus, -a, -um**:
foreign; **adorior, -īrī, adortus sum**: rise up, attack.

40.4. Livy, *ab Urbe Condita* 2.12.4: In 509 BCE, shortly after the
establishment of the Roman Republic, the city of Rome is under
siege by the Etruscans. While the Etruscan king Porsenna hopes
to bide his time until the food runs out, a young Roman noble,
Gaius Mucius Scaevola ("Lefty"), is eager for action. Scaevola first

contemplates infiltrating the Etruscan camp but fears senatorial rebuke. With the Senate's approval, Scaevola enters the camp alone and kills Porsenna's secretary (thinking him to be the king). In response to Porsenna's threats of burning at the stake, Scaevola thrusts his right hand into the altar fire (hence his cognomen). Porsenna is so impressed with Scaevola's bravery (and foolhardiness) that he opens negotiations with Rome. Here Livy recounts Scaevola's internal debate before approaching the Senate.

> Dein metuens nē, sī consulum iniussū et ignārīs omnibus īret, forte dēprehensus ā custōdibus Rōmānīs retraherētur ut transfuga, fortūnā tum urbis crīmen adfirmante, senātum adit.

Notes: **dein** = *deinde*: then, next; **metuō, -ere, metuī, metūtus**: fear, dread; **nē**: triggers a positive fear clause; **consul, consulis, m**: a high political office in Rome (*consulum*: subjective genitive with *iniussū*); **iniussū**: without orders, unbidden; **ignārīs omnibus**: ablative absolute; **ignārus, -a, -um**: ignorant, unaware; **forte**: by chance; **dēprehendō, -ere, dēprehendī, dēprehensus**: seize, arrest; **custōs, custōdis, m**: guard, attendant; **retrahō, -ere, retraxī, retractus**: drag back; **ut**: as, like; **transfuga, -ae, m**: deserter; **fortūnā…adfirmante**: ablative absolute; **tum**: then, at that time; **urbis**: with *fortūnā*; **crīmen, crīminis, n**: accusation, charge, fault, crime; **adfirmō, -āre, -āvī, -ātus**: prove; **senātum adit**: the main clause.

41. PROVISO CLAUSES

41.1. Livy, *ab Urbe Condita* 1.34.5: Livy relates the story of Lucumo, who eventually becomes Lucius Tarquinius Priscus, the fifth king of Rome (reigned 616–579 BCE). Here Lucumo's wife, Tanaquil, is ashamed of the scorn that her people, the Etruscans, have shown to Lucumo.

> Spernentibus Etruscīs Lucumōnem exsule advenā ortum, ferre indignitātem nōn potuit, oblītaque

ingenitae ergā patriam cāritātis dummodo virum
honōrātum vidēret, consilium migrandī ab Tarquiniīs
cēpit.

Notes: **spernō, -ere, sprēvī, sprētus:** scorn, spurn; **Etruscus, -a,
-um:** Etruscan (*Etruscīs:* substantive); **Lucumō, -ōnis,** m: a proper
name in this context, but usually a priestly Etruscan title; **exsul,
exsulis,** m/f: wanderer, exile (*exsule:* ablative of source; although
Lucumo was born in Etruria, his father was a political exile from
Corinth); **advena, -ae,** m/f: immigrant, foreigner (in apposition to
exsule); **orior, -īrī, ortus sum:** be born; **indignitās, -ātis,** f: humiliation, degradation; **potuit:** understand Lucumo's wife, Tanaquil,
as the subject of all the finite verbs in this passage; **oblīviscor, -ī,
oblītus sum** + genitive: forgetful of; **ingenitus, -a, -um:** innate,
natural; **ergā** + accusative: toward; **patria, -ae,** f: native land, homeland; **cāritās, -ātis,** f: esteem, favor, affection; **dummodo:** provided
that; **vir, -ī,** m: husband; **honōrō, -āre, -āvī, -ātus:** respect; **consilium capere:** form a plan; **migrō, -āre, -āvī, -ātus:** move, depart
(*migrandī:* gerund, "of moving"); **Tarquiniī, -ōrum,** m (plural): an
ancient town, giving its name to a royal Etruscan family.

41.2. Martial 2.88: Be a poet, if you like, but don't recite! Meter: elegiac couplets.

> Nīl recitās et vīs, Māmerce, poēta vidērī.
> Quidquid vīs estō, dummodo nīl recitēs.

Notes: **nīl** = *nihil;* **recitō, -āre, -āvī, -ātus:** recite, declaim;
Māmercus, -ī, m: a Roman name of Oscan origin, recalling *Māmers,*
the Oscan equivalent of the god Mars; **quisquis, quidquid:** whoever, whatever; **estō:** future imperative of *esse,* "so be it!"; **dummodo:** provided that.

41.3. Ovid, *Metamorphoses* 9.19–22: Appealing to Oeneus, his pro-
spective father-in-law, Achelous, the Calydonian river god, claims
that he will make a better husband than Hercules for Oeneus's
daughter Deianira. Meter: dactylic hexameter.

> "Nec gener externīs hospes tibi missus ab ōrīs,
> sed populāris erō et rērum pars ūna tuārum.

Tantum nē noceat, quod mē nec rēgia Iūno
ōdit, et omnis abest iussōrum poena labōrum."

Notes: **gener, generī,** m: son-in-law; **externus, -a, -um:** foreign, strange; **hospes, hospitis,** m: guest, host; **ōra, -ae,** f: shore; **populāris, -e:** of the same country; **tantum nē:** introduces a negative proviso clause; **noceō, -ēre, -uī, -itus:** harm, injure; **quod:** the fact that; **rēgius, -a, -um:** royal; **ōdī, odisse, ōsus** (no first or second principal parts): hate; **iubeō, -ēre, iussī, iussus:** order, command; **poena, -ae,** f: punishment, penalty; **labor, -ōris,** m: task, work, effort.

42. RELATIVE CLAUSES WITH SUBJUNCTIVES

42.1.   Cicero, *in Catilinam* 1.8: Catiline cannot even take a breath without Cicero's knowledge.

Nihil agis, nihil mōlīris, nihil cōgitās quod nōn ego nōn
modo audiam sed etiam videam plānēque sentiam.

Notes: notice the anaphora of *nihil;* **mōlior, -īrī, -ītus sum:** try, attempt; **cōgitō, -āre, -āvī, -ātus:** think, intend, plan; **nōn modo...sed etiam:** not only...but also; **plānē:** clearly, distinctly.

42.2.   Catullus 22.18–21: Catullus has just described the charming and sophisticated poet Suffenus, who is happy while composing his poems. When you read his awful verses, however, Suffenus seems to be a goat-milker (*caprimulgus*) and a ditchdigger (*fossor*). Here Catullus reminds us that there is a little Suffenus in each of us. Meter: limping iambics.

Nīmīrum īdem omnēs fallimur, neque est quisquam
quem nōn in aliquā rē vidēre Suffēnum
possīs. Suus cuique attribūtus est error;
sed nōn vidēmus manticae quod in tergō est.

Notes: **nīmīrum:** doubtless, truly; **īdem:** likewise, similarly; **fallō, -ere, fefellī, falsus:** deceive; **quisquam, quicquam:** any person, anything; **in aliquā rē:** in some matter; **attribuō, -ere, attribuī, attribūtus:** assign, allot; **error, -ōris, m:** mistake, fault; **mantica, -ae, f:** satchel (*manticae:* partitive genitive with *quod*); **tergum, -ī, n:** back.

42.3. Catullus 7: Catullus waxes poetic about his unquenchable passion for Lesbia. Meter: hendecasyllabics.

Quaeris, quot mihi bāsiātiōnēs
tuae, Lesbia, sint satis superque.
Quam magnus numerus Libyssae harēnae
lāsarpīciferīs iacet Cyrēnīs
ōrāclum Iovis inter aestuōsī
et Battī veteris sacrum sepulcrum;
aut quam sīdera multa, cum tacet nox,
furtīvōs hominum vident amōrēs:
tam tē bāsia multa bāsiāre
vēsānō satis et super Catullō est,
quae nec pernumerāre cūriōsī
possint nec mala fascināre lingua.

Notes: **quaerō, -ere, quaesīvī, quaesītus:** ask; **quot:** how many?; **bāsiātiō, -ōnis, f:** kiss, kissing; **satis:** enough; **super:** more; **quam magnus:** as great as, as much as; **Libyssa, -ae, f:** North African; **harēna, -ae, f:** sand; **lāsarpīcifer, lāsarpīcifera, lāsarpīciferum:** silphium-bearing (silphium was an exotic culinary seasoning and medicinal plant from Cyrene); **iaceō, -ēre, -uī, -itus:** lie, rest; **Cyrēnae, -ārum, f** (plural): Cyrene; **ōrāclum, -ī, n:** oracle; **Iuppiter, Iovis, m:** Jupiter, the supreme god of the Romans; **aestuōsus, -a, -um:** hot, sweltering; **Battus, -ī, m:** legendary founder of Cyrene; **vetus, veteris:** old; **sacer, sacra, sacrum:** sacred; **sepulc(h)rum, -ī, n:** grave; **quam multa:** as many as; **sīdus, sīderis, n:** star; **taceō, -ēre, -uī, -itus:** be silent; **furtīvus, -a, -um:** secret, furtive; **tam:** so; **bāsium, -iī, n:** kiss; **bāsiō, -āre, -āvī, -ātus:** kiss (*tē* is the subject of this infinitive); **vēsānus, -a, -um:** crazy, mad; **quae:** introduces a relative clause of purpose; **pernumerō, -āre, -āvī, -ātus:** count out, reckon up; **cūriōsus, -a, -um:** curious; **fascinō, -āre, -āvī, -ātus:** enchant, bewitch; **lingua, -ae, f:** tongue.

43. CONDITIONALS

43.1. *CIL* XIII 1983 *[ILS* 8158]: Lyon (Lugdunum, Gallia Lugdunensis). Tombstone for a beloved wife.

D(īs) et M(ānibus) memoriae aetern(ae) Blandiniae Martilōlae puellae innocentissimae quae vixit ann(ōs) XVIII m(ensēs) VIII d(iēs) V. Pompeius Catussa cīves Sēquanus tector coniugī incomparābilī et sibi benignissimē, quae mēcum vixit an(nōs) V m(ensēs) VI d(iēs) XVIII sine ul(l)ā crīminis sorde. Vī(v)us sibi et coniugī pōnendum cūrāvit et sub asciā dēdicāvit. Tū, quī legis, vāde in Apol(l)inis lavārī quod ego cum coniuge fēcī. Vellem sī ad(h)ūc possem.

Notes: **deus, -ī,** m: god; **Mānēs, -ium,** m (plural): spirits of the dead; **memoria, -ae,** f: memory, remembrance; **aeternus, -a, -um:** eternal, everlasting; **Blandinia Martilōla, Blandiniae Martilōlae,** f: a woman's name (*Blandinia*: from *blandus, -a, -um*: charming, coaxing; *Martilōla*: a diminutive of the god Mars); **innocens, innocentis:** innocent, blameless; **vīvō, -ere, vixī, victus:** live; **annus, -ī,** m: year; **mensis, -is,** m: month; **Pompeius Catussa, Pompeiī Catussae,** m: a man's name (the verb and direct object for Pompeius Catussa are missing; supply *fēcī hoc* to indicate that "I, Pompeius, built this tombstone for my wife"); **cīves** = *cīvis* from *cīvis, -is,* m/f: citizen; **Sēquanus, -a, -um:** of the Sequani, a tribe of eastern Gaul, who appealed to Caesar for help against Ariovistus but joined Vercingetorix aginst the Romans in 52 BCE; **tector, -ōris,** m: plasterer; **coniunx, coniugis,** m/f: spouse; **incomparābilis, -e:** incomparable; **benignissimē:** most generously; **sine** + ablative: without; **ullus, -a, -um:** any; **crīmen, crīminis,** n: accusation, charge, fault, crime; **sordēs, -is,** f: meanness, stinginess, humiliation; **vīvus, -a, -um:** alive; **pōnendum:** be placed (supply "*monumentum*"); **cūrō, -āre, -āvī, -ātus:** take care, pay attention to; **sub** + ablative: under; **ascia, -ae,** f: carpenter's ax, mason's trowel; **dēdicō, -āre, -āvī, -ātus:** dedicate, consecrate; **legō, -ere, lēgī, lectus:** read; **vādō, -ere, vāsī:** hasten, rush, go; **in** + accusative: into (supply "the baths of"); **Apollō, Apollinis,** m: Apollo, the Greek god of poetry, young men, and healing; **lavō, -āre, lāvī, lautus:** bathe; **quod:** a thing which (the act of bathing); **quod**...**fēcī**: communal bathing was probably a ritual act of purification; **vellem**: understand *vadere*; **adhūc**: still.

43.2. Caesar, *de Bello Gallico* 4.33.2: British chariot-fighting techniques (see 13.2).

Aurīgae interim paulātim ex proeliō excēdunt, atque ita currūs collocant, ut, sī illī ā multitūdine hostium premantur, expedītum ad suōs receptum habeant.

Notes: **aurīga, -ae,** m/f: chariot driver; **interim:** meanwhile; **paulātim:** little by little; **proelium, -iī,** n: battle; **excēdō, -ere, excessī, excessus:** go out, withdraw; **currus, -ūs,** m: chariot; **collocō, -āre, -āvī, -ātus:** set, arrange, place; **hostis, -is,** m: enemy; **multitūdō, multitūdinis,** f: crowd; **premō, -ere, pressī, pressus:** press, pursue; **expedītus, -a, -um:** light armed, ready at hand, unobstructed; **ad suōs:** "to their own lines"; **receptus, -ūs,** m: retreat.

43.3. Caesar, *de Bello Gallico* 6.13.5–6: How the Druids in Gaul adjudicate private and public disputes.

Nam ferē dē omnibus contrōversiīs pūblicīs prīvātīsque constituunt et, sī quod est admissum facinus, sī caedēs facta, sī dē hērēditāte, dē finibus contrōversia est, īdem dēcernunt, praemia poenāsque constituunt; sī quī aut prīvātus aut populus eōrum dēcrētō nōn stetit, sacrificiīs interdīcunt. Haec poena apud eōs est gravissima.

Notes: **nam:** for; **ferē:** nearly; **dē** + ablative: concerning; **contrōversia, -ae,** f: dispute, debate; **prīvātus, -a, -um:** personal, private, ordinary; **constituō, -ere, constituī, constitūtus:** establish, settle; **sī quod:** if any (take *quod* with *facinus*); **admittō, -ere, admīsī, admissus:** commit, admit; **facinus, facinoris,** n: crime; **caedēs, -is,** f: murder; **hērēditās, -ātis,** f: inheritance; **fīnis, -is,** m: border; **īdem:** "the same people"; **dēcernō, -ere, dēcrēvī, dēcrētus:** decide, resolve; **praemium, -iī,** n: reward; **poena, -ae,** f: punishment; **prīvātus, -ī,** m: individual; **populus, -ī,** m: community; **dēcrētum, -ī,** n: decision, resolution; **stō, stāre, stetī, status:** stand by, adhere to; **sacrificium, -iī,** n: sacrifice; **interdīcō, -ere, interdixī, interdictus** + dative

of the person and ablative of the thing: forbid, prohibit; **apud** +
accusative: among; **gravis, -e**: serious, severe.

43.4.   Martial 5.29: You should use your own beauty treatment. Meter:
elegiac couplets.

> Sī quandō leporem mittis mihi, Gellia, dīcis
> "Formōnsus septem, Marce, diēbus eris."
> Sī nōn dērīdēs, sī vērum, lux mea, narrās,
> ēdistī numquam, Gellia, tū leporem.

Notes: **quandō**: at any time, ever; **lepus, leporis,** m: hare; **Gellia,
-ae,** f: a woman's name; **formōnsus** = *formōsus, -a, -um*: beautiful,
handsome; **dērīdeō, -ēre, derīsī, derīsus**: mock; **vērum**: truly; **lux,
lūcis,** f: light; **edō, esse, ēdī, ēsus**: eat (some Romans believed that
eating a hare made one beautiful).

43.5.   Martial 6.17: It's all in the name. Meter: hendecasyllabics.

> Cinnam, Cinname, tē iubēs vocārī.
> nōn est hic, rogo, Cinna, barbarismus?
> Tū sī Fūrius ante dictus essēs,
> Fūr istā ratiōne dīcerēris.

Notes: Martial teases Cinnamus about his proposed nickname by
offering two plays on words, first between **cinnamum, -ī,** n: cinna-
mon, and **cinna, -ae,** f: facial distortion (see 30.2), and then between
furiōsus, -a, -um: mad, raging, and **fūr, fūris,** m: thief; **rogō, -āre,
-āvī, -ātus**: ask (final -o scans as short here in order for the meter to
work out correctly); **ante**: previously, in the past; **barbarismus, -ī,**
m: barbarism; **ratiō, -ōnis,** f: reason.

43.6.   Catullus 48: A love poem to Juventius, Catullus's young male
lover. (Catullus also eulogizes Juventius in poem 99.) Meter:
hendecasyllabics.

> Mellītōs oculōs tuōs, Iuventī,
> sī quis mē sinat usque bāsiāre,
> usque ad mīlia bāsiem trecenta
> nec numquam videar satur futūrus,

non sī dēnsior āridīs aristīs
sit nostrae seges osculātiōnis.

Notes: **mellītus, -a, -um:** honey-sweet; **oculus, -ī,** m: eye; **Iuventius, -iī,** m: a man's name derived from *iuvenis, -e:* young; **sī quis:** if anyone; **sinō, -ere, sīvī, situs:** allow; **usque:** continuously, without interruption; **bāsiō, -āre, -āvī, -ātus:** kiss; **ad milia...trecenta:** "for 300,000 times"; **numquam:** never; **satur, satura, saturum:** full, sated, well-fed; **futūrus:** understand *esse;* **dēnsus, -a, -um:** dense, closely packed; **āridus, -a, -um:** dry; **arista, -ae,** f: ear of corn; **seges, -etis,** f: crop; **osculātiō, -ōnis,** f: kissing.

43.7. Catullus 83: Catullus imagines that Lesbia insults him in front of her husband as a show of infatuation. Meter: elegiac couplets.

> Lesbia mī praesente virō mala plūrima dīcit:
> haec illī fatuō maxima laetitia est.
> Mūle, nihil sentīs? Sī nostrī oblīta tacēret,
> sāna esset: nunc quod gannit et obloquitur,
> nōn sōlum meminit, sed, quae multō ācrior est rēs,
> irātā est. Hōc est, ūritur et loquitur.

Notes: **mī** = *mihi;* **praesēns, praesentis:** present, in sight; **plūrimus, -a, -um:** very many; **illī:** dative singular (Lesbia's husband); **fatuus, -a, -um:** foolish, silly; **laetitia, -ae,** f: happiness; **mūlus, -ī,** m: mule; **oblītus, -a, -um** + genitive: forgetful of; **taceō, -ēre, -uī, -itus:** be silent, say nothing; **sānus, -a, -um:** sound, healthy; **quod:** because; **canniō, -īre** (no third or fourth principal parts): bark, snarl; **obloquor, -ī, oblocūtus sum:** speak against; **nōn sōlum:** not only; **meminī, meminisse** (no first or second principal parts): remember, recollect; **multō:** by far (ablative of degree of difference); **ācer, ācris, ācre:** sharp, fierce; **ūrō, -ere, ussī, ustus:** burn.

43.8. Vergil, *Aeneid* 6.29–33: Vergil describes how Daedalus tried to capture the death of his son, Icarus, in his engravings on the doors of the temple of Apollo at Cumae. His grief prevented him from completing his work. Meter: dactylic hexameter.

> Daedalus ipse dolōs tectī ambāgēsque resolvit,
> caeca regēns fīlō vestīgia. Tū quoque magnam

partem opere in tantō, sineret dolor, Īcare, habērēs.
Bis cōnātus erat cāsūs effingere in aurō,
bis patriae cecidēre manūs.

Notes: **dolus, -ī,** m: trick; **tectum, -ī,** n: building, structure, "maze";
ambāgēs, -is, f: winding path; **resolvō, -ere, resolvī, resolūtus:**
loosen, release; **caecus, -a, -um:** blind; **regō, regere, rexī, rec-**
tus: rule, guide; **fīlum, -ī,** n: thread; **vestīgium, -iī,** n: footprint,
track; **quoque:** also; **opus, operis,** n: work, task; **sinō, -ere, sīvī,**
situs: allow (supply *sī* before *sineret*); **dolor, -ōris,** m: grief, pain;
bis: twice; **cōnor, -ārī, -ātus sum:** try, attempt; **cāsus, -ūs,** m: misfortune, fall; **effingō, -ere, effinxī, effictus:** form, fashion; **aurum,**
-ī, n: gold; **patrius, -a, -um:** fatherly; **cadō, -ere, cecidī, cāsus:**
fall, fail.

44. GERUNDS AND GERUNDIVES

44.1. Caesar, *de Bello Gallico* 1.3.1–2: Under Orgetorix's leadership,
the Helvetians prepare to emigrate.

His rēbus adductī et auctōritāte Orgetorigis permōtī,
constituērunt ea quae ad proficiscendum pertinērent
comparāre, iūmentōrum et carrōrum quam maximum
numerum coemere, sēmentīs quam maximās facere
ut in itinere cōpia frūmentī suppeteret, cum proximīs
cīvitātibus pācem et amīcitiam confirmāre. Ad eās rēs
conficiendās biennium sibi satis esse duxērunt: in ter-
tium annum profectiōnem lēge confirmant.

Notes: **addūcō, -ere, adduxī, adductus:** lead on, induce; **auctōritās,**
-ātis, f: influence, authority; **permoveō, -ēre, permōvī, permōtus:**
influence, move deeply; **constituō, -ere, constituī, constitūtus:**
decide (+ the complementary infinitives *comparāre, coemere, facere,*
confirmāre); **proficiscor, -ī, profectus sum:** set out; **pertineō, -ēre,**
-uī, -tentus: reach, extend, pertain to; **comparō, -āre, -āvī, -ātus:**
prepare, put together; **iūmentum, -ī,** n: draft animal; **carrus, -ī,**

m: baggage-wagon; **quam maximum numerum**: the greatest possible number (*quam* + superlative expresses the highest degree possible); **coemō, -ere, coēmī, coemptus**: buy up; **sēmentēs... facere**: sow grain; **iter, itineris,** n: journey; **cōpia, -ae,** f: abundance, supply; **frūmentum, -ī,** n: grain; **suppetō, -ere, -īvī, -ītus**: be at hand, be sufficient; **cīvitās, -ātis,** f: state, tribe; **amīcitia, -ae,** f: friendship; **confirmō, -āre, -āvī, -ātus**: strengthen, confirm; **conficiō, -ere, confēcī, confectus**: complete, carry out; **biennium, -iī,** n: two-year period; **dūcō, -ere, duxī, ductus**: lead, think out, calculate, reckon; **profectiō, -ōnis,** f: departure, setting out; **lex, lēgis,** f: law, custom.

44.2. Caesar, *de Bello Gallico* 4.21.1–2: In preparation for his first invasion of Britain in 55 BCE, Caesar sends Volusenus to make a reconnaissance of the island (see 39.6).

> Ad haec cognoscenda, prius quam perīclum faceret,
> idōneum esse arbitrātus C. Volusēnum cum nāvī longā
> praemittit. Huic mandat, ut, explōrātīs omnibus rēbus,
> ad sē quam prīmum revertātur.

Notes: **cognoscō, -ere, cognōvī, cognitus**: learn, spy out; **prius quam**: before; **perīc(u)lum, -ī,** n: risk, attempt; **idōneus, -a, -um**: suitable, proper; **arbitror, -ārī, -ātus sum**: think; **Caius Volusēnus, Caiī Volusēnī,** m: known for his good sense of strategy and courage, a distinguished military officer who served Caesar for ten years in Gaul and then in the Civil Wars of the 40s BCE; **nāvis longa, nāvis longae,** f: a battleship, propelled by oars, usually with a single mast and one large sail; **praemittō, -ere, praemīsī, praemissus**: send in advance; **huic**: C. Volusenus; **mandō, -āre, -āvī, -ātus**: commit, entrust, order; **explōrō, -āre, -āvī, -ātus**: search out, investigate; **quam prīmum**: as soon as possible; **revertor, -ī, reversus sum**: return.

44.3. Caesar, *de Bello Gallico* 4.29.2: Caesar is unprepared for the effects of storms at high tide in the English Channel, and many of his ships are damaged.

> Ita ūnō tempore et longās nāvīs, quibus Caesar exercitum transportandum cūrāverat, quāsque in āridum subduxerat, aestus complēverat, et onerāriās, quae ad

ancorās erant dēligātae, tempestās adflictābat, neque
ulla nostrīs facultās aut administrandī aut auxiliandī
dabātur.

Notes: **exercitus, -ūs,** m: army; **transportō, -āre, -āvī, -ātus:** carry
across; **cūrō, -āre, -āvī, -ātus:** take care, provide for; **āridus, -a.** **-um:**
dry (*in āridum:* "onto dry land"); **subdūcō, -ere, subduxī, subduc-
tus:** haul on shore, beach; **aestus, -ūs,** m: storm, tide; **compleō, -ēre,
complēvī, complētus:** fill up; **onerāria (nāvis), onerāriae (nāvis),**
f: transport ship; **ancora, -ae,** f: anchor; **dēligō, -āre, -āvī, -ātus:**
bind, tie, fasten; **tempestās, -ātis,** f: storm; **adflictō, -āre, -āvī,
-ātus:** strike repeatedly; **facultās, -ātis,** f: opportunity, resource;
administrō, -āre, -āvī, -ātus: manage, help, assist; **auxilior, -ārī,
-ātus sum:** help, assist.

44.4. Caesar, *de Bello Gallico* 4.34.2: Caesar strategically holds his
men back from engaging the Britons in battle.

Quō factō, ad lacessendum et ad committendum proelium aliēnum esse tempus arbitrātus, suō sē locō con-
tinuit et, brevī tempore intermissō, in castra legiōnēs
reduxit.

Notes: **quō factō:** since the Romans found the British method of
fighting from chariots irksome, Caesar would arrive on the battlefield at an opportune time (*quō factō*), which always caused the
enemy to pause and allowed the Romans to recover their wits;
lacessō, -ere, -īvī, -ītus: harass, assail, attack (the enemy); **commit-
tere proelium:** join battle; **aliēnus, -a, -um:** unfavorable; **tempus,
-oris,** n: time; **arbitror, -ārī, -ātus sum:** think; **contineō, -ēre, -uī,
contentus:** hold back, keep in hand; **intermittō, -ere, intermīsī,
intermissus:** interrupt, break, allow to pass; **castra, -ōrum,** n (plural): camp; **legiō, -ōnis,** f: legion.

44.5. Caesar, *de Bello Gallico* 5.12.1–4: The people of the interior of
Britain, their origins, economy, and natural resources.

Britanniae pars interior ab eīs incolitur, quōs nātōs in
insulā ipsī memoriā prōditum dīcunt; maritima pars ab
eīs, quī praedae ac bellī īnferendī causā ex Belgiō

transiērunt (quī omnēs ferē eīs nōminibus cīvitātum
appellantur, quibus ortī ex cīvitātibus eō pervenērunt), et,
bellō inlātō, ibi permansērunt atque agrōs colere coepērunt.
Hominum est infīnīta multitūdō crēberrimaque aedifi-
cia ferē Gallicīs consimilia, pecorum magnus numerus.
Ūtuntur aut aere aut nummō aureō, aut tāleīs ferreīs ad
certum pondus exāminātis prō nummō.

Notes: **interior, interius:** remote, inland; **incolō, -ere, -uī:** live,
dwell, inhabit; **quōs nātōs** *(esse)*; **memoria, -ae,** f: memory, tradition; **prōdō, -ere, prōdidī, prōditus:** hand down (impersonal
verb governing the infintive clause *quōs nātōs in insulā*); notice the
intricate layers of subordination: the relative clause *quōs... dīcunt*
(referring back to *eīs*) triggers an indirect statement *(memoriā
prōditum [esse])*, which in turn governs a second embedded indirect statement *(quōs nātōs in insulā)*. The *quōs* does double duty
introducing the *dīcunt* clause and serving as the subject of *nātōs
(esse)*; **maritimus, -a, -um:** of the sea, by the sea; **praeda, -ae,** f:
spoil, plunder; **bellum inferre:** wage war; **causā** + genitive: for
the sake of (governing *praedae... inferendī*); **transeō, -īre, -iī,
-itus:** cross over; **ferē:** nearly; **cīvitās, -ātis,** f: state, tribe; **appellō,
-āre, -āvī, -ātus:** call; **quibus:** referring to *cīvitātum*; **orior, -īrī,
ortus sum:** arise, be born; **eō:** there, to that place; **perveniō, -īre,
pervēnī, perventus:** arrive; **permaneō, -ēre, permansī, permansus:** remain; **colō, -ere, coluī, cultus:** cultivate, till; **coepī, coepisse,
coeptus** (no first or second principal parts): begin; **infīnītus, -a,
-um:** boundless, numberless; **multitūdō, multitūdinis,** f: a large
number; **crēber, crēbra, crēbrum:** thick, crowded together; **aed-
ificium, -iī,** n: building; **consimilis, -e** + dative: exactly similar,
alike in all respects; **pecus, pecoris,** n: cattle; **ūtor, -ī, ūsus sum** +
ablative: use; **aes, aeris,** n: copper, bronze; **nummus, -ī,** m: coin,
money; **aureus, -a, -um:** of gold; **tālea, -ae,** f: stick, block; **ferreus,
-a, -um:** of iron; **pondus, ponderis,** n: weight, quantity; **exāminō,
-āre, -āvī, -ātus:** weigh.

44.6. Caesar, *de Bello Gallico* 5.17.2: The Britons attack the Roman
troops during a foraging expedition.

Sed merīdiē, cum Caesar, pābulandī causā, trīs legiōnēs
atque omnem equitātum cum C. Trebōniō lēgātō

mīsisset, repente ex omnibus partibus ad pābulātōrēs
advolāvērunt, sīc, utī ab signīs legiōnibusque nōn
absisterent.

Notes: **merīdiēs, -ēī,** m: noon, midday; **pābulor, -ārī, -ātus sum:**
forage; **legiō, -ōnis,** f: legion; **equitātus, -ūs,** m: cavalry; **Caius
Trebōnius, Caiī Trebōniī,** m: among Caesar's most trusted lieu-
tenants serving in Gaul from 55–50 BCE, he participated in the
assassination plot by detaining Marc Antony outside the Theater of
Pompey in 44 BCE; **lēgātus, -ī,** m: lieutenant, envoy; **repente:** suddenly; **pābulātor, -ōris,** m: forager (from the verb *pābulor*); **advolō,
-āre, -āvī, -ātus:** hasten to, rush upon; **utī** = *ut*; **signum, -ī,** n: military standard (see 22.1); **absistō, -ere, abstitī:** stop short of.

44.7. Caesar, *de Bello Gallico* **6.13.11:** Originating in Britain,
Druidism was later transferred to Gaul.

Disciplīna in Britanniā reperta atque inde in Galliam
translāta esse existimātur, et nunc quī dīligentius eam
rem cognoscere volunt plērumque illō discendī causā
proficiscuntur.

Notes: **disciplīna, -ae,** f: instruction, teaching; **reperta** (*esse*) from
re(p)periō, -īre, re(p)perī, re(p)pertus: find out, discover; **inde:** from
that place; **transferō, -ferre, transtulī, translātus:** transfer, carry
over; **existimō, -āre, -āvī, -ātus:** judge, consider, think; **dīligentius:**
more carefully; **cognoscō, -ere, cognōvī, cognitus:** learn, know;
plērumque: generally, for the most part; **illō:** there, to that place;
discō, -ere, didicī: learn; **proficiscor, -ī, profectus sum:** set out;
quī...volunt: subject of *proficiscuntur.*

44.8. Cicero, *in Catilinam* **1.4:** Cicero has the authority of a *senātus
consultum ultimum* (see 37.2) to take any necessary measures
against Catiline and his followers, but he hopes to be merciful.

Habēmus enim eius modī senātūs consultum, vērum
inclūsum in tabulīs, tamquam in vāgīnā recondi-
tum, quō ex senātūs consultō confestim tē interfec-
tum esse, Catilīna, convēnit. Vīvis, et vīvis nōn ad
dēpōnendam, sed ad confirmandam audāciam. Cupiō,
patrēs conscriptī, mē esse clēmentem, cupiō in tantīs reī

pūblicae perīculīs nōn dissolūtum vidērī, sed iam mē
ipse inertiae nēquitiaeque condemnō.

Notes: **modus, -ī, m:** sort, type; **consultum, -ī, n:** decree; **vērum:**
truly, to be sure, however; **inclūdō, -ere, inclūsī, inclūsus:** enclose;
tabulae, -ārum, f (plural): public records; **tamquam:** just as; **vāgīna,**
-ae, f: scabbard; **recondō, -ere, recondidī, reconditus:** hide, conceal; **confestim:** immediately; **interficiō, -ere, interfēcī, interfec-**
tus: kill; **convēnit:** it is fitting; **dēpōnō, -ere, dēposuī, dēpositus:** lay
aside; **confirmō, -āre, -āvī, -ātus:** strengthen; **audācia, -ae,** f: courage; **clēmens, clēmentis:** merciful; **dissolūtus, -a, -um:** loose, lax;
inertia, -ae, f: idleness; **nēquitia, -ae,** f: worthlessness; **condemnō,**
-āre, -āvī, -ātus: condemn.

45. FUTURE PASSIVE PERIPHRASTICS

45.1. Horace, *Carmina* 1.37.1–4: Horace urges his friends to drink,
dance, and celebrate. Meter: Alcaic strophe.

> Nunc est bibendum, nunc pede līberō
> pulsanda tellūs, nunc Saliāribus
>   ornāre pulvīnar deōrum
>   tempus erat dapibus, sodālēs.

Notes: **bibō, -ere, bibī:** drink; **pēs, pedis, m:** foot; **līber, lībera,**
līberum: free, unrestrained; **pulsō, -āre, -āvī, -ātus:** beat; **tellūs,**
-ūris, f: earth; **Saliāris, -e:** Salian (referring to an ancient priest-
hood of Mars, known for their splendid banquets and elaborate
war dances); **ornō, -āre, -āvī, -ātus:** equip, adorn; **pulvīnar, -āris,**
n: couch; **daps, dapis,** f: feast; **sodālis, -is, m:** friend, companion,
crony, buddy.

45.2. Cicero, *in Catilinam* 1.11: Thanks be to Jupiter that Rome has thus
far escaped political ruin. But we may not be so lucky this time.

> Magna dīs immortālibus habenda est atque huic ipsī
> Iovī Statōrī, antīquissimō custōdī huius urbis, grātia,

quod hanc tam taetram, tam horribilem, tamque infestam rēī pūblicae pestem totiens iam effūgimus. Nōn est saepius in ūnō homine summa salūs perīclitanda rēī pūblicae.

Notes: **magna**: modifies *grātia*; **Stator, -ōris, m**: the Stayer, an epithet of Jupiter; **custōs, custōdis, m/f**: guardian; **grātia, -ae, f**: service, kindness, here "thanks"; **taeter, taetra, taetrum**: foul, loathsome; **infestus, -a, -um**: hostile, dangerous; **pestis, -is, f**: plague, destruction; **totiens**: so many times; **saepius**: more often (comparative adverb); **salūs, salūtis, f**: safety, welfare; **perīclitor, -ārī, -ātus sum**: test, risk, endanger.

45.3. Livy, *ab Urbe Condita* 1.34.1: Lucumo's ambitions were unrealized in the place of his birth.

Ancō regnante, Lucumo, vir impiger ac dīvitiīs potens, Rōmam commigrāvit cupīdine maximē ac spē magnī honōris, cuius adipiscendī Tarquiniīs – nam ibī quoque peregrīnā stirpe oriundus erat – facultās nōn fuerat.

Notes: **Ancus, -ī, m**: the fourth king of Rome, who reigned from 640 BCE to 616 BCE, according to tradition; **regnō, -āre, -āvī, -ātus**: rule; **Lucumo**: see 41.1; **impiger, impigra, impigrum**: active, energetic; **dīvitiae, -ārum, f** (plural): wealth; **potens, potentis**: strong, powerful; **commigrō, -āre, -āvī, -ātus**: move, migrate; **cupīdō, cupīdinis, f**: desire (for gain); **maximē**: especially; **spēs, -ēī, f**: hope; **honor, -ōris, m**: honor, glory (*honōris*: objective genitive); **cuius**: refers to *spē magnī honōris*; **adipiscor, -ī, adeptus sum**: obtain (with *cuius* and depending on *facultās*); **Tarquiniī, -ōrum, m** (plural): the lands of the Tarquinii/Etruscans, a non-Italian people who lived near Rome (*Tarquiniīs*: ablative of place where); **ibī quoque**: there also (i.e., not just at Rome); **peregrīnus, -a, -um**: foreign; **stirps, stirpis, f**: family; **orior, -īrī, ortus sum**: arise, spring, be born; **facultās, -ātis, f**: opportunity, resource.

45.4. *CIL* I 2.2138: Cremona, Italy. Tombstone. One day you, too, will be like me.

M(arcus) Satius M(arcī) l(ībertīnus) Chilō hīc. Heus tū viātor lasse quī mē praetereis cum diū ambulāreis, tamen hoc veniundum est tibi.

Notes: **Marcus Satius Chilō, Marcī Satiī Chilōnis,** m: a man's name (*Chilō* derives from a Greek word for "lip" or "the brim of a drinking bowl"); **lībertīnus, -ī,** m: freedman, ex-slave; understand *est* as the verb in the first sentence; **heus:** hey there!; **viātor, -ōris,** m: traveler; **lassus, -a, -um:** tired, weary (*lasse:* vocative case); **praetereis** = *praeterīs* from *praetereō, -īre, -iī, -itus:* pass by; **cum** concessive; **diū:** for a long time; **ambulāreis** = *ambulārēs* from *ambulō, -āre, -āvī, -ātus:* walk, travel, strut; **hoc:** referring to the realm of the dead; **veniundum** = *veniendum* from *veniō, -īre, vēnī, ventus:* come, arrive; **tibi:** dative of agent.

46. SUPINES

46.1. Caesar, *de Bello Gallico* 1.30.1: Local Gallic leaders congratulate Caesar on his victory over the Helvetians.

> Bellō Helvētiōrum confectō, tōtīus ferē Galliae lēgātī, principēs cīvitātum, ad Caesarem grātulātum convēnērunt.

Notes: **bellum, -ī,** n: war; **conficiō, -ere, confēcī, confectus:** complete; **tōtus, -a, -um:** whole, entire; **ferē:** nearly; **Gallia, -ae,** f: the territory of Gaul; **lēgātus, -ī,** m: envoy; **princeps, principis,** m: leader, chieftain; **cīvitās, -ātis,** f: state, tribe; **grātulor, -ārī, -ātus sum:** congratulate, give thanks; **conveniō, -īre, convēnī, conventus:** assemble.

46.2. Vergil, *Aeneid* 2.785–787: After Troy has fallen to the Greeks, the Trojans prepare to leave, and Aeneas discovers that his wife, Creusa, is missing. Aeneas returns to the city to find her, but instead meets her ghost. The specter Creusa, after revealing her husband's fate – including trials by sea and an eventual happy ending in Italy – assures him that she was fated to die at Troy, and that it is better to die than to be a slave to the Greeks as a captive of war. Meter: dactylic hexameter.

> Nōn ego Myrmidonum sēdēs Dolopumve superbās
> aspiciam aut Grāīs servītum mātribus ībō,
> Dardanis et dīvae Veneris nurus.

Notes: **Myrmidonēs, -um,** m (plural): the Myrmidons, "ant-people," in Thessaly (northern Greece), ruled by Achilles; **sēdēs, -is,** f: seat, home; **Dolopēs, -um,** m (plural): the people of Thessaly (synonym for *Myrmidonum*); **superbus, -a, -um:** arrogant, proud, haughty (notice the synchysis in the first line); **aspiciō, -ere, aspexī, aspectus:** see, behold; **Grāius, -a, -um:** Greek; **serviō, -īre, -īvī, -ītus:** be slave to; **Dardanis, -idis,** f: a daughter of Dardanus, the mythical ancestor of the Trojan royal family; **dīvus, -a, -um:** divine; **Venus, Veneris,** f: Venus (Aeneas's mother); **nurus, -ūs,** f: daughter-in-law.

46.3. Caesar, *de Bello Gallico* 1.3.6: A Helvetian noble, Orgetorix, persuades other Gallic tribes to ally with the Helvetians against the Romans.

> Perfacile factū esse illīs probat cōnāta perficere, proptereā quod ipse suae cīvitātis imperium obtentūrus esset: nōn esse dubium quīn tōtīus Galliae plūrimum Helvētiī possent; sē suīs cōpiīs suōque exercitū illīs regna conciliātūrum confirmat.

Notes: **perfacilis, -e:** very easy (triggers the supine); **perfacile factū:** complement of *esse*; **probō, -āre, -āvī, -ātus:** prove; **cōnāta perficere:** subject of *esse*; **cōnor, -ārī, -ātus sum:** try (*cōnāta:* substantive, "attempts"); **perficiō, -ere, perfēcī, perfectus:** complete, accomplish; **proptereā quod:** because; **cīvitās, -ātis,** f: state, tribe; **imperium, -iī,** n: sovereignty; **obtineō, -ēre, obtinuī, obtentus:** obtain; **dubius, -a, -um:** doubtful; **quīn...possent:** indirect question, triggered by *dubium,* and serving as the subject of *esse* in the indirect statement *esse dubium*; **quīn:** but that; **plūrimum:** most; **possent:** here, "be powerful"; **cōpiae, -ārum,** f (plural): forces, resources, troops; **exercitus, -ūs,** m: army; **regnum, -ī,** n: kingdom; **conciliō, -āre, -āvī, -ātus:** win, procure, obtain; **confirmō, -āre, -āvī, -ātus:** assure.

46.4. Livy, *ab Urbe Condita* 4.43.1: Nothing memorable happened that year (465 BCE).

> Proximō annō, Cn. Fabiō Vibulānō T. Quinctiō Capitōlīnī filiō Capitōlīnō consulibus, ductū Fabī, cui sorte ea prōvincia ēvēnerat, nihil dignum memorātū actum.

Notes: **proximō annō**: the following year; **Cn. Fabiō Vibulānō (et) T. Quinctiō Capitōlīnī fīlio Capitōlīnō**: asyndeton. Livy establishes the year by naming the two consuls (some texts read Num. for Cn.); **Cnaius Fabius Vibulānus, Cnaiī Fabiī Vibulānī**, m: a Roman man's name, the senior consul of 465 BCE; **Titus Quinctius Capitōlīnus, Titī Quinctiī Capitōlīnī**, m: a Roman man's name (the cognomen recalls one of the seven hills of Rome, the Capitoline, from *caput, capitis*, n: head; according to legend, Rome's fifth king, Tarquinius Priscus who ruled from 616 BCE to 579 BCE, found a human skull when laying the foundations of a temple to Jupiter); **Capitōlīnī fīlio**: Titus has the same name as his father; **ductus, -ūs**, m: leadership, command; **sorte**: by lot, by chance; **prōvincia, -ae**, f: duty, command (this command entailed continuing the ongoing Roman wars against the neighboring Aequi); **ēveniō, -īre, ēvēnī, ēventus**: fall (construe with *sorte*); **nihil**: construe with *actum*; **dignus, -a, -um** + ablative: worthy (triggers the supine); **memorō, -āre, -āvī, -ātus**: mention; **agō, -ere, ēgī, actus**: do, accomplish (understand *est*).

47. INTERMEDIATE LATIN PROSE PASSAGES

47.1. Livy, *ab Urbe Condita* 22.57.2–6: In 216 BCE, early in the Second Punic War (218–201 BCE), Rome suffered from many natural disasters, boding ill for the war. In addition, two of the Vestal Virgins were accused of unchastity, and one was condemned to live burial. The Romans believed that the success of the state depended on the goodwill of the gods, who could be offended by insufficient worship or by the faulty fulfillment of rituals. After consulting the oracle at Delphi and the Sibylline books, two conduits through which deities communicated with people, the Romans hoped to appease the gods with highly unusual sacrifices, including human sacrifice by the live burial of two foreign couples.

[2] Territi etiam super tantas clades cum ceteris prodigiis, tum quod duae Vestales eo anno, Opimia atque Floronia, stupri compertae et altera sub terra, uti

mos est, ad portam Collinam necata fuerat, altera sibimet ipsa mortem consciverat;

[3] L. Cantilius scriba pontificius, quos nunc minores pontifices appellant, qui cum Floronia stuprum fecerat, a Pontifice Maximo eo usque virgis in Comitio caesus erat ut inter verbera exspiraret.

[4] Hoc nefas cum inter tot, ut fit, clades in prodigium versum esset, decemviri libros adire iussi sunt

[5] et Q. Fabius Pictor Delphos ad oraculum missus est sciscitatum quibus precibus suppliciisque deos possent placare et quaenam futura finis tantis cladibus foret.

[6] Interim ex fatalibus libris sacrificia aliquot extraordinaria facta, inter quae Gallus et Galla, Graecus et Graeca in foro bovario sub terram vivi demissi sunt in locum saxo consaeptum, iam ante hostiis humanis, minime Romano sacro, imbutum.

Notes:

22.57.2: **territi** (*sunt*): understand *populi Romani* as the subject; **terreo, -ere, -ui, -itus:** frighten, terrify; **super** + accusative: in addition to; **clades, -is,** f: calamity, natural disaster; **cum...tum:** not only...but also; **ceterus, -a, -um:** other, remaining; **prodigium, -ii,** n: portent, prodigy, wonder, supernatural phenomena that the Romans believed to be messages from the gods; **quod:** because; **eo anno:** in that same year; **Opimia atque Floronia:** the names of the Vestals, in apposition to *Vestales*; **stuprum, -i,** n: indecency, disgrace, sexual intercourse (*stupri:* genitive of the charge; the Vestals took a vow of chastity, and any breech was punishable by burial alive); **compertae** (*sunt*) from *comperio, -ire, comperi, compertus:* find guilty; **alter...alter:** the one...the other; **uti** = *ut*; **mos, moris,** m: habit, custom; **Porta Collina, Portae Collinae,** f: the gate in the fourth-century-BCE Servian Wall at the northern end of the city where the *viae Saleria* and *Nomentana* met, hence making the Vestal's execution very public; **neco, -are, -avi, -atus:** put to death; **sibimet:** *sibi* + the enclitic intensifier *-met* ("her very own self"); **mors, mortis,** f: death; **conscisco, -ere, conscivi, conscitus:** inflict, bring on oneself.

22.57.3: Lucius Cantilius, Lucii Cantilii, m: known only for debauching the Vestal Floronia; **scriba, -ae,** m: scribe, clerk; **pontificius, -a, -um:** priestly, pontifical; **minor, minus:** lesser, subordinate; **pontifex, -ficis,** m: official Roman religion was overseen by a number of different priestly colleges, all of which were under the authority of the *Pontifex Maximus*, who served for life and held great political authority; (*populi Romani*) **appellant; eo:** there; **usque:** continuously; **virga, -ae,** f: twig, "lash"; **Comitium, -ii,** n: political center of ancient Rome, where stood the *Curia* (Senate House) and *Rostrum* (speaker's platform); **caedo, -ere, cecidi, caesus:** cut down, execute; **ut:** introduces a result clause; **verber, verberis,** n: flogging, beating; **exspiro, -are, -avi, -atus:** expire, die, cease.

22.57.4: **nefas,** n (indeclinable): a violation of divine law, an impious act; **ut fit:** a parenthetical clause that interrupts Livy's prepositional phrase; **verto, -ere, verti, versus:** turn, convert (*versum esset*: "since this violation had been turned into a prodigy…"); **decemviri, -orum,** m (plural): one of the priestly colleges at Rome, with ten members during the Punic Wars, but growing to sixteen by the late Republic. The *decemviri* were responsible for guarding, consulting, and interpreting the Sibylline books as requested by the Senate during times of political emergencies and natural disasters; **liber, libri,** m: book, here the Sibylline books, a collection of ritual texts in hexameters, supposedly dating from the reign of Tarquinius Superbus (534–510 BCE); **adeo, -ire, -ii, -itus:** approach, consult; **iubeo, -ere, iussi, iussus:** order, command.

22.57.5: Quintus Fabius Pictor, Quinti Fabii Pictoris, m: a senator and Rome's first historian, who wrote an annalistic (year-by-year) account in Greek that is now lost; **Delphos ad oraculum:** the famous shrine at Delphi in Boeotia in Greece, where people from across the Mediterranean came to consult Apollo's oracle; **sciscitor, -ari, -atus sum:** consult (*sciscitatum*: supine of purpose); **prex, precis,** f: prayer, request; **supplicium, -ii,** n: entreaty, supplication; **placo, -are, -avi, -atus:** appease, placate, reconcile; **quaenam:** what, just what; **finis, -is,** m: end; **foret** = *futurus esset*; **tantis cladibus:** dative of reference.

22.57.6: **fatalis, -e:** fated, relating to destiny (the Sibylline books were believed to be prophetic); **sacrificium, -ii,** n: offering, sacrifice; **aliquot** (indeclinable): some, several; **extraordinarius, -a, -um:** extraordinary, irregular; **facta** (*sunt*); **quae** (*sacrificia*); **Gallus**

et Galla: a man and a woman from Gaul; **Graecus et Graeca**: a man and a woman from Greece; **in foro bovario**: the marketplace where cattle (*bos, bovis*, m/f) were sold; **sub** + accusative: beneath; **vivus, -a, -um**: alive; **demitto, -ere, demisi, demissus**: lower, send down, drop; **saxum, -i**, n: rock, cliff, crag; **consaepio, -ire, consaepsi, consaeptus**: surround, seal off, shut in; **ante**: previously, i.e., before the Romans occupied Latium; **hostia, -ae**, f: sacrificial offering (construe with *imbutum*); **minime**: not at all (Livy tells us that the practice is *Greek* not *Roman*); **minime... sacro**: take in apposition to *hostiis humanis*; **sacrum, -i**, n: religious rite; **imbuo, -ere, imbui, imbutus**: saturate, steep, taint (*imbutum* modifies *locum*).

47.2. Petronius, *Satyricon* 39.4–15: In this section of the novel, Trimalchio, an affluent freedman, is hosting an outlandish banquet at which each course is more elaborate than the previous one. Just brought out for the amusement of the guests is a dish representing the twelve signs of the zodiac, for which the host gives hilariously fallacious explanations. Trimalchio's posturing, just like that of his guests, often results in grammatical errors. We pick up in the middle of a longer speech.

[4] "...Patrono meo ossa bene quiescant, qui me hominem inter homines voluit esse. Nam mihi nihil novi potest afferri, sicut ille fer[i]culus †ta mel habuit praxim†.

[5] Caelus hic, in quo duodecim dii habitant, in totidem se figuras convertit, et modo fit aries. Itaque quisquis nascitur illo signo, multa pecora habet, multum lanae, caput praeterea durum, frontem expudoratam, cornum acutum. Plurimi hoc signo scholastici nascuntur et arietilli." laudamus urbanitatem mathematici; itaque adiecit:

[6] "Deinde totus caelus taurulus fit. Itaque tunc calcitrosi nascuntur et bubulci et qui se ipsi pascunt.

[7] In geminis autem nascuntur bigae et boves et colei et qui utrosque parietes linunt.

[8] In cancro ego natus sum: ideo multis pedibus sto, et in mari et in terra multa possideo; nam cancer et hoc et illoc quadrat. Et ideo iam dudum nihil supra illum posui, ne genesim meam premerem.

[9] In leone cataphagae nascuntur et imperiosi.

[10] In virgine mulierosi et fugitivi et compediti; in libra laniones et unguentarii et quicumque aliquid expendunt;

[11] in scorpione venenarii et percussores; in sagittario strabones, qui holera spectant, lardum tollunt;

[12] in capricorno aerumnosi, quibus prae mala sua cornua nascuntur; in aquario copones et cucurbitae;

[13] in piscibus obsonatores et rhetores. Sic orbis vertitur tamquam mola, et semper aliquid mali facit, ut homines aut nascantur aut pereant.

[14] Quod autem in medio caespitem videtis et super caespitem favum, nihil sine ratione facio.

[15] Terra mater est in medio quasi ovum corrotundata, et omnia bona in se habet tamquam favus."

Notes:

39.4: **patronus, -i**, m: patron; **os, ossis**, n: bone; **quiesco, -ere, quievi, quietus**: rest; **novi**: partitive with *nihil;* **affero, -ferre, attuli, allatus**: bring; **sicut**: just as; **fericulum, -i**, n: dish, course (Trimalchio has converted the usual neuter form to a masculine); † **ta mel habuit praxim** †: the phrase as preserved in the manuscript does not make sense, so editors have offered various "corrections" to the text. Perhaps the most convincing emendation is *iam semel habuit apodexin* (*apodexin*: a Greek word meaning "demonstration," "proof"); **habuit praxim**: "has given proof" (*praxim*: a Greek accusative; *praxis* is not used elsewhere in Latin literature).

39.5: **caelus, -i**, m: sky (this word is usually neuter); **totidem**: as many; **se**: direct object of *convertit;* **figuras**: object of the preposition *in*, taken with *totidem;* **modo**: just now (we imagine Trimalchio pointing to the relevant components of the dish as he explains the signs of the zodiac); **aries, -etis,** m: ram; **nascor, -i, natus sum:** be born, spring forth; **pecus, pecoris,** n: herd, flock; **lana, -ae,** f: wool (*lanae:* partitive with *multum*); **praeterea:** moreover; **durus, -a, -um:** hard, inflexible; **frons, frontis,** f: forehead, brow; **expudoratus, -a, -um,** lacking shame, brazen; **cornu, -us,** n: horn (the accusative singular is usually *cornu*); **acutus, -a, -um:** sharp; **scholasticus, -i,** m: teacher, rhetorician; **arietillus, -a, -um:** ram-like, shameless (*arietilli:* substantive, "shameless people"); **urbanitas, -atis,** f: sophistication, wit; **mathematicus, -i,** m: astrologer; **adicio, -ere, adieci, adiectus:** add, proceed, go on.

39.6: **taurulus, -a, -um:** like a bull; **calcitrosus, -a, -um:** inclined to kick with the heels (Taurus is the only sign that is represented facing backward and thus seems to go through the night sky unwillingly); **bubulcus, -i,** m: cattle driver, farm laborer, "cowboy"; **pasco, -ere, pavi, pastus:** feed, pasture, support (*pascunt* refers to people who are perceived to be self-reliant or independent).

39.7: **in** + ablative: here, "under the sign of"; **geminus, -a, -um:** twin-born, twin (referring to Castor and Pollux, the adventuring twin brothers of Helen: they protected horses, the Roman *equites* who were originally a class of mounted knights, and shipwrecked sailors; they also brought favorable winds to their worshippers; Pollux, son of Zeus, was so grieved at the death of Castor, the mortal son of Tyndareus, that he shared half of his immortality with Castor; thus the twins, splitting their time between the realm of the gods on Olympus and the world of the dead in Hades, are always together); **bigae, -arum,** f (plural): brace of horses, two-horse team; **bos, bovis,** m/f: ox (here, two oxen yoked together); **coleus, -i,** m: testicle (which also come in a pair); **uterque, utraque, utrumque:** each, both; **paries, -etis,** m: wall; **lino, -ere, levi, litus:** plaster, smear (as typical of a duplicitous politician).

39.8–9: **cancer, cancri,** m: crab; **ideo:** therefore; **possideo, -ere, possedi, possessus:** be master of, occupy, possess; **et hoc et illoc** = *et huc et illuc*; **quadro, -are, -avi, -atus:** square up, suit (the crab is amphibious, dwelling both on land and in water); **dudum:** just now; **illum** (*cancrum*); **genesis, -is,** f: horoscope (*genesim*: Greek accusative); **premo, -ere, pressi, pressus:** cause to sink; **leo, leonis,** m: lion; **cataphagas, -ae,** m: glutton (a Greek word); **imperiosus, -a, -um:** domineering, dictatorial, imperious.

39.10: virgo, virginis, f: maid, virgin; **mulierosus, -a, -um**: fond of women; **fugitivus, -a, -um**: fugitive, runaway (originally the constellation Virgo was connected with Erigone, who fled the earth after the Golden Age; hence, she was a *fugitiva*); **compeditus, -i,** m: shackled slave (the constellation Virgo appears near one of the cardinal points [knot/*nodus*] of the zodiac, and her feet thus seem to be bound by this *nodus*); **libra, -ae,** f: scale, balance; **lanio, -onis,** m: butcher; **unguentarius, -ii,** m: perfume dealer; **expendo, -ere, expendi, expensus:** weigh.

39.11: scorpio, -onis, m: scorpion (a poisonous animal); **venenarius, -ii,** m: poisoner; **percussor, -oris,** m: murderer, assassin; **sagittarius, -ii,** m: archer, bowman; **strabo, -onis,** m: squinter (like an archer as he aims his bow); **holus, holeris,** n: vegetable; **lardum, -i,** n: bacon; **tollo, tollere, sustuli, sublatus:** lift, raise, steal (thieves focus their attention in one direction, their gaze in another).

39.12: capricornus, -i, m: goat horn (this sign fell under the astrological "House" of Saturn, and thus is associated with people who endure hardships); **aerumnosus, -a, -um:** afflicted with troubles; **prae mala sua cornua nascuntur:** an obscure phrase that may refer to cuckolds or pushovers ("whose horns spring up when faced with their evils"); **quibus:** dative of possession; **prae** + ablative (in classical Latin): before, in front of, faced with (here with the accusative, as is common in later Latin; this may be the earliest example of *prae* + accusative); **aquarius, -ii,** m: water carrier (Ganymede or Hebe); **copo, -onis,** m: salesman, tavern keeper, huckster (the classical spelling is *caupo*; innkeepers were often accused of mixing too much water into the wine to save money or increase profits); **cucurbita, -ae,** f: gourd, cupping glass for bleeding (a medical practice), a "gourd-headed person" (i.e., someone with "water on the brain" – gourds were among the materials used to store and transfer water).

39.13: piscis, -is, m: fish; **obsonator, -oris,** m: caterer (who would deal in fish; the word derives from Greek *opsoneo*, which refers particularly to the purchase of fish); **rhetor, -oris,** m: rhetor, teacher of rhetoric (because Pan, closely associated with Mercury, the god of eloquence and persuasion, once turned himself into the Capricorn to escape danger); **orbis, -is,** m: circle (here, world), subject of *vertitur* and *facit*; **verto, -ere, verti, versus:** turn; **tamquam:** just like; **mola, -ae,** f: millstone; **mali:** partitive with *aliquid*; **pereo, -ire, -ivi, -itus:** die, pass away.

39.14–15: **quod**: the fact that; **in medio** (of the dish representing the zodiac); **caespes, -itis**, m: ground, turf; **favus, -i**, m: honeycomb (symbolizing growth); **quasi**: as if (construe with *ovum*); **ovum, -i**, n: egg; **corrotundo, -are, -avi, -atus**: make round; **bona, -orum**, n (plural): "property".

47.3. Pliny the Younger, *Epistulae* 6.16.15–20: In this letter to the historian Tacitus, Pliny describes how his uncle, Pliny the Elder, was stationed at Misenum in August of 79 CE when Mount Vesuvius erupted. His uncle rushed toward the blast and initiated heroic rescue efforts that resulted in his death. Here, Pliny describes the final moments of his uncle's life. After receiving this letter, Tacitus asks Pliny to describe his own reaction to the eruption, and Pliny complies with another harrowing description of the natural disaster (*Epistulae* 6.20).

[15] In commune consultant, intra tecta subsistant an in aperto vagentur. Nam crebris vastisque tremoribus tecta nutabant, et quasi emota sedibus suis nunc huc nunc illuc abire aut referri videbantur.

[16] Sub dio rursus quamquam levium exesorumque pumicum casus metuebatur, quod tamen periculorum collatio elegit; et apud illum quidem ratio rationem, apud alios timorem timor vicit. Cervicalia capitibus imposita linteis constringunt; id munimentum adversus incidentia fuit.

[17] Iam dies alibi, illic nox omnibus noctibus nigrior densiorque; quam tamen faces multae variaque lumina solvebant. Placuit egredi in litus, et ex proximo adspicere, ecquid iam mare admitteret; quod adhuc vastum et adversum permanebat.

[18] Ibi super abiectum linteum recubans semel atque iterum frigidam aquam poposcit hausitque. Deinde flammae flammarumque praenuntius odor sulpuris alios in fugam vertunt, excitant illum.

[19] Innitens servolis duobus adsurrexit et statim concidit, ut ego colligo, crassiore caligine spiritu obstructo,

clausoque stomacho qui illi natura invalidus et angustus et frequenter aestuans erat.

[20] Ubi dies redditus (is ab eo quem novissime viderat tertius), corpus inventum integrum inlaesum opertumque ut fuerat indutus: habitus corporis quiescenti quam defuncto similior.

Notes:

6.16.15: in **commune:** "for a common purpose"; **consulto, -are, -avi, -atus:** deliberate, take counsel (triggers an indirect question); **intra** + accusative: within; **tectum, -i,** n: house, building, shelter; **subsisto, -ere, substiti:** stand still, remain standing; **an:** whether... or; **in aperto:** "in the open air"; **vagor, -ari, -atus sum:** wander; **creber, crebra, crebrum:** frequent, numerous; **tremor, -oris,** m: tremor, quaking (*tremoribus:* ablative of means); **nuto, -are, -avi, -atus:** shake; **quasi:** as if; **emoveo, -ere, emovi, emotus:** move away, dislodge; **sedes, -is,** f: base, foundation; **nunc huc nunc illuc:** now this way, now that way; **abeo, -ire, -ii, -itus:** go away; **refero, -ferre, rettuli, relatus:** bring back, return.

6.16.16: **sub dio:** "in the open air"; **rursus:** on the one hand; **quamquam:** although (qualifies *levium exesorumque*); **levis, -e:** light; **exesus, -a, -um:** corroded; **pumex, pumicis,** m: stone; **casus, -us,** m: falling; **metuo, -ere, metui, metutus:** fear; **quod:** "this route/ course of action" (refers to entire previous clause); **periculum, -i,** n: danger (*periculorum:* partitive genitive with *quod*); **collatio, collationis,** f: comparison, combination; **eligo, -ere, elegi, electus:** choose; **apud** + accusative: in the case of; **illum:** Uncle Pliny; **ratio, -onis,** f: calculation, reasoning, judgment; **timor, -oris,** m: fear; **vinco, -ere, vici, victus:** overcome, conquer; **cervicalium, -ii,** n: cushion; **caput, capitis,** n: head; **linteum, -i,** n: linen cloth, sail; **impono, -ere, imposui, impositus:** place upon; **constringo, -ere, constrinxi, constrictus:** bind, tie; **munimentum, -i,** n: defense, protection; **adversus** + accusative: against; **incido, -ere, incidi, incasus:** fall (*incidentia:* substantive, "the things falling").

6.16.17: **iam:** now; **dies, -ei,** m: day; **alibi:** elsewhere; **illic:** there; **nox, noctis,** f: night; **omnibus noctibus:** ablative of comparison; **niger, nigra, nigrum:** black, dark; **densus, -a, -um:** thick, close; **quam:** it (night); **fax, facis,** f: torch; **lumen, luminis,** n: light; **solvo, -ere,**

solvi, solutus: release, weaken; placeo, -ere, placui, placitus: be pleasing; egredior, -i, egressus sum: set out, depart; litus, litoris, n: shore; ex proximo: "from the nearest point"; adspicio, -ere, adspexi, adspectus: look at (triggers an indirect question); ecquid: whether anything; if anything; mare, maris, n: sea; admitto, -ere, admisi, admissus: allow, permit; quod: it (the sea); adversus, -a, -um: hostile, adverse, unfavorable; permaneo, -ere, permansi, permansus: hold out, be permanent, remain.

6.16.18: super + accusative: over, upon, on; abicio, -ere, abieci, abiectus: throw away, throw down; recubo, -are: lie down, recline; semel atque iterum: once and a second time; posco, -ere, poposci: demand, request (understand Uncle Pliny as the subject); haurio, -ire, hausi, haustus: drink up, drain; flamma, -ae, f: flame; praenuntius, -ii, m: foreteller, harbinger; odor, -oris, m: smell, odor; sulpur, sulpuris, n: sulphur; fuga, -ae, f: flight, panic, escape; verto, -ere, verti, versus: turn; excito, -are, -avi, -atus: wake up, rouse (note the asyndeton in this clause); illum: Uncle Pliny.

6.16.19: innitor, -i, innixus sum: lean upon; servolus, -i, m: young slave; adsurgo, -ere, adsurrexi, adsurrectus: rise up, stand up; concido, -ere, concidi: fall down; ut: as; colligo, -ere, collegi, collectus: gather, deduce; crassus, -a, -um: fat, thick, solid; caligo, caliginis, f: thick air, mist, fog; spiritus, -us, m: breath; obstruo, -ere, obstruxi, obstructus: block, stop up; claudo, -ere, clausi, clausus: restrict, shut down; stomachus, -i, m: windpipe, esophagus; illi: dative case (Uncle Pliny); natura: ablative of cause; invalidus, -a, -um: weak; angustus, -a, -um: contracted; frequenter: often; aestuo, -are, -avi, -atus: burn.

6.16.20: ubi: when; redditus (est); reddo, -ere, reddidi, redditus: return, restore; is (dies erat)...tertius: it (was) the third (day); novissime: most recently; is ab eo quem novissime viderat tertius: "it was the third day from that which Uncle Pliny had seen most recently" (Uncle Pliny was dead two days later); corpus, corporis, n: body; inventum (est) from invenio, -ire, inveni, inventus: find; integer, integra, integrum: whole, intact; inlaesus, -a, -um: unharmed; operio, -ire, operui, opertus: cover over; indutus, -a, -um: clothed; habitus, -us, m: condition, appearance; quiesco, -ere, quievi, quietus: rest; quam: than; defunctus, -a, -um: dead, finished off; similis, -e + dative: similar.

48. INTERMEDIATE LATIN POETRY PASSAGES

48.1. Vergil, *Georgics* 4.485–503: Vergil ends this didactic poem on farming with an *epyllion*, or "little epic," that relates the story of the famous musician Orpheus and his beloved wife, Eurydice. Shortly after their wedding, Eurydice dies from a poisonous snakebite, and Orpheus journeys to the underworld to plead for the return of his wife. His lyre playing so moves Proserpina, the queen of the underworld, that she grants Eurydice's return – provided that Orpheus not look upon his wife until they are both in the light of the upper world. They are almost home, when Orpheus gives into temptation and steals a glance at Eurydice, who in turn vanishes into thin air. Later in his career, Vergil composed a similar passage to describe Aeneas's anguish at the loss of his wife Creusa in the flames of Troy (see *Aeneid* 2.768–795). Meter: dactylic hexameter.

Iamque pedem referens casus evaserat omnis;   485
redditaque Eurydice superas veniebat ad auras,
pone sequens (namque hanc dederat
    Proserpina legem),
cum subita incautum dementia cepit amantem,
ignoscenda quidem, scirent si ignoscere Manes.
Restitit, Eurydicenque suam iam luce sub ipsa   490
immemor – heu! – victusque animi
    respexit. Ibi omnis
effusus labor atque immitis rupta tyranni
foedera, terque fragor stagnis auditus Avernis.
Illa, "Quis et me," inquit, "miseram et te
    perdidit, Orpheu,
quis tantus furor? En iterum crudelia retro   495
Fata vocant, conditque natantia lumina somnus.
Iamque vale: feror ingenti circumdata nocte
invalidasque tibi tendens, heu non tua, palmas!"
Dixit et ex oculis subito, ceu fumus in auras
commixtus tenuis, fugit diversa, neque illum,   500

prensantem nequiquam umbras et multa volentem
dicere, praeterea vidit, nec portitor Orci
amplius obiectam passus transire paludem.

Notes:

4.485–489: **iamque:** and now, at this precise moment; **pes, pedis,**
m: foot; **refero, -ferre, rettuli, relatus:** bring back, carry back (with
pedem: go back, withdraw, retreat: *referens* modifies an understood
Orpheus); **casus, -us,** m: misfortune, mishap; **evado, -ere, evasi,**
evasus: escape, pass beyond; **reddo, -ere, reddidi, redditus:** return,
restore; **superus, -a, -um:** upper, higher; **aura, -ae,** f: air, breeze;
pone: behind; **sequor, -i, secutus sum:** follow; **Proserpina, -ae,** f:
queen of the underworld; **lex, legis,** f: condition, regulation, stipula-
tion; **cum:** when; **subitus, -a, -um:** sudden, unexpected; **incautus,**
-a, -um: incautious, reckless; **dementia, -ae,** f: madness, insanity;
capio, -ere, cepi, captus: take, seize; **subita incautum dementia**
amantem: synchises; **ignosco, -ere, ignovi, ignotus:** forgive, over-
look (*ignoscenda:* gerundive with *dementia*); **quidem:** indeed; **scio,**
-ire, scivi, scitus: know (*scirent:* subjunctive in the protasis of a con-
trary-to-fact conditional); **Manes, -ium,** m (plural): shades, spirits.

4.490–493: **resto, restare, restiti:** stand still; **Eurydicen:** Greek
accusative singular of *Eurydice;* **suam:** his (Orpheus's) own; **luce sub**
ipsa: at daybreak itself; **immemor, immemoris:** forgetful, unmind-
ful: **heu:** alas; **vinco, -ere, vici, victus:** overcome, overpower; **animi:**
objective genitive, "by his soul"; **respicio, -ere, respexi, respectus:**
look back; **ibi:** there, in that place; **effusus** (*est*) from *effundo, -ere,*
effudi, effusus: pour out, squander, waste; **labor, -oris,** m: effort,
work; **immitis, -e:** harsh, severe, stern; **rupta** (*sunt*); **rumpo, -ere,**
rupi, ruptus: break, burst, tear apart; **tyrannus, -i,** m: king (here,
Pluto, the king of the underworld); **foedus, foederis,** n: treaty, alliance; **immitis rupta tyranni foedera:** synchises; **ter:** three times;
fragor, -oris, m: crash, loud noise; **stagnum, -i,** n: lake, pool; **audi-**
tus (*est*); **Avernus, -a, -um:** of the underworld, infernal regions.

4.494–498: **Illa:** Eurydice; **Quis:** who? what? (pronoun used as an
adjective with *tantus furor* and repeated in the next line for poetic
emphasis [anaphora]); **et...et:** both...and; **perdo, -ere, perdidi,**
perditus: destroy, ruin; **Orpheu:** vocative singular; **furor, -oris,**
m: madness, passion, rage; **En:** behold; **iterum:** again; **crudelis,**

-e: cruel, severe, fierce; **retro**: back; **Fata, -orum**, n (plural): Fates; **vocant**: supply Euridyce as the direct object; **condo, -ere, condidi, conditus**: put together, close, shut; **nato, -are, -avi, -atus**: swim; **lumen, luminis**, n: light, eye; **somnus, -i**, m: sleep; **ingens, ingentis**: huge, vast; **circumdo, -are, circumdedi, circumdatus**: surround, encircle; **nox, noctis**, f: night; **invalidus, -a, -um**: weak, feeble; **tendo, -ere, tetendi, tentus**: stretch; **heu non tua** (*sum*): "alas, (I am) no longer yours"; **palma, -ae**, f: palm (of a hand); **invalidas...palmas**: hyperbaton.

4.499–503: Euridyce is the subject of *dixit* and *fugit*; **ex oculis**: refers to Orpheus's eyes; **ceu**: just as; **fumus, -i**, m: smoke; **commisceo, -ere, commiscui, commixtus**: mix, mingle together; **tenuis, -e**: thin; **fugio, -ere, fugi**: flee, escape; **diversus, -a, -um**: turned in different directions; **neque...nec**: neither...nor; **illum**: Orpheus; **prenso, -are, -avi, -atus**: grasp; **nequiquam**: in vain; **umbra, -ae**, f: shadow, shade; **praeterea**: besides, moreover; **vidit**: the subject is still Eurydice; **portitor, -oris**, m: ferryman (here, Charon); **Orcus, -i**, m: underworld; **amplius**: further, besides, a second time; **obicio, -ere, obieci, obiectus**: throw before, spread before; **passus** (*est*) from *patior, -i, passus sum*: allow (take Orpheus as the understood direct object); **transeo, -ire, -ii, -itus**: cross; **palus, paludis**, f: swamp, marsh, pool.

48.2. Sulpicia 2 and 3: Sulpicia is one of the only Roman women whose writings survive to the present day. Her elegiac poems rival those of her male counterparts (Catullus, Propertius, Tibullus, and Ovid) and feature her "literary boyfriend," Cerinthus. In the first poem, Sulpicia is disappointed because her guardian, Messalla, has made plans for them to spend her birthday in the country. She would rather stay in Rome and celebrate with Cerinthus. If forced to go on the trip, she plans to leave her heart and mind in the city. In the second poem, Sulpicia informs Cerinthus that her plans have changed and that she can spend her birthday with him. Sulpicia is not the only Roman poet to compose birthday poems (*genethliaca*). See also Tibullus 1.7 and 2.2. Meter: elegiac couplets.

> Invisus natalis adest, qui rure molesto
> et sine Cerintho tristis agendus erit.

Dulcius urbe quid est? An villa sit apta puellae
atque Arretino frigidus amnis agro?
Iam, nimium Messalla mei studiose, quiescas,
non tempestivae saepe, propinque, viae!
Hic animum sensusque meos abducta relinquo,
arbitrio quamvis non sinit esse meo.

***

Scis iter ex animo sublatum triste puellae?
natali Romae iam licet esse suo.
Omnibus ille dies nobis natalis agatur,
qui nec opinanti nunc tibi forte venit.

Notes:

Poem 2: **invisus, -a, -um:** hateful, detested; **natalis** (*dies*): birthday; **adsum, -esse, affui:** be at hand, be here; **rus, ruris,** n: country;
molestus, -a, -um: annoying; **sine** + ablative: without; **tristis, -e:**
sad, unhappy (here, adverbial, "unhappily"); **ago, -ere, egi, actus:**
spend (*agendus erit:* will have to be spent); **dulcis, -e:** sweet; **urbe:**
ablative of comparison; **an:** or; **villa, -ae,** f: country house; **sit:** delib-
erative subjunctive; **aptus, -a, -um** + dative: fitting (for); **Arretino
frigidus amnis agro:** chiasmus; **Arretinus, -a, -um:** of Arretium;
frigidus, -a, -um: cold, cool; **amnis, -is,** m: river, stream (here, the
Arno); **nimium:** too much, too; **mei:** objective genitive; **studiosus,
-a, -um:** anxious, devoted, attached; **quiesco, -ere, quievi, quietus:**
keep quiet, stop (*quiescas:* hortatory subjunctive); **tempestivus, -a,
-um:** opportune, seasonsable; **propinquus, -i,** m: relative; **via, -ae,**
f: road; **hic:** here; **abduco, -ere, abduxi, abductus:** lead away, carry
off; **relinquo, -ere, reliqui, relictus:** leave behind, abandon; **arbi-
trium, -i,** n: judgment, power, free will (ablative of specification);
quamvis: although (here "since"); **sino, -ere, sivi, situs:** allow, permit (understand Messalla as subject of *sinit*).

Poem 3: **scio, -ire, scivi, scitus:** know; **iter, itineris,** n: journey;
sublatum (*esse*) from *tollo, -ere, sustuli, sublatus:* take away, remove;
Romae: locative case; **licet, -ere, licuit:** it is allowed; **suo:** her own
(Sulpicia's); some texts read *tuo* for *suo;* **agatur:** jussive subjunctive;
omnibus nobis: by us all (dative of agent); **qui:** antecedent is *dies;*
opinor, -ari, -atus sum: think, expect; **forte:** by chance.

48.3. Ovid, *Metamorphoses* 8.796–813: Erysichthon dishonors the goddess Ceres by chopping down her sacred oak, even after his workmen warn him to refrain from such impiety. A nymph of Ceres, who lives in the oak, curses him for this crime. When Ceres hears what has happened, she decides to torment Erysichthon with insatiable hunger. She orders one of her mountain nymphs to drive her dragon-led chariot and enlist the help of Hunger because Ceres herself cannot come in contact with such an inauspicious goddess. In this passage, the mountain nymph has arrived at Hunger's lair, and Ovid provides a vivid description of Hunger's physical qualities and the nymph's dread as she executes Ceres' mandate. Meter: dactylic hexameter.

> Illa dato subvecta per aera curru
> devenit in Scythiam rigidique cacumine montis
> (Caucason appellant) serpentum colla levavit
> quaesitamque Famem lapidoso vidit in agro
> unguibus et raras vellentem dentibus herbas.   800
> Hirtus erat crinis, cava lumina, pallor in ore,
> labra incana situ, scabrae rubigine fauces,
> dura cutis, per quam spectari viscera possent;
> ossa sub incurvis exstabant arida lumbis,
> ventris erat pro ventre locus; pendere putares   805
> pectus et a spinae tantummodo crate teneri.
> Auxerat articulos macies, genuumque tumebat
> orbis, et immodico prodibant tubere tali.
> Hanc procul ut vidit (neque enim est accedere iuxta
>   ausa), refert mandata deae paulumque morata,   810
> quamquam aberat longe, quamquam modo
>   venerat illuc,
> visa tamen sensisse famem est, retroque dracones
> egit in Haemoniam versis sublimis habenis.

Notes:

8.796–800: **illa:** Ceres' nymph; **subveho, -ere, subvexi, subvectus:** convey, transport; **aer, aeris,** m: air (*aera:* accusative singular); **currus, -us,** m: chariot (*dato…curru:* ablative absolute); **devenio, -ire,**

deveni, deventus: come down, arrive; **Scythia, -ae,** f: Scythia; **rigidus, -a, -um:** rough, rocky; **cacumen, cacuminis,** n: peak, summit; **mons, montis,** m: mountain; **Caucasus, -i,** m: mountains between the Caspian and Black seas (*Caucason:* Greek accusative singular); **serpens, serpentis,** m: snake, serpent (here, the dragons pulling the chariot); **collum, -i,** n: neck; **levo, -are, -avi, -atus:** release, free; **quaero, -ere, quaesivi, quaesitus:** seek, look for; **Fames, -is,** f: Hunger; **lapidosus, -a, -um:** full of stones; **ager, agri,** m: field; **unguis, -is,** m: nail; **rarus, -a, -um:** few, scarce, scattered; **vello, -ere, velli, vulsus:** pluck, pull out; **dens, dentis,** m: tooth; **herba, -ae,** f: grass.

8.801–806: **hirtus, -a, -um:** rough, shaggy; **crinis, -is,** m: hair; **cavus, -a, -um:** hollow; **lumen, luminis,** n: light, eye; **pallor, -oris,** m: paleness; **os, oris,** n: mouth; **labrum, -i,** n: lip; **incanus, -a, -um:** gray; **situs, -us,** m: inactivity, neglect; **scaber, scabra, scabrum:** rough; **rubigo, rubiginis,** f: rust, mildew, mold; **fauces, -ium,** f (plural): throat, jaws; **durus, -a, -um:** rough, harsh; **cutis, -is,** f: skin; **viscera, -um,** n (plural): entrails; **ossa incurvis arida lumbis:** synchises; **os, ossis,** n: bone; **incurvus, -a, -um:** crooked, curved; **exsto, -are, exstiti:** stand out; **aridus, -a, -um:** dry; **lumbus, -i,** m: loin; **ventris erat pro ventre locus:** "the place for a belly was instead of belly"; **pendeo, -ere, pependi:** hang; **puto, -are, -avi, -atus:** think (*putares:* "you would have thought"); **pectus, pectoris,** n: chest; **spina, -ae,** f: spine; **tantummodo:** only, merely; **cratis, -is,** f: rib.

8.807–813: **augeo, -ere, auxi, auctus:** enlarge, augment, exaggerate; **articulus, -i,** m: joint; **macies, -ei,** f: thinness; **genu, -us,** n: knee; **tumeo, -ere, -ui:** swell; **orbis, -is,** m: orb, knob; **immodicus, -a, -um:** excessive; **prodeo, -ire, -ii, -itus:** go forth, come forth; **tuber, tuberis,** n: lump, swelling; **talus, -i,** m: ankle; **hanc:** this woman (Hunger); **procul:** at a distance; **ut:** when (understand Ceres' nymph as the subject of *vidit*); **accedo, -ere, accessi:** come near, approach; **iuxta;** close, nearby; **audeo, -ere, ausus sum:** dare; **refero, -ferre, rettuli, relatus:** announce, report; **mandatum, -i,** n: command, order; **paulum:** a little; **moror, -ari, -atus sum:** delay; **quamquam:** although; **absum, -esse, afui, afuturus:** be away; **longe:** far off; **modo:** just now, recently; **illuc:** to that place; **visa est:** she seemed; **sentio, -ire, sensi, sensus:** perceive, feel; **retro:** back; **draco, -onis,** m: dragon, huge serpent; **ago, -ere, egi, actus:** do, drive; **Haemonia, -ae,** f: Thessaly; **verto, -ere, verti, versus:** turn; **sublimis, -e:** raised up; **habenae, -arum,** f (plural): reins.

49. ADVANCED LATIN PROSE PASSAGES

49.1. Sallust, *Bellum Catilinae* 60.1–7: Following the example of his model, the Greek historian Thucydides, Sallust wrote in a complex and compressed style. He aimed to treat history selectively and realistically, and he succeeded in painting psychological studies that emphasized the personality and morals of the primary actors. Sallust favored archaisms, employing ancient grammatical constructions and spellings, of which there are four examples in our passage: *maxumo* for *maximo*, *vorsari* for *versari*, *relicuom* for *relictum*, and *confertissumos* for *confertissimos*.

Sallust provides an alternate account of the Catilinarian conspiracy, although it is likely that he used Cicero's speeches as a source for his work. Here, he describes the final battle of the Catilinarian conspiracy at Pistorium, in Etruria north of Rome, January of 62 BCE.

[1] Sed ubi omnibus rebus exploratis Petreius tuba signum dat, cohortis paulatim incedere iubet; idem facit hostium exercitus.

[2] Postquam eo ventum est, unde a ferentariis proelium conmitti posset, maxumo clamore cum infestis signis concurrunt: pila omittunt, gladiis res geritur.

[3] Veterani pristinae virtutis memores comminus acriter instare, illi haud timidi resistunt: maxuma vi certatur.

[4] Interea Catilina cum expeditis in prima acie vorsari, laborantibus succurrere, integros pro sauciis arcessere, omnia providere, multum ipse pugnare, saepe hostem ferire: strenui militis et boni imperatoris officia simul exsequebatur.

[5] Petreius ubi videt Catilinam, contra ac ratus erat, magna vi tendere, cohortem praetoriam in medios

hostis inducit, eosque perturbatos atque alios alibi resistentis interficit. Deinde utrimque ex lateribus ceteros adgreditur.

[6] Manlius et Faesulanus in primis pugnantes cadunt.

[7] Catilina postquam fusas copias seque cum paucis relicuom videt, memor generis atque pristinae suae dignitatis, in confertissumos hostis incurrit ibique pugnans confoditur.

Notes:

60.1: **res, rei,** f: preparation; **exploro, -are, -avi, -atus:** test, investigate; **(Marcus) Petreius, (Marci) Petreii,** m: the Roman general leading the troops against Catiline. Praised by Cicero for his actions at this battle (*Sest.* 12), he was later loyal to Pompey when civil war broke out, and committed suicide after the Republican defeat at Thapsus in 46 BCE; **tuba, -ae,** f: war trumpet; **signum, -i,** n: sign; **cohors, cohortis,** f: cohort; **paulatim:** little by little; **incedo, -ere, incessi:** advance; **iubeo, -ere, iussi, iussus:** order, command; **idem, eadem, idem:** the same; **hostis, -is,** m/f: enemy; **exercitus, -us,** m: army.

60.2: **postquam:** after; **eo:** to that place; **ventum est** from *venio* (impersonal, "there was a coming" or "they came"); **unde:** from where; **ferentarius, -ii,** m: light-armed soldier, skirmisher; **proelium, -ii,** n: battle; **conmitto, -ere, conmisi, conmisus:** engage, bring about; **maxumo** = *maximo*; **infestus, -a, -um:** hostile, dangerous; **signum, -i,** n: military standard (see 22.1); **concurro, -ere, concurri, concursus:** charge, rally, engage in battle; **pilum, -i,** n: a heavy iron-tipped throwing spear (usually the Romans volleyed these spears after the skirmishes by the *ferentarii*, and then fought at close quarters with swords. But Catiline's forces have jumped straight into hand-to-hand combat); **omitto, -ere, omisi, omissus:** disregard, lay aside, leave out; **gladius, -i,** m: sword; **gero, -ere, gessi, gestus:** carry on, manage.

60.3: **veteranus, -a, -um:** old, veteran, experienced; **pristinus, -a, -um:** former, original; **virtus, virtutis,** f: excellence, manliness, moral excellence, virtue (*virtutis:* objective genitive); **memor, -oris** + genitive: remembering, mindful; **comminus:** hand to hand, in close quarters; **acriter:** fiercely; **insto, -are, -stiti:** press upon, pursue, harass (*instare:* historical infinitive); **haud:** by no means; **resisto, -ere, restiti:** resist, oppose; **maxuma** = *maxima*; **vis, vis,** f (irregular noun): strength, force, power; **certo, -are, -avi, -atus:** struggle, fight (*certatur:* impersonal passive, "it is fought," "they fight").

60.4: Sallust employs additional historical infinitives, making the action seem even faster, crisper, and more vivid. Translate the historical infinitives (*vorsari, succurrere, arcessere, providere, pugnare, ferire*) as regular verbs; **interea:** meanwhile; **expeditus, -a, -um:** light-armed (here, used as a substantive, "light-armed troops"); **acies, -ei,** f: sharp edge, battle line; **vorsari** = *versari* from *verso, -are, -avi, -atus:* turn, twist around; **laboro, -are, -avi, -atus:** be in trouble, be in distress, be overwhelmed (*laborantibus:* substantive, "those in distress"): **succurro, -ere, succurri, succursus** + dative: run to the aid of, help; **integer, integra, integrum:** fresh (troops), vigorous; **saucius, -a, -um:** wounded; **arcesso, -ere, arcessivi, arcessitus:** send for; **provideo, -ere, provisi, provisus:** foresee, make provisions; **hostem:** Sallust here speaks from Catiline's point of view: the enemy is Petreius's army; **ferio, -ire** (no third and fourth principal parts): strike; **strenuus, -a, -um:** active, vigorous; **miles, militis,** m: soldier; **imperator, -oris,** m: title usually reserved for a victorious Roman general; **officium, -ii,** n: duty; **simul:** at the same time; **exsequor, -i, -secutus sum:** carry out, perform, accomplish.

60.5: **videt:** governs an indirect statement (*Catilinam...tendere*); **contra ac:** otherwise than; **reor, -i, ratus sum:** think, suppose, believe (Petreius is the subject); **tendo, -ere, tetendi, tentus:** strive, exert; **praetorius, -a, -um:** praetorian, relating to the military commander (here, Petreius); **in** + accusative: into, against; **induco, -ere, induxi, inductus:** lead in; **eos:** Catiline's forces; **perturbo, -are, -avi, -atus:** disturb thoroughly, throw into complete confusion; **alibi:** elsewhere; **interficio, -ere, interfeci, interfectus:** kill; **utrimque:** on both sides; **latus, lateris,** n: side, flank; **ceterus, -a, -um:** the other(s), the remaining; **adgredior, -i, aggressus sum:** approach, attack, assail.

60.6: **(Caius) Manlius, (Caii) Manlii,** m: Catiline's ally and general in charge of the right flank at the final battle. Manlius raised an army in Etruria, north of Rome, organized the revolt for Catiline, and was in charge of Catiline's left flank at Pistorium (*Bellum*

Catilinae 59.3; see also *Bellum Catilinae* 33 for Manlius's pep talk to his troops, full of righteous indignation on behalf of the lower classes who had been denied the right of appeal and had been victimized by moneylenders); **Faesulanus, Faesulani,** m: otherwise unknown, but perhaps a soldier from Faesulae (Fiesoli, in Etruria); **in primis**: among the first; **cado, cadere, cecidi, casus**: fall, die.

60.7: **fusas** (*esse*) from *fundo, -ere, fudi, fusus*: rout, scatter; **copiae, -arum**, f (plural): forces, resources, troops; **paucus, -a, -um**: few, little; **relicuom** = *relictum* (*esse*), from *relinquo, relinquere, reliqui, relictus*: leave behind; Sallust compares Catiline to the Roman veterans. Notice the repetition of vocabulary from 60.3; **genus, generis**, n: birth, descent, "nobility"; **dignitas, -atis**, f: excellence, dignity, worth; **confertus, -a -um**: crowded, pressed together, in close order (*confertissumos*: superlative); **incurro, -ere, incurri, incursus**: rush in, attack; **confodio, -ere, confodi, confossus**: stab, run through, wound fatally.

49.2.   Tacitus, *Annales* 1.5.1–3: Tacitus's literary style is highly elliptical: he usually omits forms of the verb "to be," and his ablatives absolute are frequently single words; he also values variation of syntactical structure (balancing historical infinitives with imperfect indicatives, as below in 1.5.1) and vocabulary (in our passage, employing five separate words for "death" or "dying").

Here, Tacitus describes Augustus's rumored reconciliation with his grandson, the brutish Postumus Agrippa, the son of Augustus's daughter Julia, and his friend and advisor Marcus Vipsanius Agrippa. Augustus had adopted Postumus Agrippa as his co-heir with Tiberius, but banished the youth to the small island of Planasia (southwest of Elba, east of Corsica) ostensibly for unpleasantness and rudeness but more likely for a conspiracy against Augustus. Soon after the reconciliation, the emperor died under suspicious circumstances. Tacitus implies that Augustus's wife Livia orchestrated the death to ensure that her son, Tiberius, would succeed Augustus to the throne.

[1] Haec atque talia agitantibus, gravescere valetudo Augusti, et quidam scelus uxoris suspectabant. Quippe rumor incesserat, paucos ante mensis Augustum, electis

consciis et comite uno Fabio Maximo, Planasiam vectum ad visendum Agrippam; multas illic utrimque lac-
rimas et signa caritatis spemque ex eo fore ut iuvenis
penatibus avi redderetur:

[2] quod Maximum uxori Marciae aperuisse, illam
Liviae. Gnarum id Caesari; neque multo post extincto
Maximo, dubium an quaesita morte, auditos in funere
eius Marciae gemitus semet incusantis, quod causa
exitii marito fuisset.

[3] Utcumque se ea res habuit, vixdum ingressus
Illyricum Tiberius properis matris litteris accitur;
neque satis conpertum est, spirantem adhuc Augustum
apud urbem Nolam an exanimem reppererit. Acribus
namque custodiis domum et vias saepserat Livia, laet-
ique interdum nuntii vulgabantur, donec provisis quae
tempus monebat simul excessisse Augustum et rerum
potiri Neronem fama eadem tulit.

Notes:

1.5.1: **haec**: direct object of *agitantibus*, referring to the deteriorat-
ing state of the morals of Augustus's family; **talia**: a second direct
object of *agitantibus*, referring to the perceived haughtiness and
savagery of Tiberius, Augustus's stepson and heir; **agito, -are, -avi,
-atus**: consider (*agitantibus*: one-word ablative absolute; supply
"Roman citizens" to complete the construction); **gravesco, -ere** (no
third or fourth principal parts): grow worse (*gravescere*: historical
infinitive); **valetudo, valetudinis**, f: health, good health, sound-
ness; **quidam** (*cives*): certain (citizens); **scelus, sceleris**, n: crime;
uxor, -oris, f: wife (Livia, Augustus's wife and Tiberius's mother);
suspecto, -are, -avi, -atus: be suspicious of (note the lack of parallel structure, characteristic of Tacitus's literary style: he employs
a historical infinitive, *gravescere*, and then a finite verb, *suspectabant*); **quippe**: naturally, of course; **incedo, -ere, incessi**: advance;
Augustum vectum (*esse*): indirect statement following *rumor*; **electis...Maximo**: ablative absolute; **eligo, -ere, elegi, electus**: pick out,
choose; **conscius, -ii**, m/f: accomplice, accessory, partner; **comes,
comitis**, m/f: comrade, companion; **(Paullus) Fabius Maximus,
(Paulli) Fabii Maximi**, m: married to Augustus's maternal aunt

Atia, served as consul in 11 BCE and proconsul of Asia in 10 BCE; **veho, -ere, vexi, vectus:** convey, carry; **ad visendum:** gerund expressing purpose; **illic:** there; **utrimque:** on both sides; **lacrima, -ae,** f: tear; **signum, -i,** n: sign, indication; **caritas, -atis,** f: esteem, favor, affection; **spes, -ei,** f: hope (triggers an indirect command); **ex eo:** from Augustus; **fore** = *esse* ("that it would happen"); **iuvenis, -is,** m: young man (Postumus Agrippa); **penates, -ium,** m (plural): gods of the home, hearth, or family line; **avus, -i,** m: grandfather, ancestor; **reddo, -ere, reddidi, redditus:** return; restore; deliver.

1.5.2: **quod:** "an event that" (that is, Augustus's trip to Planasia); **Maximum aperuisse:** indirect statement (depending on *rumor*, above); **aperio, -ire, aperui, apertus:** disclose, recount; **illam:** Marcia; **gnarum** (*factum esse*) from *gnarus, -a, -um:* known; **Caesari:** Tiberius; **multo post:** much later; **extincto Maximo:** ablative absolute; **extinguo, -ere, extinxi, extinctus:** extinguish, kill, destroy; **dubium** (*esse*): impersonal construction (triggers an indirect question); **dubius, -a, -um:** doubtful, uncertain; **an:** whether, if; **quaero, -ere, quaesivi, quaesitus:** ask, seek; **mors, mortis,** f: death; **auditos** (*esse*); **funus, funeris,** n: burial, funeral; **eius:** Maximus; **gemitus, -us,** m: groan, sigh; **semet:** Marcia herself (direct object of *incusantis*); **incuso, -are, -avi, -atus:** blame, condemn (*incusantis:* present participle); **quod:** that; **exitium, -ii,** n: death; **maritus, -i,** m: husband (*marito:* dative of disadvantage).

1.5.3: **utcumque:** in whatever manner; **res, rei,** f: affair, course of events; **vixdum:** scarcely yet, only just; **ingredior, -i, ingressus sum:** advance, enter; **Illyricum, -i,** n: a Roman province in the Balkans; **properus, -a, -um:** hasty, speedy; **litterae, -arum,** f (plural): letter, literature; **accio, -ire, -ivi, -itus:** send for, summon; **conperio, -ire, conperi, conpertus:** learn, verify (*conpertum est:* impersonal); (*utrum*)...**an:** (whether)...or; **spiro, -are, -avi, -atus:** breathe; **Nola, -ae,** f: a city in southern Italy near Naples; **exanimis, -e:** dead, lifeless; **re(p)perio, -ire, re(p)peri, re(p)pertus:** find, discover (Tiberius is the subject of *reppererit*); **acer, acris, acre:** sharp, fierce; **custodia, -ae,** f: guard; **saepio, -ire, saepsi, saeptus:** surround, seal off, shut in; **laetus, -a, -um:** cheerful, favorable; **interdum:** meanwhile; **nuntius, -ii,** m: message; **vulgo, -are, -avi, -atus:** publish, circulate; **donec:** as long as; **provideo, -ere, providi, provisus:** foresee, provide for, make provision (*provisis:* one-word ablative absolute governing *quae...monebat*, "as long as the things, which the time advised, were being provided for"); **moneo, -ere, -ui**: advise, warn; **excedo, -ere, excessi, excessus**: withdraw (from life), die; **potior, -iri, potitus sum** + genitive or ablative: obtain, seize, control; **Neronem**: Tiberius; **idem, eadem, idem**: the same; **fama, -ae**, f: rumor; **fero, ferre, tuli, latus**: tell, convey.

49.3. Suetonius, *de Vita Neronis* 22.1–2: In his *de Vitis Caesarum*, Suetonius explores not only the public images of the emperors but also their private lives. His literary style is reminiscent of Tacitus's with its compressed clauses and lack of parallel structure. What distinguishes Suetonius from other Latin prose authors is his lively vocabulary and biting insight into human behavior, the result of which is popular biography at its best.

Here, Suetonius describes Nero's lifelong passion for chariot racing, an obsession that Nero developed in childhood and maintained throughout his life. This "hobby" even inspired Nero to stage mock chariot races in his garden and eventually to drive his own chariot in the Circus Maximus.

[1] Equorum studio vel praecipue ab ineunte aetate flagravit plurimusque illi sermo, quanquam vetaretur, de circensibus erat; et quondam tractum prasini agitatorem inter condiscipulos querens, obiurgante paedagogo, de Hectore se loqui ementitus est. Sed cum inter initia imperii eburneis quadrigis cotidie in abaco luderet, ad omnis etiam minimos circenses e secessu commeabat, primo clam, deinde propalam, ut nemini dubium esset eo die utique affuturum.

[2] Neque dissimulabat velle se palmarum numerum ampliari; quare spectaculum multiplicatis missibus in serum protrahebatur, ne dominis quidem iam factionum dignantibus, nisi ad totius diei cursum, greges ducere. Mox et ipse aurigare atque etiam spectari saepius voluit positoque in hortis inter servitia et sordidam plebem rudimento universorum se oculis in Circo Maximo praebuit, aliquo liberto mittente mappam unde magistratus solent.

Notes:

22.1: **equus, -i,** m: horse (*equorum*: objective genitive with *studio*); **studium, -ii,** n: zest, zeal, enthusiasm; **vel praecipue:** chiefly, especially; **ab ineunte aetate:** "from his childhood" (literally, "from his beginning life"); **aetas, -atis,** f: lifetime, age; **flagro, -are, -avi, -atus:** burn, be inflamed; **illi:** dative of possession; **sermo, sermonis,** m: talk, conversation; **quanquam** = *quamquam*: although (triggers a concessive clause with a subjunctive verb); **veto, -are, vetui, vetitus:** forbid; **Circensis, -e:** of the circus (*circensibus*: substantive, "Circus [Maximus] races"); **quondam:** once; **tractum** (*esse*) **agitatorem:** indirect statement depending on *querens*; **traho, -ere, traxi, tractus:** drag; **prasini** (*factionis*): of the green team, of the green political faction (see 38.1); **agitator, -oris,** m: driver; **condiscipulus, -i,** m: fellow pupil, schoolmate; **queror, -i, questus sum:** lament, complain; **obiurgante paedagogo:** ablative absolute; **obiurgo, -are, -avi, -atus:** scold, rebuke; **paedagogus, -i,** m: tutor; **de Hectore:** about Hector, the Trojan hero, whom Achilles killed and whose corpse the Greek hero dragged around the walls of Troy, the worst humiliation for a fallen enemy foe; **loquor, -i, locutus sum:** talk, speak; **ementior, -iri, ementitus sum:** lie, pretend (Nero is the subject; *ementitus est* triggers an indirect statement); **cum...luderet:** describes attendant circumstances; **initium, -ii,** n: beginning; **imperium, -ii,** n: command, reign (Nero reigned from 54–68 CE); **eburneus, -a, -um:** ivory; **quadrigae, -arum,** f (plural): four-horse chariot(s); **cotidie:** everyday, daily; **abacus, -i,** m: table, gaming board; **ludo, -ere, lusi, lusus** + ablative: play (with); **minimus, -a, -um:** smallest, most insignificant (superlative of *parvus, -a, -um*); **secessus, -us,** m: retreat, solitude; **commeo, -are, -avi:** go; **clam:** secretly; **propalam:** openly, publicly; **ut:** introduces a result clause; **nemini:** dative singular; **dubius, -a, -um:** doubtful; **eo die:** on that day; **utique:** certainly, in any case; **affuturum** (*esse*): one-word indirect statement, "that he would be present."

22.2: **neque:** and...not; **dissimulo, -are, -avi, -atus:** disguise (triggers an indirect statement *velle...ampliari*); **palma, -ae,** f: prize, mark of victory; **amplio, -are, -avi, -atus:** increase; **quare:** wherefore; **spectaculum, -i,** n: show, spectacle; **multiplicatis missibus:** ablative absolute; **multiplico, -are, -avi, -atus:** multiply, increase; **missus, -us,** m: course, heat, "number of races"; **in serum:** "until late at night" (literally, "[in]to a late hour); **protraho, -ere, protraxi, protractus**: drag out; produce; **ne...quidem**: not even; **dominis...dignantibus**: ablative absolute; **dominus, -i**, m: commander, leader, manager; **factio, -onis**, f: political party, faction (*factionum*: objective genitive with *dominis*); **dignor, -ari, -atus sum**: deem worthy (construe with *ducere*, "to produce"); **nisi**: unless; **totius**: genitive singular; **cursus, -us**, m: course, passage; **grex, gregis**, m: company (of charioteers; *greges* is the direct object of *ducere*); **et**: even; **ipse**: (Nero) himself; **aurigo, -are, -avi, -atus**: be a charioteer, drive a chariot; **saepius**: comparative of *saepe*; **posito...rudimento**: ablative absolute; **hortus, -i**, m: garden; **servitium, -ii**, n: group of slaves; **sordidus, -a, -um**: squalid, dirty, foul; **plebes, -ei** f: rabble, common people; **rudimentum, -i**, n: trial, first attempt; **universi, -orum**, m (plural): everyone; **praebeo, -ere, praebui, praebitus**: offer, exhibit; **aliquo liberto mittente**: ablative absolute; **libertus, -i**, m: freedman; **mappa, -ae**, f: signal cloth; **unde**: from the place where; **magistratus, -us**, m: magistrate; **soleo, -ere, solitus sum**: be accustomed (to give the signal).

50. ADVANCED LATIN POETRY PASSAGES

50.1.   Horace, *Carmina* 3.30: Building on the artistry of Catullus and the other neoteric poets, Horace continues the tradition of composing Latin lyric poems in meters that were, for the most part, originally Greek. His poetic style is highly elevated, combining brevity and simplicity with intricate word order and a rich poetic vocabulary.

Here, Horace proudly declares that his poems will stand as an everlasting monument and offer him a chance to evade death and the constraints of mortality. Other Augustan poets express similar sentiments about their literary achievements (see, for example, Ovid, *Amores* 3.15). Meter: first Asclepiadean.

> Exegi monumentum aere perennius
> regalique situ Pyramidum altius,

quod non imber edax, non Aquilo impotens
possit diruere aut innumerabilis
annorum series et fuga temporum.   5
Non omnis moriar multaque pars mei
vitabit Libitinam; usque ego postera
crescam laude recens, dum Capitolium
scandet cum tacita virgine Pontifex.
Dicar, qua violens obstrepit Aufidus   10
et qua pauper aquae Daunus agrestium
regnavit populorum, ex humili potens
princeps Aeolium carmen ad Italos
deduxisse modos. Sume superbiam
quaesitam meritis et mihi Delphica   15
lauro cinge volens, Melpomene, comam.

Notes:

3.30.1–5: **exigo, -ere, exegi, exactus:** finish, complete; **monumentum, -i,** n: monument, memorial; **aes, aeris,** n: bronze (*aere:* ablative of comparison with *perennius*); **perennis, -e:** enduring, everlasting; **regalis, -e:** royal, splendid; **situs, -us,** m: site, structure (*situ:* ablative of comparison with *altius*); **pyramis, -idis,** f: pyramid; **altus, -a, -um:** high, lofty; **quod:** which (referring to *monumentum*); **imber, imbris,** m: rain; **edax, edacis:** destructive, devouring; **Aquilo, -onis,** m: north wind; **impotens, impotentis:** unrestrained, violent; **possit:** present subjunctive in a relative clause of characteristic; **diruo, diruere, dirui, dirutus:** demolish, destroy; **innumerabilis, -e:** immeasurable; **series, -ei,** f: sequence, chain, series; **fuga, -ae,** f: flight.

3.30.6–9: **omnis:** here, adverbial, "completely" (*omnis* modifies the subject of *moriar*); **morior, -i, mortuus sum:** die; **mei:** genitive singular; **vito, -are, -avi, -atus:** avoid, escape, evade; **Libitina, -ae,** f: goddess of corpses; **usque:** continuously; **posterus, -a, -um:** ensuing, subsequent; **cresco, -ere, crevi, cretus:** grow; **laus, laudis,** f: praise; **recens, recentis:** fresh; **dum:** while, as long as; **Capitolium, -ii,** n: Capitoline Hill in Rome as well as the Temple of Jupiter located there (see also 46.4); **scando, -ere, scandi:** climb, ascend; **tacitus, -a, -um:** quiet, reverent; **virgo, virginis,** f: (Vestal) Virgin; **pontifex, pontificis,** m: chief high priest of Rome (see 47.1);

dum... pontifex: in other words, as long as Roman institutions and the city of Rome survive.

3.30.10–16: **qua**: where; **violens, violentis**: furious, violent; **obstrepo, -ere, obstrepui, obstrepitus**: resound, roar; **Aufidus, -i**, m: river in Apulia; **pauper, pauperis** + genitive: poor (in), scant (in); **Daunus, -i**, m: father of Turnus, king in Apulia; **agrestis, -e**: belonging to the country, rustic; **regno, -are, -avi, -atus** + genitive: rule over; **ex humili**: "from humble origin"; **potens, potentis**: powerful (*potens* modifies the subject of *dicar*); **princeps, principis**: first (*princeps* modifies the subject of *dicar* and triggers the infinitive *deduxisse*); **Aeolius, -a, -um**: of the Aeolian poets, Aeolian; **carmen, carminis**, n: song (*carmen*: direct object of *deduxisse*); **Italus, -a, -um**: Italian, Latin; **deduco, -ere, deduxi, deductus**: divert, draw out; **modus, -i**, m: measure, meter; **sumo, -ere, sumpsi, sumptus**: take up, claim; **superbia, -ae**, f: pride, arrogance; **quaero, -ere, quaesivi, quaesitus**: seek, acquire, earn; **meritum, -i**, n: merit, worth (*meritis*: ablative of cause); **Delphicus, -a, -um**: Delphic, of Apollo; **laurus, -i**, f: laurel branch; **cingo, -ere, cinxi, cinctus**: gird, wreathe, crown; **volens, volentis**: willingly, voluntarily; **Melpomene, -es**, f: Muse of tragedy (and by extension poetry in general); **coma, -ae**, f: hair.

50.2.   Germanicus, *Aratea* 328–342: The *Aratea* is a Latin adaptation of Aratus's (300–240 BCE) Greek hexameter poem, the *Phaenomena*, which gave a versified account of the constellations. Aratus's *Phaenomena* significantly influenced subsequent Greek and Latin poets, and it quickly became one of the most widely read poems in antiquity. It was translated and adapted into Latin four times, with versions by Cicero, the polymath Varro (116–27 BCE), the astronomer Avienus (fl. 340–380 CE), and by Germanicus. Germanicus's version falls into three parts: a description of the constellations, which mixes astronomy and mythology (lines 24–445); a description of the different circles of the heavens (lines 446–572); and an explanation of how to estimate the passage of time according to the rise of zodiacal constellations (lines 573–725).

Here, Germanicus gives a vivid description of the constellation of the mighty Greek hunter Orion. Easily distinguished by his sword belt, Orion is accompanied by his trusty hunting dog, Canis Major, who eternally appears to be chasing a rabbit through the night sky. Meter: dactylic hexameter.

Primus in obliquum rapitur sub pectore Tauri
Orion. Non ulla magis vicina notabit
stella virum, sparsae quam toto corpore flammae: 330
tale caput, magnique umeri sic balteus ardet,
sic vagina ensis, pernici sic pede lucet.
Talis ei custos aderit Canis ore timendo.
Ore vomit flammam, membris contemptior ignis.
Sirion hunc Grai proprio sub nomine dicunt.   335
Cum tetigit solis radios, accenditur aestas,
discernitque ortu longe sata, vivida firmat
at, quibus astrictae frondes aut languida radix,
exanimat. Nullo gaudet maiusve minusve
agricola et sidus primo speculatur ab ortu.   340
Auritum Leporem sequitur Canis et fugit ille,
sic utrumque oritur, sic occidit in freta sidus.

Notes:

328–332: **obliquus, -a, -um**: slanting (angle); **rapio, -ere, rapui, raptus**: drag off, hurry off; **pectus, -oris**, n: chest; **Taurus, -i**, m: bull (the constellation Taurus); **ullus, -a, -um**: any; **magis…quam**: more…than; **vicinus, -a, -um**: neighboring; **noto, -are, -avi, -atus**: here, "trace"; **stella, -ae**, f: constellation; **spargo, -ere, sparsi, sparsus**: scatter, sprinkle; **toto corpore**: on the entire body (of the constellation Orion); **flamma, -ae**, f: individual star; **talis, -e**: so great, such; **umerus, -i**, m: shoulder; **balteus, -i**, m: shoulder-belt; **ardeo, -ere, arsi, arsus**: burn, sparkle; **vagina, -ae**, f: sheath, scabbard; **ensis, -is**, m: sword; **pernix, pernicis**: swift, nimble; **luceo, -ere, luxi**: shine, be bright.

333–334: **ei**: dative of reference (Orion); **custos, custodis**, m: guardian, watchman; **adsum, -esse, affui**: be in attendance, be near; **Canis, -is**, m: referring to the constellation Canis Major, Orion's hunting dog; **os, oris**, n: mouth (twice referring to the dog's mouth, lines 333 and 334); **timeo, -ere, timui**: fear (*timendo*: gerundive in an ablative absolute with *ore*); **vomo, -ere, vomui, vomitus**: discharge, spew forth; **flamma, -ae**, f: flame (i.e., Sirius, the brightest star in Canis Major); **membrum, -i**, n: limb (metonymy for the dog's body, and ablative of place where); **contemptus, -a, -um**: faint (the comparison is between the brightness of the dog's mouth and the faintness of its body); **ignis, -is,** m: fire, light (*ignis*: in apposition to Canis Major).

335–340: **Sirion**: Greek accusative of *Sirius*; **hunc**: referring to the bright star in Canis Major's mouth; **Grai, -orum,** m (plural): Greeks; **proprius, -a, -um**: very own, particular; **sub** + ablative: here, "by"; **cum**: when; **tango, -ere, tetigi, tactus**: touch, border on (take *Sirius* as the subject); **sol, solis,** m: sun; **radius, -ii,** m: ray, **accendo, -ere, accendi, accensus**: ignite, set on fire; **aestas, -atis,** f: summer; **discerno, -ere, discrevi, discretus**: see, discern (take *Sirius* as the subject); **ortus, -us,** m: rising; **longe**: at a distance; **sata** from *sero, -ere, sevi, satus*: sow (substantive, "crops"); **vivida** (*sata*) from *vividus, -a, -um*: vigorous; **firmo, -are, -avi, -atus**: strengthen; **quibus** (*satis*): dative of possession; **astrictus, -a, -um**: constricted, dense, restrained; **frons, frondis,** f: foliage; **languidus, -a, -um**: sluggish, listless; **radix, radicis,** f: root; **exanimo, -are, -avi, -atus**: kill; **nullo** (*sidere*); **gaudeo, -ere, gavisus sum**: rejoice; **-ve…-ve**: either…or; **agricola, -ae,** m: farmer; **sidus, sideris,** n: star, constellation; **speculor, -ari, speculatus sum**: observe, examine.

341–342: **auritus, -a, -um**: long-eared; **lepus, leporis,** m: hare, rabbit (here, the constellation Lepus below Orion); **canis**: Canis Major; **fugio, fugere, fugi**: flee; **ille**: *lepus*; **utrumque…sidus**: hyperbaton; **uterque, utraque, utrumque**: each (of two), both; **orior, -iri, ortus sum**: rise; **occido, -ere, occidi, occisus**: fall; **fretum, -i,** n: sea. The Greeks and Romans believed that the earth did not move, but instead that the heavens revolved around the earth. Hence, the constellations appeared to rise in the east and then dip into the sea to the west at the end of their transit through the night sky.

50.3.   Statius, *Silvae* 2.5.1–19: Statius was a great admirer of Vergil, whose *Aeneid*, as he claims, he dared to follow only from a distance (*Thebaid* 12.816–819). The style of the *Silvae*, a three-book collection of short occasional poems, is lighter. Statius's literary expression is highly compressed with layers of subordination, and he relies heavily on participial clauses and the liberal use of hyperbaton.

In 80 CE, Statius's contemporary Martial wrote *Liber Spectaculorum*, an entire collection of epigrams about the arena, in honor of the opening of the Colosseum. Many of these poems feature the animals of the gladiatorial combats. (Poem 18, for example, describes a tigress tearing apart a lion.) In *Silvae* 2.5, Statius takes up this idea from the perspective of the animal itself: a tame lion, who died in the arena, elicits anguish from the other captive lions as well as from the hard-hearted Domitian (reigned 81–96 CE). Statius's poem is full of hyperbole, and he personifies the lion in religious and heroic terms, lamenting that such a wonderful animal, skilled at all sorts of organized combat, has met so tragic an end. The Greeks and Romans emphasized the similiarities between humans and animals, and the literary personification of animals has a long tradition dating back to the earliest literature. For example, Achilles' horses mourned the death of Patroclus, the Greek hero's best friend (*Iliad* 17.426–439). Meter: dactylic hexameter.

> Quid tibi constrata mansuescere profuit ira?
> Quid scelus humanasque animo dediscere caedis
> imperiumque pati et domino parere minori?
> Quid? Quod abire domo rursusque in
>   claustra reverti
> suetus et a capta iam sponte recedere praeda   5
> insertasque manus laxo dimittere morsu?
> Occidis, altarum vastator docte ferarum,
> non grege Massylo curvaque indagine clausus,
> non formidato supra venabula saltu
> incitus aut caeco foveae deceptus hiatu,   10
> sed victus fugiente fera. Stat cardine aperto
> infelix cavea, et clausas circum undique portas
> hoc licuisse nefas placidi tumuere leones.
> Tum cunctis cecidere iubae, puduitque relatum
> aspicere et totas duxere in lumina frontis.   15
> At non te primo fusum novus obruit ictu
> ille pudor: mansere animi, virtusque cadenti
> a media iam morte redit, nec protinus omnes
> terga dedere minae.

Notes:

1–6: Statius addresses the lion directly; notice the preponderance of vocatives and second-person pronouns and verbs;

constrata...ira: ablative absolute; **consterno, -ere, constravi, constratus**: cover, calm; **mansuesco, -ere, mansuevi, mansuetus**: become tame, become gentle; **prosum, prodesse, profui, profuturus**: be advantageous, benefit, profit; **ira, -ae, f**: anger, wrath; **scelus, sceleris, n**: crime, evil actions; **animus, -i, m**: soul, spirit; **dedisco, -ere, dedidici**: unlearn, forget; **caedes, -is, f**: slaughter; **imperium, -ii, n**: command, control; **patior, -i, passus sum**: suffer, endure; **dominus, -i, m**: master; **pareo, -ere, -ui, -itus** + dative: obey; **quid** (*profuit*); **quod**: the fact that; **domo**: "from your cage"; **rursus**: again; **claustrum, -i, n**: enclosure, barrier; **revertor, -i, reversus sum**: go back, return; **suetus** (*es*) from *suesco, -ere, suevi, suetus*: become accustomed; **sponte**: voluntarily; **recedo, -ere, recessi**: retreat, withdraw; **capta**...**praeda**: hyperbaton; **praeda, -ae, f**: plunder, prey; **insero, -ere, inserui, insertus**: thrust in; **manus, -us, f**: hand; **laxus, -a, -um**: relaxed, gaping; **dimitto, -ere, dimisi, dimissus**: forsake, give up; **morsus, -us, m**: jaws, teeth.

7–11: **occido, occidere, occidi, occisus**: perish, be slain; **altarum vastator docte ferarum**: chiasmus; **altus, -a, -um**: tall, lofty; **vastator, -oris, m**: destroyer, ravager; **doctus, -a, -um**: learned, skilled, well-trained (*docte*: vocative singular); **fera, -ae, f**: wild beast; **grege Massylo curvaque indagine**: chiasmus; **grex, gregis, m**: crowd, company; **Massylus, -a, -um**: relating to a tribe from Numidia, whose king Jugurtha fought against Rome, 112–105 BCE (the poets perpetuated the reputation of the Massylians as savage and barbaric); **indago, indaginis, f**: ring of huntsmen; **claudo, -ere, clausi, clausus**: besiege, enclose, confine; **formido, -are, -avi, -atus**: dread, fear; **supra** + accusative: above, beyond; **venabulum, -i, n**: hunting spear; **saltus, -us, m**: leap; **incitus, -a, -um**: headlong, swift; **caecus, -a, -um**: blind, hidden, secret; **fovea, -ae, f**: pit; **decipio, -ere, decepi, deceptus**: cheat, deceive, mislead; **hiatus, -us, m**: jaw, chasm, cleft; **vinco, vincere, vici, victus**: conquer, overcome; **fugio, fugere, fugi**: flee; **fera**: ablative of cause with *fugiente* (perhaps referring to a hunting expedition during which our lion haplessly went after some imperial prey).

11–15: **cardo, cardinis, m**: hinge, pole, axis; **apertus, -a, -um**: open, exposed; **infelix, infelicis**: unfortunate, unhappy, unlucky; **cavea, -ae, f**: hollow enclosure, crate; **undique**: from all sides; **porta, -ae, f**: gate, entrance; **hoc licuisse nefas**: indirect statement depending on *tumuere*, "because this *nefas* has been permitted"; **hoc**: construe with *nefas*; **licet, -ere, licuit**: it is allowed, permitted; **nefas**, n (indeclinable): a violation of divine law, an impious act (Statius heightens the sense of pathos and hyperbole by using religiously charged vocabulary); **tumuere** = *tumuerunt* from *tumesco, -ere, tumui*: become enflamed; **cunctis** *(leonibus)*: dative of possession; **cecidere** = *ceciderunt* from *cado, -ere, cecidi, casus*: fall; **iuba, -ae**, f: mane, crest; **pudeo, -ere, -ui, -itu**s: be ashamed (often impersonal); **refero, -ferre, rettuli, relatus**: bring back (our lion, of course); **aspicio, -ere, aspexi, aspectus**: behold, observe; **duxere** = *duxerunt*; **lumen, luminis**, n: light, eye; **frons, frontis**, f: brow, forehead.

16–19: **at**: but, on the other hand; **fundo, -ere, fudi, fusus**: rout, defeat (*fusum* modifies *te*); **obruo, -ere, obrui, obrutus**: overwhelm, ruin; **ictus, -us**, m: blow, stroke; **pudor, -oris**, m: shame; **mansere** = *manserunt* from *maneo, -ere, mansi, mansus*: remain; **virtus, virtutis**, f: excellence, manliness, virtue; **cadenti** *(tibi)*: dative of disadvantage; **mors, mortis**, f: death; **redeo, -ire, redii, reditus**: return; **protinus**: immediately; **tergum, -i**, n: back; **dedere** = *dederunt*; **terga dedere**: "turn tail"; **minae, -arum**, f (plural): warning signs, threats.

BIOGRAPHICAL SKETCHES

Caesar: Gaius Julius Caesar (100–15 March 44 BCE) was an accomplished author, politician, and military general who was famously murdered by a senatorial faction. His patrician family, ancient but undistinguished for several generations, traced its lineage back to the goddess Venus. Caesar pursued a traditional political and military career, serving in Asia in the 70s BCE where he received the *corona civica* for saving the lives of fellow Roman citizens at Miletos (western Turkey) in 75 BCE (the *corona civica* was the second-highest military decoration, after the *corona obsidionalis* reserved for generals whose actions had saved an entire legion or army). Captured by Cilician pirates on his return to Rome, Caesar, already estimating his own worth very high and offering 50 talents in lieu of the usual ransom of 20, lived amicably with the pirates for thirty-eight days until the ransom was raised; whereupon Caesar paid it but then soon captured and executed the pirates. After serving as *tribunus militum* in 73 BCE, and quaestor and praetor in Hispania Ulterior (Further Spain), Caesar was elected consul in 59 BCE. After his consulship he assumed the governorship of three provinces (Illyricum, Gallia Cisalpina, and Gallia Transpadana) for an unprecedented ten years. *de Bello Gallico* records his own account of his governorship, including campaigns against the Helvetians, expeditions into Germany and Britain, the famous war against the Arveni and Vercingetorix, and the battle at Alesia (52 BCE). *de Bello Civile* records the war against Pompeius Magnus and senatorial forces from 48–47 BCE. Accounts of the Alexandrine, African, and Spanish Wars, although credited to Caesar, were probably penned by his generals. As dictator, Caesar reformed the tax system to protect against extortion, attempted to ameliorate the debt problem, and sponsored public works at Rome (including the *Forum Caesaris*). His calendrical revisions, executed by the Egyptian astronomer Sosigenes, were not substantially revised until 1582. Caesar also commissioned a map of the world, unfinished at his death, but completed under his grandnephew Augustus.

Caesar's writings were intended to communicate with the Senate and upper classes while he was away from Rome. He also wished to maintain his popularity with the common people, whose causes he sought to advance by increasing the authority of the popular assemblies (hence Caesar's designation as a *Popularis,* in contrast with the *Optimatis* Cicero, who favored the preeminence of the Senate as a governing body). Cicero praised Caesar's lucid, pure, and straightforward style (*Brutus* 261). Nonetheless, Caesar's writings are artful, replete with rhetorical devices; vocabulary is carefully chosen, and phrases skillfully arranged. His ablatives absolute and layers of subordination often dazzle.

Catiline: Lucius Sergius Catilina (108–62 BCE) pursued a political career at Rome, serving as praetor in 68 BCE, after which he was accused of misconduct in office and barred from standing for office in 67 BCE. Feeling that his honor was impugned, Catiline plotted the murder of the consuls (the so-called first Catilinarian conspiracy), for which he was tried and acquitted. He ran for the consulship in 63 BCE but was defeated by Cicero. Catiline then demanded the office, gathering troops in Etruria (with the help of Gaius Manlius) and making lavish promises to the people in Rome. With information from a mistress of one of the conspirators, Cicero made a public accusation in the Senate on 8 November 63 BCE (*in Catilinam* 1). Although Catiline fled to his army in Etruria, his co-conspirators continued to plot at Rome, seeking an alliance with the Allobroges (a Celtic tribe who dwelled between the Rhone and Lake Geneva, in modern Switzerland), who in turn revealed the plans to Cicero. The Senate arrested the conspirators on December 3, condemning them to death and executing them two days later. Julius Caesar made an eloquent appeal for mercy (see Sallust, *Bellum Catilinae* 51), leading later to charges that Cicero had denied due process to Roman citizens, for which he was exiled from Rome in 58 BCE. Catiline's forces did not disband after the execution of the conspirators at Rome. Catiline and his generals fell in pitched battle at Pistorium in January 62 BCE. An account of the conspiracy survives in the *Bellum Catilinae* of Sallust (see 49.1), who is far more sympathetic to Catiline than Cicero.

Catullus: Gaius Valerius Catullus was born in Verona, northern Italy, ca. 84 BCE, and, as a young man, made his way to Rome. Little is known about his public life except that he served under the governor of Bithynia from 57–56 BCE. Unfortunately, Catullus died very young (ca. 54 BCE) and left us with only 116 poems. It is unclear whether he published any of them during his lifetime, or even whether he organized them into the format we have inherited. Catullus is considered one of the neoteric poets, who adopted a Hellenistic vision for their creative works and composed Latin verses in meters that were originally Greek. Catullus's collection can be divided into three sections: short lyric poems (1–60); long poems (61–68, including Poem 64 with its *epyllion* featuring the abandonment of Ariadne by the hero Theseus); and elegiac poems (69–116). Catullus's most famous poems explore his love affair with Lesbia, a married woman whom many believe to be Clodia, the sister of Publius Clodius Pulcher and the wife of Quintus Caecilius Metellus Celer, who features prominently as an object of derision and the subject of scandal in Cicero's *pro Caelio*. Recent scholarship prefers to see Lesbia as a literary construction rather than a historical figure. Regardless, Catullus's mistress served as the inspiration for a host of other elegiac *femmes fatales*: Propertius's Cynthia, Tibullus's Delia, and Ovid's Corinna.

Cicero: Marcus Tullius Cicero (3 January 106–7 December 43 BCE) was a statesman, constitutionalist, and philosopher seminal in establishing Greek philosophy in Roman intellectual culture and in coining Latin philosophical terms (e.g., *essentia, moralis, qualitas*). He was born in Arpinum, south of Rome, to a well-off but politically undistinguished equestrian family. Always ambitious and sorely sensitive about his ancestry, Cicero studied philosophy, rhetoric, and jurisprudence. By 75 BCE, he began to climb the *cursus honorum*, successfully standing for the office of quaestor at the youngest legal age (thirty-one). Admiring his probity as quaestor, the people of Sicily asked Cicero to lead the prosecution against their corrupt ex-governor Gaius Verres, who had notoriously mismanaged the province. Cicero's dazzling speeches to the senatorial jury secured his reputation as the greatest speaker in Rome. His lightning-fast ascent of the *cursus* continued with the aedileship in 69 BCE (age thirty-seven), praetorship in 66 BCE (age forty), and consulship in 63 BCE (age forty-three). As the first member of his family to hold that high office, he was rightly proud of his accomplishment as a *novus homo*. During his consulship, he thwarted the Catilinarian conspiracy (see the biographical sketch for Catiline), claiming to have saved the Republic single-handedly, exaggerating the extent of the crisis and the magnitude of his own success. In 62 BCE, Cicero secured a particularly spiteful enemy when Publius Clodius Pulcher was brought up on charges of violating the sacred festival of the *Bona Dea*, celebrated exclusively by aristocratic women. The rites were held at the *Regia*, the home of the Pontifex Maximus (Julius Caesar), and Clodius was caught dressed in drag, presumably to keep a dalliance with Caesar's wife Pompeia. When the case came to trial, Cicero destroyed Clodius's alibi (of being absent from Rome on the day of the festival). Clodius's acquittal was secured only when Crassus bribed the jury. Adopted into a plebeian family in order to be elected to the powerful office of the *tribunus plebis* (58 BCE), Clodius retroactively enacted a law aimed at Cicero and his execution of Roman citizens without trial in connection with the Catilinarian conspiracy. Cicero's property was confiscated and he was barred from living within 500 miles of Rome. Amid riots and physical attacks, Cicero left Rome for Greece, where he studied philosophy. In August 57 BCE, Cicero returned to Rome with the support of the *tribunus plebis* Titus Annius Milo (and Caesar, Pompey, and Crassus, "the first triumvirate," who had invited Cicero to join their informal alliance in 60 BCE). Landing at Brundisium, he was greeted by cheering crowds, and he declared, with typical Ciceronian hyperbole, that the Republic was restored to him. Prohibited from participating in politics, Cicero continued his rhetorical career, speaking in court to the Senate and Roman people. He was unsuccessful in defending his friend Milo for the murder of his enemy Clodius in 52 BCE. At the end of the Civil War, Caesar pardoned Cicero for backing Pompey but blocked him from politics. After Caesar's murder, Cicero composed fourteen vitriolic speeches calling for the senatorial support of the adolescent (and malleable) Octavian, Caesar's heir, against Caesar's lieutenant, Antony (*Philippicae*, the title evokes the *Philippics* of Greek orator Demosthenes, who roused the Athenians to fight Alexander's father, Philip of Macedon). All but the *Second Philippic* were delivered publicly. When Octavian, Lepidus, and Antony agreed to share power, Antony took steps to eliminate his enemy Cicero, whom Octavian refused to protect despite Cicero's role in advancing Caesar's young heir. Fleeing Rome, Cicero was overtaken on Antony's orders. His throat was cut, and his head and hands were cut off and then nailed to the senatorial *Rostrum* in Rome.

Cicero was a prolific writer. We have the texts of fifty-seven speeches, twenty-one works on philosophy (Stoicism and Academic skepticism), some poetry, and a compendious collection of letters to friends (especially Atticus and Brutus), family, and enemies (including Caesar). The letters, never intended for publication, are colloquial, light, and informal. The model of the flowery "Asiatic" style, Cicero's speeches are highly wrought *tours de force*.

Germanicus: Germanicus Julius Caesar (15 BCE–19 CE) was the nephew and adopted son of Tiberius (emperor of Rome 14–37 CE), chosen by Augustus as Tiberius's imperial successor. Well educated, Germanicus earned a reputation as a fine orator, and he composed comedies in Greek, as well as epigrams and a short epic poem (our *Aratea*) in Latin. He married Augustus's granddaughter Agrippina, with whom he fathered nine children, six of whom reached adulthood (including the notorious emperor Caligula and his equally disreputable sisters, Livilla, Drusilla, and Agrippinilla/Agrippina II, mother of Nero). Germanicus led campaigns in Germany from 11–16 CE, for which he celebrated a triumph in 17 CE. In 18 CE, he campaigned in Cappadocia and Commagene, both territories then becoming Roman provinces, and next toured Egypt and Syria, where he died suddenly and mysteriously at Antioch in October of 19 CE. Germanicus's immense popularity with the Roman people only increased after his death, which left the unpopular Tiberius with a public relations nightmare, as he and his governor of Syria were implicated in conspiring to assassinate Germanicus.

Horace: Quintus Horatius Flaccus (8 December 65–27 November 8 BCE) was one of the leading poets of the Augustan Age. The son of a freedman, Horace was educated in Rome and Athens. As a young man, he supported Brutus after Julius Caesar's assassination, but suffered the consequences when Brutus lost to Antony and Octavian at the battle of Philippi in eastern Macedonia in 42 BCE. Despite that setback, Horace returned to Rome and began writing. Maecenas, Augustus's cultural advisor and Vergil's patron, asked Horace to join his circle of writers and helped the young poet acquire his Sabine farm, near Rome. In 35 BCE, Horace published his first book of poetic satires, or *Sermones*. Soon afterward, in 30 BCE, a second book of satires appeared as well his *Epodes*, a collection of somewhat provocative poems, many of which were written in iambic strophe. For the next decade, Horace devoted himself to lyric poetry, publishing eighty-eight poems in three books of *Carmina* (23 BCE); the *Carmen Saeculare*, a centennial hymn for the *Ludi Saeculares* in 17 BCE; and a fourth book of *Carmina* in 15 BCE. At the end of his career, Horace produced two books of literary epistles in dactylic hexameter, the second of which contains the *Ars Poetica*, a poetic essay of literary criticism that analyzes the characteristics of Roman poetry, epic and drama in particular.

Livy: Titus Livius was born in 64 or 59 BCE in northern Italy at Patavium (Padua), a city renowned for stern morality and conservative politics, siding with the Senate against Marc Antony in the 40s BCE. Livy married and had children, a son who wrote a geographical work and a daughter who married a rhetorician. It is unknown when Livy came to Rome, but he was friendly with the emperor Augustus, and he encouraged young Claudius, the future emperor, to write history. Livy's own great history of Rome, *ab Urbe Condita*, began with the Aeneas legend and treated Roman history from its foundation in 753 BCE down to 9 BCE. Of the original 142 books, only 1–10 (foundation to 292 BCE) and 21–45 (222–167 BCE, including the Second Punic War) survive, along with some fragments of other books, as well as later summaries. The *Oxyrhynchus Epitome* covers books 37–40 and 48–55; the *Periochae* preserve summaries of all the books except 136 and 137. Livy's varied style is rhetorical and rich, employing poetical and archaic words, mixing direct and indirect speech, shifting seamlessly from short, vivid sentences to extensive, almost Ciceronian, periods. Concentrating on major episodes, Livy weaves a colorful narrative full of emotion, mythology, and ambiance.

Martial: Marcus Valerius Martialis was born in Bilbilis, Hispania Tarraconensis, between 38 and 41 CE. As a young man, he came to Rome and possibly became part of Seneca's circle. In 80 CE, he published his first collection of poems, *Liber Spectaculorum*, to commemorate the opening of the Colosseum. Around 83 CE, he published the *Xenia* and the *Apophoreta*, books of two-line poems to accompany presents. Over the next fifteen years, he wrote eleven books of epigrams. In style, these verses reflect the spirit of Catullus's short, witty poems. At times, Martial even parodies his work. Returning to Spain in 98 CE, Martial published a last book of epigrams. His later work indicates that he idealized his homeland, but, after reestablishing himself in Spain, he missed the excitement of Rome and grew frustrated with life outside the city. He died in Bilbilis around 104 CE.

Ovid: Publius Ovidius Naso was born in Sulmo in the Apennine Valley in 43 BCE. After his formal education and a brief attempt at political life, Ovid quickly rose to literary fame in Rome. He published six major works before his exile in 8 CE: *Amores*, three books of elegiac poems, many of which chronicle Ovid's affair with his literary mistress Corinna; *Heroides*, twenty-one literary epistles that feature famous mythological heroines writing to their lovers or husbands (in three cases the men write back!); *Medicamina Faciei Femineae*, a didactic poem about cosmetics; *Ars Amatoria*, a didactic poem in three books about the art of seduction; *Remedia Amoris*, a didactic poem on ending and recovering from a love affair; and the *Metamorphoses*, Ovid's epic masterpiece detailing the changes of the world from the beginning of time to Augustan Rome and serving as one of the most comprehensive sources for Greco-Roman mythology. Shortly after the publication of the *Metamorphoses*, having incurred the wrath of Augustus, Ovid was exiled to Tomis on the Black Sea. There he worked on his *Fasti*, a didactic poem on holidays and customs related to the Roman calendar (of which only six books, treating January to June, survive). In Tomis, he also composed two collections of poems, *Tristia* and *Epistulae ex Ponto*, both of which explore the devastation of his exile and his fervent desire to return to Rome, and the *Ibis*, a curse poem attacking some unnamed enemy. Ovid died in exile around 17 CE.

Petronius: Scholars debate whether our Petronius, the author of the *Satyricon*, is identifiable with the Petronius who served as the arbiter of elegance (*arbiter elegantiae*) of Nero's court whom Tacitus describes as self-indulgent, witty, and amoral (*Annales* 16.17–20). Implicated in a plot against Nero (reigned 54–68 CE), the Pisonian conspiracy led by the senator Gaius Calpurnius Piso in 65 CE, Petronius was forced to commit suicide in 66 CE. According to Tacitus, the suicide was capricious: Petronius severed his veins then bound them back up; as the mood struck him, he engaged in frivolous conversations with his friends, and arbitrarily rewarded or beat his slaves.

The *Satyricon* is a curious and fragmentary novel, combining prose and poetry. The title refers to the influence of Roman satire as well as to the satyr-like sexual exploits of Encolpius, the primary character. The *Satyricon* traces the adventures of Encolpius and his homosexual lover Giton in southern Italy. Among the episodes is the *Cena Trimalchionis*, which describes an absurdly elaborate banquet hosted by an ex-slave who attained indescribable wealth. Several minor characters try to seduce Giton (who is not especially faithful) away from Encolpius. The *Satyricon* seems to parody life at Nero's court, and it may also be a burlesque of the boy-meets-girl ideal in Roman comedy and Greek novels.

Pliny the Younger: Gaius Plinius Caecilius Secundus was born at Comum (Como) on Lake Larius in northern Italy in 61/62 CE. His father passed away when Pliny was still a child, and he was raised and eventually adopted by his uncle, Pliny the Elder, author of *Naturalis Historia*, a vast encyclopedia covering geography, anthropology, zoology, botany, pharmacology, and mineralogy, among other things. Pliny the Younger eventually settled in Rome and took advantage of all the opportunities the city had to offer, including studying rhetoric under Quintilian (who wrote, among other things, handbooks on rhetoric and education). After serving as a military tribune in Syria (82 CE), Pliny decided to pursue a career in a Roman political life, being elected quaestor, tribune, praetor, and, eventually, consul.

During his consulship (100 CE), Pliny delivered the *Panegyricus Traiani* to the Roman Senate. In addition to that text, Pliny wrote nine books of *Epistulae* that he edited for publication and one book of letters to the emperor Trajan. Lost to us are his volumes of poetry. In 110 CE, Pliny became the governor of Bithynia-Pontus. He is thought to have died while on that post somewhere around 112 CE.

Sallust: Gaius Sallustius Crispus of Amiternum in the Sabine territory near Rome (87/86–35 BCE) pursued a traditional political career at Rome, serving as *tribunus plebis* in 52 BCE (see the biographical sketch for Cicero). He was expelled from the Senate in 50 BCE by the censor Appius Claudius Pulcher, ostensibly on trumped-up charges of adultery, but more likely because of his support of Caesar over Pompey. As Caesar's military lieutenant, Sallust served as praetor in 47 BCE and governor of Africa Nova (Numidia) in 46 BCE. On retiring from politics, Sallust devoted himself to writing, producing two historical monographs, the *Bellum Catilinae* (covering the same Catilinarian conspiracy that occupied Cicero's consulship) and the *Bellum Iugurthinum* (Jugurtha was the king of Numidia who went to war with Rome, 112–105 BCE). In both monographs, Sallust explored the moral decay in Roman society. Sallust then set to work composing the *Historiae,* an annalistic history of Rome from 78 BCE. He completed the first four books (up to 72 BCE) and part of the fifth before his death. Sallust was widely praised as a writer commensurate with Cicero, Horace, Terence, and Vergil, and Martial (14.191) tells us that he was considered the best of the Roman historians. Sallust's works were translated into Greek by Zenobius under Hadrian (reigned 117–138 CE).

Statius: Publius Papinius Statius was born in Naples ca. 50 CE, the son of a teacher who was also an acclaimed poet (*Silvae* 5.3). Statius, like his father, won victories for his compositions at the *Augustalia* in Naples. He also won at the Alban Festival (instituted by Domitian, reigned 81–96 CE) with a poem on the emperor's German and Dacian campaigns (of which only four hexameter lines survive). Statius moved to Rome where he competed in the prestigious Capitoline Festival in 90 CE but suffered a devastating loss. He returned to Naples, and there he died ca. 96 CE. Although he married Claudia (*Silvae* 3.5), the widow of a famous singer and mother of a musically gifted girl, Statius had no children of his own. His works include two epics: the twelve-book *Thebaid,* treating the myth of the Seven against Thebes, published after twelve long years of composition and excruciating revision (*Silvae* 4.7.26); and the *Achilleid,* on the Greek hero Achilles, unfinished at the poet's death. His *Silvae,* thirty-two poems in four books of light verse, occasionally autobiographical and mostly in hexameters, are a miscellany of praise poems to the *glitterati* at Rome in the early 90s CE.

Suetonius: Gaius Suetonius Tranquillus was born ca. 70 CE. He spent his formative years in Rome under Domitian's rule (81–96 CE). As a young man, Suetonius earned the patronage of Pliny the Younger, who helped him secure land and minor political postings. Under Trajan's reign, Suetonius was in charge of all Roman public libraries, and several years later he was appointed imperial secretary to Hadrian, a position that likely gave him access to archives that were instrumental in his research for the *de Vitis Caesarum*. Sometime in 121–122 CE, Hadrian dismissed him from this office, and Suetonius never returned to political life. He died around 130 CE.

Suetonius wrote two major sets of biographies: *de Viris Illustribus*, which explored the lives of famous literary figures; and *de Vitis Caesarum*, twelve biographies of the Roman emperors from Julius Caesar to Domitian. Suetonius wrote other works, now lost, on kings, famous courtesans, Greek games, Roman spectacles, Roman public offices, the Roman calendar, Cicero's *de Republica*, and various lexigraphical matters. Although Suetonius is often criticized for historical imprecision, his lively biographies provide us with engaging snapshots of prominent Romans of the first century CE.

Sulpicia: Sulpicia was the daughter of Servius Sulpicius Rufus, a lawyer who prosecuted Lucius Licinius Murena (whom Cicero defended in his *pro Murena*) in 62 BCE and who served as consul in 51 BCE, and the niece of Marcus Valerius Messalla Corvinus (64 BCE–8 CE), who, after a distinguished military career, became the patron of Tibullus, Lygdamus, and Ovid. Sulpicia is the only female writer from the Augustan Age whose writings survive. Preserved in the *Corpus Tibullianum*, six poems ascribed to her chronicle her love affair with Cerinthus. Five additional poems speak about these two lovers, but are attributed to another poet, known as *auctor de Sulpicia* or *amicus Sulpiciae*. For years, Sulpicia's poems were largely ignored, but recently they have enjoyed scholarly acclaim, and Sulpicia is now thought to have been a credible part of Messalla's literary circle.

Tacitus: Born ca. 55–58 CE, Cornelius Tacitus pursued a traditional political career at Rome, serving as praetor in 88 CE, consul in 97 CE, and proconsul in 112/113 CE. He wrote five books: the *Agricola*, a biography of his father-in-law, Gnaeus Julius Agricola, who was largely responsible for the Roman conquest of Britain during his governorship (77–85 CE); the *Germania*, an ethnography of the German people, published ca. 98 CE; the *Historia* (mostly lost), covering Roman history from the end of Nero's reign in 69 CE to about 110 CE; the *Annales*, treating Roman imperial history from the death of Augustus (14 CE) to the end of Nero's reign (69 CE); and a dialogue on oratory, dedicated to Fabius Justus, consul 102 CE. Tacitus died early in Hadrian's reign (117–138 CE).

Vergil (Virgil): Publius Vergilius Maro was born on 15 October 70 BCE on the family estate in the little village of Andes near Mantua in northern Italy. Broadly educated, Vergil studied rhetoric in Mediolanum (Milan) and Rome, and he joined the Epicurean school at Naples. His family lands were confiscated during the veteran resettlement program of 42–40 BCE, but then restored. In 37 BCE, Vergil published as a set his *Eclogues*, ten pastoral pieces inspired by the Greek poet Theocritus (third century BCE). He soon came to the attention of Maecenas, Octavian's trusted advisor and an important patron of the arts at Rome. By 29 BCE, the poet completed his *Georgics*, a versified agricultural account, in four books, in the tradition of Hesiod's *Works and Days*. Vergil then spent the remainder of his life on the *Aeneid*. A Roman national epic celebrating her legendary founder, Aeneas, it is perhaps the greatest poem in Latin and Rome's answer to Homer's *Iliad* and *Odyssey*. Returning from Greece, Vergil died of illness at Brundisium (a natural and major port on the heel of Italy's south-eastern Adriatic Coast) on 21 September 19 BCE before completing his masterpiece (although he did leave instructions for the manuscript to be burned if he died before finishing it!).

BASIC GUIDE TO LATIN METER AND SCANSION

L atin poetry follows a strict rhythm based on the quantity of the vowel in each syllable. Each line of poetry divides into a number of feet (analogous to the measures in music). The syllables in each foot scan as "long" or "short" according to the parameters of the meter that the poet employs.

A vowel scans as "long" if (1) it is long by nature (e.g., the ablative singular ending in the first declension: *puellā*); (2) it is a diphthong: AE (*saepe*), AU (*laudat*), EI (*deinde*), EU (*neuter*), OE (*poena*), UI (*cui*); (3) it is long by position – these vowels are followed by double consonants (*cantātae*) or a consonantal I (*Trōia*), X (*flexibus*), or Z. All other vowels scan as "short."

A few other matters often confuse beginners: (1) QU and GU count as a single consonants (*sīc aquilam*: 1.5; *linguā*: 13.1); (2) H does NOT affect the quantity of a vowel (*Bellus homō*: 10.1); (3) if a mute (B, C, D, G, K, Q, P, T) is followed by L or R, the preceding vowel scans according to the demands of the meter, either long (*omnium patrōnus*: 25.1, the -a in *patrōnus* scans as long to accommodate the hendecasyllabic meter) OR short (*prō patriā*: 2.2, the first -a in *patriā* scans as short to accommodate the Alcaic strophe).

Two vowels may elide, and the first vowel drops out and does not affect the quantity of the elided syllable. Elision in Latin occurs if (1) one word ends in a vowel or diphthong and the next one begins in a vowel (*Lesbia, atque amēmus*: 6.3); (2) one word ends in a vowel or diphthong and the next one begins in H (*Atque hīc*: 8.3); or (3) one word ends in –UM, –AM, or –EM and the next word begins in a vowel (*quantum est*: 4.2). An elided syllable scans according to the quantity of the **second** vowel. A hiatus (or very abrupt break in the line) results from a failure to elide.

Most Latin meters utilize five different types of measures:

- dactyl: — ∪ ∪   (example: *Lesbia*)
- spondee: — —   (example: *quārē*)
- iamb: ∪ —   (example: *regō*)
- trochee: — ∪   (example: *praeda*)
- choriamb: — ∪ ∪ —   (example: *dēliciae*)

Note the following conventions:

- | marks the division between feet in dactylic lines
- || marks the pause within a line
- x marks a syllable that can scan either long or short

There are eight meters represented in *A Little Latin Reader*:

Dactylic hexameter: six feet of dactyls. The first four feet can be either dactyls or spondees; the fifth foot is usually a dactyl; and the last foot scans as a spondee whether the last syllable is short or long.

$$ - \overline{\cup \cup} \mid - \overline{\cup \cup} \mid - \overline{\cup \cup} \mid - \overline{\cup \cup} \mid - \cup \cup \mid - x $$

Elegaic couplets: alternating lines of dactylic hexameter and dactylic pentameter. In the pentameter line, the first two feet may be dactyls or spondees, but the rest of the line follows a set pattern.

$$ - \overline{\cup \cup} \mid - \overline{\cup \cup} \mid - \overline{\cup \cup} \mid - \overline{\cup \cup} \mid - \cup \cup \mid - x $$
$$ - \cup \cup \mid - \cup \cup \mid - \parallel - \cup \cup \mid - \cup \cup \mid x $$

Hendecasyllabics: lines of eleven syllables in five feet. The first foot may be a spondee, iamb, or trochee, followed by a dactyl, two trochees, and finally a spondee or trochee.

$$ \underline{\cup} \overline{\cup} - \cup \cup - \cup - \cup - x $$

Limping iambics (known also as choliambics or scazons): five iambs capped off with a trochee or spondee. A spondee may be substituted in the first and third foot.

$$ \overline{\cup} - \cup - \overline{\cup} - \cup - \cup - - x $$

Iambic strophe: alternating lines of iambic trimeter (three pairs of iambs) and iambic dimeter (two pairs of iambs) with flexibility to substitute spondees in the first, third, and fifth foot of the trimeter line, and in the first and third foot of the dimeter line.

$$\bar{\cup} - \cup - \bar{\cup} \,\|\, - \cup - \bar{\cup} - \cup\, x$$
$$\bar{\cup} - \cup - \bar{\cup} - \cup\, x$$

Sapphic strophe (in honor of Sappho of Lesbos, fl. seventh-sixth century BCE): a four-verse stanza, with the same metrical pattern in the first three lines.

$$- \cup - - - \,\|\, \cup\cup - \cup - x$$
$$- \cup - - - \,\|\, \cup\cup - \cup - x$$
$$- \cup - - - \,\|\, \cup\cup - \cup - x$$
$$- \cup\cup - x$$

Alcaic strophe (in honor of the Greek poet Alcaeus of Lesbos, born ca. 630 BCE): a four-verse stanza, with the same metrical pattern in the first two lines.

$$x - \cup - - \,\|\, - \cup\cup - \cup\, x$$
$$x - \cup - - \,\|\, - \cup\cup - \cup\, x$$
$$x - \cup - - - \cup - x$$
$$- \cup\cup - \cup\cup - \cup - x$$

First Asclepiadean (in honor of the Greek poet Asclepiades of Samos, fl. 290 BCE): a spondee followed by two choriambs, capped off with an iamb.

$$- - - \cup\cup - \,\|\, - \cup\cup - \cup\, x$$

BASIC GUIDE TO LATIN EPIGRAPHY

Complementing the rich, though limited and skewed, literary tradition is an equally rich collection of messages painted onto walls or etched in stone, metal, bricks, glass, pottery, mosaic *tesserae*, and wooden tablets. Epigraphy, from the Greek *epigraphein* ("to write on"), is the study of these inscriptions that were left for us by a variety of people, from humble provincials at the furthest reaches of the Roman Empire (Britain and Turkey), to self-promoting local politicians throughout the Empire, to the emperors themselves. Epigraphy preserves for us a record of idle musing (1.2, 1.3), personal vendettas (1.1, 5.5), sporting rivalries (38.1), election campaigns (1.4), and poignant epitaphs for deceased loved ones (34.4, 43.1). Inscriptions clarify the intended purpose of smaller items including altars (6.1) and votives (as payment for an answered prayer). Some inscriptions even take the form of curses, which were almost always inscribed on lead tablets (33.1, 38.1). Most visible and well-known are the monumental public inscriptions, including those on buildings, milestones, and temples. Inscriptions are a valuable resource for Roman social history, helping us piece together at least a small part of the lives of people who otherwise had no voice. These documents also help us flesh out legal codes and religious mandates, both of which were commonly displayed prominently and publicly in metal or wood. The fifth-century-BCE *Twelve Tables*, Rome's first codified system of law, was displayed in the Roman forum on bronze tablets (Livy 3.34; the originals were destroyed in 387 BCE when the Gauls sacked the city). During Caesar's triumphal parade in 47 BCE, a placard, inscribed *veni, vidi, vici*, preceded the victorious *imperator* (Suetonius, *de Vita Caesaris* 37.2). The text was probably painted on wood.

About 180,000 inscriptions have been collected in twenty volumes of the *Corpus Inscriptionum Latinarum* (*CIL*), the first of which was published in 1893. Other valuable collections of inscriptions include *Inscriptiones Latinae Selectae* (*ILS*), three large volumes published from 1892 to 1916, and *Roman Inscriptions of Britain* (*RIB*), an ongoing project with the first volume apprearing in 1965. Inscriptions have been discovered in the context of formal archaeological digs, city infrastructure improvement (the temple to the popular Eastern god Mithras in London was discovered in 1954 during reconstruction in the Walbrook district), and even in backyards. New inscriptions continue to come to light every year.

Inscriptions date back to the earliest known written languages (e.g., Babylonian cuneiform tablets on baked clay). Roman-era inscriptions are recorded in several languages. In the western provinces and Italy, most inscriptions are in Latin, the common language of business and politics. In the East, where Greek was more widely known, inscriptions were etched in that language. Many inscriptions, especially official ones, were cut bilingually. Augustus's autobiography, *Res Gestae Divi Augusti,* was erected at Rome, Apollonia in Illyricum and Antioch in Pisidia, and elsewhere, in both Greek and Latin. No single inscription is complete, but the Latin and Greek versions complement each other and thus have facilitated a reconstruction of the whole. Trilingual inscriptions also survive, rendering monumental messages in Latin, Greek, and local languages, especially in Tunisia, Thrace, and Palmyra in Syria, where Latin was the "official" language but Greek remained the *de facto* language of business. Hence, all literate residents could know the contents of an inscription regardless of ethnic background or level of education. Many inscriptions reflect local pronunciation (33.1: *anilum* for *anulum*; 34.4: *anc* for *hanc*) and interesting grammatical anomalies and errors (1.4).

In *A Little Latin Reader*, the inscriptions are neatly typed. The actual artifacts, however, are anything but regular. Public inscriptions on buildings, milestones, and honorific dedications to flatter the current emperor were usually done at great expense. The lettering was regular and blocky. Words would be etched deeply and then painted red for contrast and ease of reading, or bronze letters would be attached with pins (on the Arch of Titus, the careful observer can still see the holes where the bronze lettering was attached). An individual might hire a stonecutter to inscribe a tombstone, and the lettering could fall anywhere within the range from elegant to crude. Personal votives and simple objects dedicated by ordinary people were frequently inscribed more crudely, painted, scratched, or incised with rough and barely legible cursive characters.

Also fully expanded in *A Little Latin Reader* are the abbreviations in the inscriptions. Abbreviations were, for the most part, regularized and would be used to shorten inscriptions, perhaps to reduce the cost associated with having inscriptions cut. In addition to the *praenomines*, common abbreviations include conventional phrases, such as *v.s.l.m.* (*votum solvit libens merito*: 6.1) and *I.O.M.* (*Iovi Optimo Maximo*, almost always in the dative: 7.5). Also common is the omission of a direct object after *fecit* and other verbs of dedication or restoration (7.1–3, 18.1, 19.1, 20.1). Finally, although punctuation is missing, many monumental inscriptions do retain word division with the use of interpuncts, little dots, triangles, or flourishes etched between words.

Speaking to a widely held assumption that inscriptions are permanent, Horace claims to have created in his poetry a record "more lasting than bronze" (*aere perennius*: 50.1). Much of the epigraphical record has been lost, however, owing to the vulnerable nature of the materials on which messages were written. Bronze was a valuable commodity, melted down for reuse. Wood burns. Papyrus deteriorates. And even stone can be erased. During the Empire, as one regime replaced another, the names of unpopular emperors, who had suffered condemnation of memory (*damnatio memoriae*) – among them probably Caligula, certainly Nero – were literally chiseled off hundreds of stones. Some of these stones were broken down into rubble. In contrast, because of the great durability and utility of stone, many stone altars, in particular, were repurposed as sundials or fountains, or as building materials, including fences for livestock, houses, and even Christian churches. Consequently, much of the pagan religious record that the Christians sought to destroy from the fourth through sixth centuries CE has, in fact, been preserved by the would-be destroyers.

The Latin epigraphical record spans a milennium, but the great majority of the surviving inscriptions date to the first three centuries CE. Among the many clues that help scholars date Latin inscriptions are lettering styles, variations in abbreviations, irregularities in spelling and grammar, materials, and references to people and groups known from other contexts (emperors, politicians, military units: e.g., the Sixth Legion was sent to York in Britain around 120 CE. Thus, any inscriptions erected by members of the Sixth Legion date to after that time).

For a more complete introduction accessible to the nonspecialist, see Lawrence Keppie, *Understanding Roman Inscriptions*, Johns Hopkins, 1991.

INDEX OF LATIN GRAMMAR AND SYNTAX

We have organized the selections in *A Little Latin Reader* to highlight specific examples of Latin grammar and syntax. Since many passages could have appeared under more than one heading, we include here a list of cross-references so that instructors and students can reconfigure the passages in the reader for whatever review of Latin grammar and syntax they envision.

Subjunctive, Independent Uses, 6.3, 29.2, 33.1–5, 47.2, 48.2, 48.3, 50.1

Substantives, 12.1–3, 18.1, 22.6, 22.7, 29.1, 30.5, 38.1, 39.1, 41.1, 46.3, 47.2, 47.3, 49.1, 49.3, 50.2

Superlatives, Section 25

    Adjectives, 13.1, 14.1, 16.1, 18.2, 19.1, 19.4, 20.3, 22.4, 25.1–3, 26.2, 28.7, 29.1, 29.3, 30.7, 35.2, 35.3, 36.1, 37.1, 37.2, 39.1, 40.1, 43.1, 43.3, 43.7, 44.1, 44.5, 45.2, 47.1, 47.2, 49.1, 49.3

    Adverbs, 17.3, 19.4, 29.1, 43.1, 45.3, 46.3, 47.1, 47.3

Supines, 46.1–4, 47.1

Syncopated Forms

    Nouns, 19.4, 27.3, 29.3
    Pronouns, 29.3, 30.6, 41.2, 43.7
    Verbs, 15.1, 20.3, 21.4, 28.5, 30.3, 30.6, 33.3, 33.5, 38.3

Vocative Case, 1.5, 3.4, 4.1–3, 9.1, 10.1, 10.2, 11.3, 12.1, 12.3, 13.1, 15.1–3, 17.3, 18.3, 19.5, 20.2, 21.1–3, 24.1, 25.1, 25.2, 28.1, 28.2, 28.4, 28.5, 29.3, 30.1, 30.2, 30.4, 30.6, 31.2, 33.2, 34.1, 36.1, 36.2, 37.3, 38.1, 38.3, 39.3–5, 40.2, 41.2, 42.3, 43.6–8, 44.8, 45.1, 45.4, 48.1, 48.2, 50.1, 50.3

Volo, Nolo, and Malo, 10.1–3, 17.3, 22.2, 24.1, 30.6, 33.1, 39.3, 39.4, 41.2, 43.1, 44.7, 47.2, 48.1, 49.3

INDEX OF ROMAN CULTURE

This index is designed primarily for instructors and students who want to use the selections in the reader to become acquainted with various aspects of Roman history, culture, and civilization.

GUIDE TO PLACES AND PEOPLES ASSOCIATED WITH THE READINGS

This appendix notes the places and peoples associated with the selections in the reader and their authors whose geographical landscape undoubtedly influenced their work. We hope that students and instructors use this index and the accompanying maps to contextualize the readings within the ancient world.

Map 1: Roman Empire at its Greatest Extent, ca. 112 CE

Provinces

Africa: 2.1, 19.1, 22.5, 28.6, 28.7, 31.6, 31.7, 33.4, 34.4, 35.4, 38.1, 42.3, Sallust Biographical Sketch, Appendix C

Britannia: 6.1, 7.1–5, 13.2, 16.1, 17.3, 18.2, 19.1, 20.1, 22.1, 23.1–3, 26.3, 31.3, 32.1–3, 33.1, 35.2, 37.1, 38.2, 39.6, 43.2, 44.2–7, Caesar Biographical Sketch, Tacitus Biographical Sketch, Appendix C

Bythinia-Pontus: Catullus Biographical Sketch, Pliny Biographical Sketch

Cappadocia: Germanicus Biographical Sketch

Cilicia: Caesar Biographical Sketch

Commagene: Germanicus Biographical Sketch

Cyrene: 42.3

Egypt (Aegyptia): 10.2, 50.1, Germanicus Biographical Sketch

Gallia (Lugdunensis, Belgica, Aquitania, Narbonensis): 7.1, 8.3, 9.2, 14.1, 14.2, 19.3, 19.4, 21.4, 25.3, 26.1, 26.2, 26.4, 28.1, 28.3, 30.5, 40.1, 43.1, 43.3, 44.1, 44.5, 44.7, 46.1, 46.3, 47.1, Caesar Biographical Sketch

Gallia Cisalpina: 26.2, Caesar Biographical Sketch
Germania: 7.1, 13.3, 14.2–4, 20.3, 24.4, 26.2, 26.5, 29.1, 35.3, Caesar
  Biographical Sketch, Germanicus Biographical Sketch, Tacitus
  Biographical Sketch
Graecia: 29.3, 46.2, 47.1, 50.2
Hispania: 31.1, Caesar Biographical Sketch
Italia: 7.1
Sardinia: 5.8
Scythia: 48.3
Sicilia: 12.2, Cicero Biographical Sketch
  Scylla and Charybdis: 28.5
Syria: 6.1, Germanicus Biographical Sketch
Thessalia: 48.3
Thrace: Appendix C

Cities

Alesia, Gallia Lugdunensis: Caesar Biographical Sketch
Antioch, Syria: Germanicus Biographical Sketch, Appendix C
Apollonia, Illyricum: Appendix C
Bilbilis, Hispania Tarraconensis: Martial Biographical Sketch
Carthago: 12.2, 22.5, 24.2, 28.5–7, 31.6, 31.7, 33.4, 34.4, 35.4, 39.1
Delphi, Graecia: 47.1, 50.1
Hadrumetum, Africa: 38.1
Lugdunum (Lyon), Gallia Lugdunensis: 28.1, 43.1
Miletos, Mysia (western Turkey): Caesar Biographical Sketch
Palmyra, Syria: Appendix C
Philippi, eastern Macedonia: Horace Biographical Sketch
Thelepte, Tunisia: 34.4
Tudrus (Thysdrus), Tunisia: 19.1
Timgad, North Africa: 2.1
Tomis, Black Sea: 33.5, Ovid Biographical Sketch
Troia (Troy): 28.5, 29.3, 30.7, 33.4
Tyria (Tyre): 28.6, 31.7

Natural Landmarks

Caucasus Mountains: 48.3
Cythera: 35.4
Hercynian Forest, Germania: 13.3, 14.4, 20.3, 24.4
Jura Mountains: 26.2

Lesbos, Aeolia: 15.2, 50.1
Lacus Lemannus, Gallia Narbonensis: 26.2
Mare Adriaticum (Adriatic Sea): 24.3, Vergil Biographical Sketch
Nile River (Nilus): 10.2
Pontus (Black Sea): 33.5
Rhenus (Rhine River): 26.2
Rhodanus (Rhone River): 26.2
Samos: 5.5
Simois River, Troia: 29.3
Syrtis Major (Gulf of Sidra): 28.7
Syrtis Minor (Gulf of Gabès): 28.7

Peoples

Allobroges, Gallia Narbonensis: Catiline Biographical Sketch
Aquitani, Gallia Aquitania: 26.1
Atrebates, Gallia Belgica and Britannia: 26.3
Belgae, Gallia Belgica: 26.1, 44.5
Helvetii, Gallia Narbonensis: 9.2, 25.3, 26.2, 44.1, 46.1, 46.3
Massilii (Massylii), Numidia: 50.3
Morini, Gallia Belgica: 16.1
Myrmidones and Dolopes, Thessalia: 46.2
Sebusiani, Gallia Lugdunensis: 32.1
Sequani, Gallia Narbonensis: 26.2, 43.1
Veneti, Gallia Lugdunensis: 16.1

Map 1 Inset: Italia

Arno River: 48.2
Alba Longa: 16.2, 36.3
Apulia: 50.1
Arretium: 48.2
Aufidus River, Apulia: 50.1
Caralis, Sardinia: 5.8
Comum (Como), northern Italy: Pliny Biographical Sketch
Cremona: 45.4
Cumae: 43.8
Etruria: 27.3, 31.4, 40.4, 41.1, 49.1, Catiline Biographical Sketch
Formiae: 13.1
Latium: 28.5
Mantua, northen Italy: Vergil Biographical Sketch

Mount Vesuvius: 47.3
Naples (Neapolis): 47.3
Nola: 49.2
Nomentum: 39.5, Statius Biographical Sketch
Osci (Oscans), Campania: 41.2
Pistorium, Etruria: 49.1, Catiline Biographical Sketch
Planasia: 49.2
Pompeii: 1.1–4, 3.1, 5.1–5, 12.1, 18.1, 30.1, 34.3
Roma: see Map 2
Sabini (Sabines): 11.2, 18.1, 18.2, 39.5, Horace Biographical Sketch
Sulmo: Ovid Biographical Sketch
Verona: Catullus Biographical Sketch

Map 2: Rome in the Early Empire

Roma: 5.6, 8.3, 15.1, 17.1, 31.1, 34.4, 45.3, 48.2
Amphitheatrum Flavii (Colosseum): 50.3, Martial Biographical
  Sketch
Arch of Titus: Appendix C
Capitolinus (Capitoline Hill): 46.4, 50.1
Circus Maximus: 49.3
Comitium: 47.1
Pons Mulvius (Mulvian Bridge): 31.1
Horti Neronis (Nero's gardens): 49.3
Porta Collina: 47.1
Tiberis (Tiber River): 38.1
Via Flaminia: 10.2
Via Saleria: 47.1
Via Nomentana: 47.1

Map 3: Roman Britain

Bath (Aquae Sulis): 18.2
Benwell (Condercum), a Roman fort on Hadrian's Wall: 7.4
Bollihope Common, Stanhope, County Durham: 32.1
Carvoran (Magnis), a Roman fort on Hadrian's Wall: 6.1
Custom Scrubs: 7.3
English Channel: 37.1, 44.3
London (Londinium Augusta): 7.2, Appendix C

Lydney Park, Gloucestershire: 33.1
Martlesham, Suffolk: 20.1
Newcastle-upon-Tyne (Pons Aelius): 7.5
Old Carlisle (Maglona): 19.1
Winchester (Venta Belgarum): 7.1

Map 1: Roman Empire at its Greatest Extent, ca. 112 CE

KEY

1 Saepta Julia	7 Porta Collina
2 Theatrum Pompeii	8 Comitium
3 Theatrum Marcelli	9 Forum Caesaris
4 Amphitheatrum Flavium	10 Forum Augusti
5 Castra Praetoria	11 Forum Vespasiani
6 Circus Maximus	12 Arcus Titi

Map 2: Rome in the Early Empire

Map 3: Roman Britain

SUGGESTIONS FOR FURTHER READING

These sources provide an excellent starting point for students and instructors who want to learn more about the topics featured in *A Little Latin Reader*. In the interest of space, we have refrained from including books limited to one Roman author or genre.

Bonner, Stanley F. *Education in Ancient Rome: From the Elder Cato to the Younger Pliny*. University of California, 1977. An account of intellectual training in Rome, both informal and formal, contextualizing the curriculum and process of education within the larger scope of Roman culture.

Casson, Lionel. *Everyday Life in Ancient Rome*. Johns Hopkins, 1999. An engagingly succinct introduction to Roman social history, including chapters on the family, agriculture, city life, sports, and engineering.

Connolly, Peter, and Hazel Dodge. *The Ancient City: Life in Classical Athens and Rome*. Oxford, 2000. A beautifully illustrated book synthesizing many facets of life in the ancient world, including daily life and public and private infrastructure. The illustrations are a mix of actual remains and artistic reconstructions.

Conte, Gian Biagio. *Latin Literature: A History*. Trans. Joseph B. Solodaw. Johns Hopkins, 1994. A comprehensive handbook discussing all of the major authors and genres from the early Republic to the late Empire.

Dixon, Suzanne. *The Roman Family*. Johns Hopkins, 1992. A scholarly account of the social and legal aspects of the family unit at Rome.

Fantham, Elaine, Helene Peet Foley, Natalie Boymel Kampien, Sarah B. Pomeroy, and H. Alan Shapiro, eds. *Women in the Classical World*. Oxford, 1994. An informative and readable survey of women of all classes in public and private life in the ancient world, including their concerns and contributions.

Harrison, Stephen, ed. *A Companion to Latin Literature* (Blackwell Companions to the Ancient World). Wiley-Blackwell, 2007. An excellent collection of essays, divided into sections on periods (from the early Republic to the high Empire), genres, and themes (including chapters on friendship and patronage as well as slavery and class).

LeGlay, Marcel, Jean-Louis Voisin, Yan Le Bohec, David Cherry, Donald G. Kyle, and Eleni Manolaraki. *A History of Rome*. 4th ed. Wiley-Blackwell, 2009. A solid introduction to Roman history, synthesizing historical, political, military, social, and economic aspects.

Reynolds, L. D., and N. G. Wilson. *Scribes and Scholars: A Guide to the Transmission of Greek and Latin Literature*. 3rd ed. Oxford, 1991. A fascinating narrative about the history of scholarship, the book, how ancient texts were preserved, and why some texts survived while others were lost.

Salway, Peter. *Roman Britain: A Very Short Introduction*. Oxford, 2002. A concise, informative distillation of the history of Roman Britain and its significance within the Roman Empire.

Shelton, Jo-Ann. *As the Romans Did: A Sourcebook in Roman Social History*. 2nd ed. Oxford, 1998. A lively collection of passages from ancient authors illustrating numerous aspects of daily life, including work, religion, and entertainment.

Taylor, Lily Ross. *Party Politics in the Age of Caesar*. University of California, 1949. A wonderfully readable account of Roman political life in the final years of the Republic.

Warry, John Gibson. *Warfare in the Classical World: An Illustrated Encyclopedia of Weapons, Warriors and Warfare in the Ancient Civilisations of Greece and Rome*. University of Oklahoma, 1995. A richly illustrated account of the armies of Greece and Rome, and their cultural, historical, and political significance.

Wells, Colin. *The Roman Empire*. 2nd ed. Harvard, 1995. A concise history of the Roman Empire from Octavius's birth to the fragmentation of the Empire in the West.

Wilkinson, L. P. *Golden Latin Artistry*. University of Oklahoma, 1985 (reprint of the 1963 Cambridge edition). A thorough guide to Latin meter and poetic structure.

Zanker, Paul. *Pompeii: Public and Private Life*. Harvard, 1998. An introduction to the city, including its origins, history, and archaeological remains.

GLOSSARY

Below are listed words that appear in more than one selection. Proper names and words that occur only in one passage are glossed beneath the relevant selections. As in the main text, we have used the *Oxford Latin Dictionary* as a guide for the macrons and abbreviations.

ā/ab + ablative: away from, by
abdūcō, -ere, abduxī, abductus: lead away, carry off
abeō, -īre, -iī, -itus: go away
absistō, -ere, abstitī: stop short of
absum, -esse, āfuī, āfutūrus: be away, be absent
ac: and also
accēdō, -ere, accessī, accessus: approach, reach, come near
accīdō, -ere, accīdī, accīsus: cut, weaken
accipiō, -ere, accēpī, acceptus: take, receive
ācer, ācris, ācre: sharp, fierce
aciēs, -ēī, f: edge, piercing look, battle line
ācriter: fiercely
acūtus, -a, -um: sharp, pointed
ad + accusative: to, toward, near

addūcō, -ere, adduxī, adductus: lead on, induce
adeō, -īre, -iī, -itus: approach, consult
adeō: so, very, even, right up to
adflīgō, -ere, adflixī, adflictus: shatter, damage
adhūc: thus far, yet, still, even now
adiciō, -ere, adiēcī, adiectus: join, add to, proceed
adiūrō, -āre, -āvī, -ātus: swear
admittō, -ere, admīsī, admissus: commit, admit, allow, permit
adorior, -īrī, adortus sum: attack, assail, rise up
adsum, -esse, affuī: be at hand, be near, be in attendance
adulescens, adulescentis, m/f: youth, young person

171

advena, -ae, m/f: immigrant, foreigner
adversus + accusative: against
adversus, -a, -um: hostile, adverse, unfavorable
aequor, -oris, n: sea, ocean, level surface
aes, aeris, n: copper, bronze
aestus, -ūs, m: storm, tide, heat
aeternus, -a, -um: eternal, everlasting
afferō, -ferre, attulī, allātus: bring, convey, allege
ager, agrī, m: field, land, farm
agitātor, -ōris, m: driver
agna, -ae, f: lamb
agō, -ere, ēgī, actus: do, drive, accomplish, guide, spend
ait: he/she says, affirms
āla, -ae, f: wing, squadron
albus, -a, -um: white
alibī: elsewhere
aliēnus, -a, -um: other, unfavorable
alius, alia, aliud: other, some
alter, altera, alterum: another, the other (of two)
altum, -ī, n: the deep (sea)
altus, -a, -um: deep, high, severe
amans, amantis, m/f: lover
ambāgēs, -is, f: devious tale, double talk, evasion
ambulō, -āre, -āvī, -ātus: walk, travel, strut
amīca, -ae, f: girlfriend
amīcitia, -ae, f: friendship
amō, -āre, -āvī, -ātus: like, love
amor, -ōris, m: love
an: whether... or, if, or
anima, -ae, f: breath, life, soul
animadvertō, -ere, animadvertī, animadversus: notice

animus, -ī, m: soul, mind
annus, -ī, m: year
apertus, -a, -um: open, exposed
appellō, -āre, -āvī, -ātus: call
apud + accusative: among, in the case of
aqua, -ae, f: water
aquila, -ae, f: eagle, military standard
arbitror, -ārī, -ātus sum: think
arbor, -oris, f: tree
āridus, -a, -um: dry
arma, -ōrum, n (plural): arms, equipment
ars, artis, f: art, craft, skill
articulus, -ī, m: joint, knuckle, toe
aspiciō, -ere, aspexī, aspectus: see, behold, observe
at: but, however, moreover, on the other hand
atque: and also
attribuō, -ere, attribuī, attribūtus: assign, allot
auctōritās, -ātis, f: influence, authority
audācia, -ae, f: courage, audacity, recklessness
audeō, -ēre, ausus sum (semi-deponent): dare
audiō, -īre, -īvī, -ītus: hear
augustus, -a, -um: solemn, venerable, "of the emperor"
aura, -ae, f: air, breeze
auris, -is, f: ear
aurum, -ī, n: gold
aut: or
aut... aut: either... or
autem: moreover

bāsiō, -āre, -āvī, -ātus: kiss
bāsium, -iī, n: kiss
beātus, -a, -um: blessed

bellē: prettily

bellum, -ī, n: war

bellus, -a, -um: pretty, handsome, beautiful

bene: well

bis: twice

bonus, -a, -um: good, honest, brave, noble

bōs, bovis, m/f: ox, bull, cow

brevis, -e: small, short

cadō, -ere, cecidī, cāsus: fall, fail, die

caecus, -a, -um: blind, hidden, secret

caedēs, -is, f: murder, slaughter

caelum, -ī, n: sky, heaven

caespes, caespitis, m: ground

cantō, -āre, -āvī, -ātus: sing

capillus, -ī, m: hair

capiō, -ere, cēpī, captus: take, seize, capture

caput, capitis, n: head

cardō, cardinis, m: hinge, pole, axis

cāritās, -ātis, f: esteem, favor, affection

carmen, carminis, n: song, poem, verse, poetry

cārus, -a, -um + dative: dear, valued

castra, -ōrum, n (plural): camp

cāsus, -ūs, m: fall, misfortune

causa, -ae, f: cause, reason

causā + genitive (post-positive preposition that follows its object): for the sake of

caveō, -ēre, cāvī, cautus: beware

cavus, -a, -um: hollow

cēnō, -āre, -āvī, -ātus: dine

centum (indeclinable): one hundred

certē: certainly, at least

certus, -a, -um: certain, definite

cēterus, -a, -um: the other, the remaining

ceu: as if, as though

circā: around, nearby

cīvitās, -ātis, f: state, tribe

clāmō, -āre, -āvī, -ātus: shout

classis, -is, f: fleet

claudō, -ere, clausī, clausus: besiege, enclose, confine, restrict, shut down

claustrum, -ī, n: enclosure, barrier

coepī, coepisse, coeptus (no first or second principal parts): begin

cōgitō, -āre, -āvī, -ātus: think, intend, plan

cognoscō, -ere, cognōvī, cognitus: learn, know, spy out, recognize

cōgō, -ere, coēgī, coactus: compel, force

cohors, cohortis, f: troop, company, cohort

cōiciō, -ere, cōiēcī, cōiectus: throw together, hurl, toss, cast

colligō, -ere, collēgī, collectus: gather, collect, deduce

collis, -is, m: hill

collum, -ī, n: neck

color, -ōris, m: color, tint, hue

columba, -ae, f: dove

coma, -ae, f: hair

comes, comitis, m/f: companion, partner, devotee

commoveō, -ēre, commōvī, commōtus: disturb

comparō, -āre, -āvī, -ātus: compare, prepare, put together

complūrēs, -a: several, many

concidō, -ere, concidī: fall down

concurrō, -ere, concurrī, concursus: charge, rally, engage in battle

condō, -ere, condidī, conditus: put together, hide, plunge, bury

conferō, -ferre, contulī, collātus: bring together

confestim: immediately

confirmō, -āre, -āvī, -ātus: strengthen, assure, confirm

coniunx, coniugis, m/f: spouse

cōnor, -ārī, -ātus sum: try, attempt

consilium, -iī, n: assembly, council, plan, counsel, good judgment

consimilis, -e + dative: exactly similar, alike in all respects

consistō, -ere, constitī: consist of, be formed of, be taken up with

conspiciō, -ere, conspexī, conspectus: catch sight of, perceive

constituō, -ere, constituī, constitūtus: establish, resolve, decide

consuescō, -ere, consuēvī, consuētus: be accustomed

consuētūdō, consuētūdinis, f: custom, habit

consultum, -ī, n: decree

contineō, -ēre, continuī, contentus: hold back, detain, keep in hand

contrōversia, -ae, f: dispute, debate

conveniō, -īre, convēnī, conventus: convene, assemble, meet

convenit: it is fitting

convīva, -ae, m/f: banquet guest

cōpia, -ae, f: abundance, supply; (in plural) forces, resources, troops

cornū, -ūs, n: horn

corpus, corporis, n: body

cōtīdiē: every day, daily

crēber, crēbra, crēbrum: thick, crowded together, frequent, numerous

creō, -āre, -āvī, -ātus: produce, give birth to

crescō, -ere, crēvī, crētus: grow, increase

crīmen, crīminis, n: accusation, charge, fault, crime

crīnis, -is, m: hair

crūdēlis, -e: cruel, harsh, severe, fierce

cum + ablative: with

cum: when, since, because, although

cum...tum: not only...but also

cupīdō, cupīdinis, m: desire; Cupid, son of Venus

cupidus, -a, -um: desirous, eager, zealous

cupiō, -ere, -īvī/iī, -ītus: desire, long for, wish for

cūrō, -āre, -āvī, -ātus: take care, pay attention to, provide for

currō, -ere, cucurrī, cursus: run

currus, -ūs, m: chariot

cursus, -ūs, m: course, direction, passage

custōdia, -ae, f: protection, charge, defense

custōs, custōdis, m/f: guardian

dē + ablative: from, about, concerning

dēbeō, -ēre, debuī, debitus: owe

dēclāmō, -āre, -āvī, -ātus: declaim, give oratorical speeches

dēdicō, -āre, -āvī, -ātus: dedicate, consecrate

dēdō, -ere, dēdidī, dēditus: devote

dēdūco, -ere, dēduxī, dēductus: lead down, bring down, divert, draw out

dēferō, -ferre, dētulī, dēlātus: carry away, confer upon

deinde: then, next, afterward

dēliciae, -ārum, f (plural): delight, darling

dens, dentis, m: tooth

densus, -a, -um: thick, close, closely
packed

deus, -ī, m: god

dexter, dextra, dextrum: right
(hand)

dīcō, -ere, dixī, dictus: say, speak,
speak of, mention

diēs, diēī, m (rarely f): day

dignitās, -ātis, f: excellence, dignity,
worth

dīligenter: carefully

dīligō, -ere, dīlexī, dīlectus: love,
esteem, value

dīmidius, -a, -um: half

dīmittō, -ere, dīmīsī, dīmissus: send
forth, forsake, give up

disciplīna, -ae, f: instruction,
teaching

dissimulō, -āre, -āvī, -ātus: conceal,
disguise

diū: for a long time

dīvēs, dīvitis: rich, wealthy

dīvidō, -ere, dīvīsī, dīvīsus: divide

dīvīnus, -a, -um: divine, noble

dīvitiae, -ārum, f (plural): wealth

dīvus, -a, -um: divine

dō, dare, dedī, datus: give

dolor, -ōris, m: pain, grief

dominus, -ī, m: commander, leader,
manager, master

domus, -ūs, f: house, home,
household

dōnec: while, as long as, until

dōnō, -āre, -āvī, -ātus: give as a present, present

dōnum, -ī, n: gift

druidēs, -um, m (plural): Druids

dūcō, -ere, duxī, ductus: lead, consider, think out

dulcis, -e: sweet

dum: while, as long as

dummodo: provided that

duo, duae, duo: two

dūrus, -a, -um: hard, inflexible,
harsh

dux, ducis, m: leader

ē /ex + ablative: from, out of

efferō, -ferre, extulī, ēlātus: raise up

efficiō, -ere, effēcī, effectus: produce,
make, effect

effundō, -ere, effūdī, effūsus: pour
out, squander, waste

ego: I

ēgredior, -ī, ēgressus sum: step out,
set out, depart

ēligo, -ere, ēlēgī, ēlectus: pick out,
choose

enim: for, in fact

eō, īre, iī or īvī, itus: go

eō: there, to that place

eques, equitis, m: horseman, cavalryman, knight, man of the equestrian rank; (in plural) cavalry

equitātus, -ūs, m: cavalry

equus, -ī, m: horse

ergō: therefore, well now

ēripiō, -ere, ēripuī, ēreptus: snatch,
take away by force

essedum, -ī, n: a Celtic war chariot

et: and, even

et...et: both...and

etiam: also, even, yet again

ēveniō, -īre, ēvēnī, ēventus: turn out,
result, happen

excēdō, -ere, excessī, excessus: go
out, go away, die

excitō, -āre, -āvī, -ātus: arouse,
attract, wake up, rouse

exercitus, -ūs, m: army

exigō, -ere, exēgī, exactus: finish, complete, discover

exitium, -iī, n: ruin, destruction, death

expedītus, -a, -um: light armed

explōrō, -āre, -āvī, -ātus: search out, test, investigate

externus, -a, -um: foreign

faciēs, -ēī, f: face, appearance, shape

facilis, -e: easy

faciō, -ere, fēcī, factus: make, do

factiō, -ōnis, f: political party, faction

facultās, -ātis, f: opportunity, resource

fallō, -ere, fefellī, falsus: deceive, trick

fāma, -ae, f: rumor, reputation

famēs, -is, f: hunger

fateor, -ērī, fassus sum: confess, acknowledge

fātum, -ī, n: fate, destiny; (in plural) the Fates

faucēs, -ium, f (plural): throat, jaws, mountain pass

febris, -is, f: fever

fēlix, fēlīcis: bringing good luck, lucky

fēmina, -ae, f: woman

fera, -ae, f: wild beast

ferē: nearly

feriō, -īre (no third or fourth principal parts): strike, beat

ferō, ferre, tulī, lātus: bear, endure, carry, convey, hold, tell, speak of

fidēs, -ēī, f: faith, trust, loyalty, honesty

figūra, -ae, f: image, shape, form

fīlia, -ae, f: daughter

fīlius, -iī, m: son

fīnis, -is, m: border, boundary, end; (in plural) territory

fīō, fierī, factus sum: become, happen

flamma, -ae, f: fire, flame, blaze

fluctus, -ūs, m: wave, flood, sea, tide

flūmen, flūminis, n: stream, river

foedus, foederis, n: treaty, alliance

forma, -ae, f: form, shape, beauty

fors, fortis, f: chance, luck

forte: by chance

fortis, -e: strong, courageous

fortūna, -ae, f: fortune, luck (good and bad)

forum, -ī, n: forum, open square, marketplace

frāter, frātris, m/f: brother

frīgidus, -a, -um: cold

frons, frontis, f: brow, forehead

fuga, -ae, f: flight, panic, escape

fugiō, -ere, fūgī: flee, escape, run away

funda, -ae, f: sling

fundō, -ere, fūdī, fūsus: rout, scatter, defeat

furor, -ōris, m: fury, passion, madness, rage

garriō, -īre, -īvī: chatter, babble

geminus, -a, -um: twin-born, twin

gener, generī, m: son-in-law

gens, gentis, f: nation, people, race, clan

genus, generis, n: type, kind, birth, descent, "nobility"

gerō, -ere, gessī, gestus: carry on, manage

gnātus, -ī, m: son

grātia, -ae, f + dative: charm, beauty, grace, service, kindness

gravis, -e: dignified, serious, severe

grex, gregis, m/f: flock, herd, crowd,
company

habeō, -ēre, -uī, -itus: have, consider,
wear

habitō, -āre, -āvī: live, dwell

harēna, -ae, f: sand, the arena of the
amphitheater

haud: by no means

hauriō, -īre, hausī, haustus: drink
up, drain

hērēditās, -ātis, f: inheritance

heu: alas

hic, haec, hoc: this (person or thing)

hīc: here

homō, hominis, m: human being,
mankind, person

honor, -ōris, m: honor, glory, reward,
respect, distinction

horridus, -a, -um: rough, shaggy,
bristly, wild, frightful

hospes, hospitis, m/f: guest, stranger,
host

hostis, -is, m/f: enemy

hūc: here, to this place

hūmānus, -a, -um: human, civilized,
refined

humilis, -e: humble

iaceō, -ēre, iacuī, iacitus: lie, rest, lie
dead

iactō, -āre, -āvī, -ātus: throw away,
cast, hurl

iam: now, already

ibi/ibī: there, in that place

īdem, eadem, idem: the same

īdem: likewise, similarly

idōneus, -a, -um: suitable, proper

ignārus, -a, -um: inexperienced,
ignorant, unaware

ignis, -is, m: fire, flame

ille, illa, illud: that, that well-known
(person or thing)

illīc: there

illūc: to that place

immō: no indeed, by no means,
rather, on the contrary, more
precisely

immolō, -āre, -āvī, -ātus: sacrifice

immortālis, -e: deathless, immortal

imperātor, -ōris, m: general, emperor,
victorious Roman general

imperium, -iī, n: command, control,
dominion, power, sovereignty,
reign

in + ablative: in, on

in + accusative: into, to, toward,
against

incēdō, -ere, incessī: advance, come
over

incipiō, -ere, incēpī, inceptus: begin

incitō, -āre, -āvī, -ātus: urge on, hasten, enrage

incolō, -ere, incoluī: live in, inhabit,
dwell

inde: from that place

infestus, -a, -um: hostile, dangerous

ingens, ingentis: huge, vast

ingredior, -ī, ingressus sum:
advance, enter

initium, -iī, n: beginning, element,
first principles

iniūria, -ae, f: insult, injustice

inquit: he/she says

insequor, -ī, insecūtus sum: follow,
pursue

institūtum, -ī, n: undertaking,
arrangement, institution

instō, -āre, institī: press upon, pursue, harass, solicit

insula, -ae, f: island

integer, integra, integrum: whole, intact, vigorous
inter + accusative: between, among, within
intereā: meanwhile
interficiō, -ere, interfēcī, interfectus: kill
interim: meanwhile
intermittō, -ere, intermīsī, intermissus: interrupt, break, discontinue
intrā + accusative: within, before
invalidus, -a, -um: weak, feeble
inveniō, -īre, invēnī, inventus: find, come upon
invictus, -a, -um: unconquered, invincible
ipse, ipsa, ipsum: himself, herself, itself, themselves
īra, -ae, f: anger, wrath
īrascor, -ī, īrātus sum: be angry
is, ea, id: he, she, it
iste, ista, istud: that of yours, of such a kind
ita: thus, to such an extent
itaque: and thus, and so
item: likewise
iter, itineris, n: journey, march
iterum: again
iubeō, -ēre, iussī, iussus: order, command
iūcundus, -a, -um: pleasant, agreeable
iūs, iūris, n: right, justice, law
iuvenis, -is, m/f: young man/woman
iuvō, -āre, iūvī, iūtus: aid, support, help, assist, please

labor, -ōris, m: work, labor, effort
labrum, -ī, n: lip
lacessō, -ere, -īvī, -ītus: harass, assail, attack
lacrima, -ae, f: tear

laetus, -a, -um: cheerful, favorable, happy
lāna, -ae, f: wool
latus, lateris, n: side, flank
laurus, -ī, f: laurel tree or branch
laus, laudis, f: praise
lavō, -āre, lāvī, lautus: bathe
lēgātus, -ī, m: lieutenant, envoy
legiō, -ōnis, f: body of soldiers, legion
legō, -ere, lēgī, lectus: gather, collect, read
lēnis, -e: smooth, gentle
leō, -ōnis, m: lion
lepus, leporis, m: hare, rabbit
levis, -e: light, swift
lēvis, -e: smooth, delicate
levō, -āre, -āvī, -ātus: lift, raise, release, free
libellus, -ī, m: little book
libens, libentis: willing, joyful
liber, librī, m: book
līber, lībera, līberum: free, unrestrained
līberī, -ōrum, m (plural): children
licet, -ēre, licuit + dative: it is permitted
lignum, -ī, n: wood
līmen, līminis, n: threshold, entrance
lingua, -ae, f: tongue, language
lītus, lītoris, n: seashore, beach
locus, -ī, m: place, region, area
longē: by far, far off
longus, -a, -um: long
lucrum, -ī, n: profit
lūdō, -ere, lūsī, lūsus + ablative: play, sport, mock, toy with
lūmen, lūminis, n: light, eye
lūna, -ae, f: moon
lux, lūcis, f: light, dawn

maestus, -a, -um: sad, mournful, gloomy

magis: more

magistrātus, -ūs, m: magistrate, state official

magnitūdō, magnitūdinis, f: size

magnus, -a, -um: great, large, vast, illustrious

māiōres, -ium, m/f (plural): ancestors

mālō, malle, māluī: prefer, be more willing

malum, -ī, n: evil, misfortune

malus, -a, -um: bad, evil

maneō, -ēre, mansī, mansus: stay, remain

mānēs, -ium, m (plural): the spirits of the dead

manus, -ūs, f: hand

mare, -is, n: sea

maritimus, -a, -um: of the sea, by the sea

marmor, -oris, n: marble

māter, mātris, f: mother

maximē: especially

maximus, -a, -um (superlative of magnus): greatest

medicus, -ī, m: physician, surgeon

medius, -a, -um: middle, midmost

melior, melius (comparative of bonus): better

membrum, -ī, n: limb

meminī, meminisse (no first or second principal parts): remember, recollect

memor, -oris + gentive: remembering, mindful

memoria, -ae, f: memory, remembrance, by tradition

mercātor, -ōris, m: merchant

meritō: deservedly, rightly

-met (intensive enclitic): very, self

metuō, -ere, metuī, metūtus: fear, dread

metus, -ūs, m (rarely f): fear, apprehension, dread

meus, -a, -um: my

micō, -āre, micuī: twinkle, dart, glitter

mīles, mīlitis, m: soldier

minimus, -a, -um (superlative of parvus): smallest, very small

minor, minus (comparative of parvus): lesser, subordinate

miser, misera, miserum: wretched, pitiable

mittō, mittere, mīsī, missus: send, let go

moderātius: with more restraint

modo: just now, a moment ago

modus, -ī, m: method, way, sort, type, measure, meter

moenia, -ium, n (plural): walls, city walls

molestus, -a, -um: annoying, bothersome, troublesome

mōlior, -īrī, -ītus sum: try, attempt

mons, montis, m: mountain

morbus, -ī, m: disease

morior, -ī, mortuus sum: die

moror, -ārī, -ātus sum: delay

mors, mortis, f: death

mortuus, -a, -um: dead

mōs, mōris, m: habit, custom, law; (in plural) character, morals

mōtus, -ūs, m: motion, movement

mulier, mulieris, f: woman

multitūdō, multitūdinis, f: crowd, a large number

multum: much

multus, -a, -um: great, many

mundus, -ī, m: universe, world
nam: for
namque: for, seeing that
narrō, -āre, -āvī, -ātus: tell, report, relate
nascor, -ī, nātus sum: be born, arise, spring forth
nāsus, -ī, m: nose
nātiō, -ōnis, f: tribe, race, people
nātūra, -ae, f: nature
nātus, -ī, m: son, child
nāvis, -is, f: ship
nāvis onerāria, nāvis onerāriae, f: transport ship
nē: lest
-ne: whether, or
nē... quidem: not even
nec: and... not
nefās, n (indeclinable): a violation of divine law, an impious act
negō, -āre, -āvī, -ātus: deny, refuse
negōtium, -iī, n: business
nēmō, nēminis, m/f: no one
nepōs, -ōtis, m: grandson, descendant
neque: nor, and... not
neque... nec: neither... nor
nervus, -ī, m: muscle, string of a musical instrument
niger, nigra, nigrum: black, dark
nihil, n (indeclinable): nothing
nimium: too much, too
nisi: unless, except
nōbilis, -e: well-known, famous
nōlō, nolle, nōluī: be unwilling, refuse
nōmen, nōminis, n: name
nōminō, -āre, -āvī, -ātus: call
nōn: not
noscō, -ere, nōvī, nōtus: know, be familiar with

noster, nostra, nostrum: our
nōtō, -āre, -āvī, -ātus: observe, mark, note
nōtus, -a, -um: well-known, famous, esteemed
novus, -a, -um: new
nox, noctis, f: night
nullus, -a, -um: no, none, not any
nūmen, nūminis, n: divine spirit
numerus, -ī, m: account, estimation, esteem, number
nummus, -ī, m: coin, money
numquam: never
nunc: now
nuptiae, -ārum, f (plural): marriage, wedding, nuptials
ō!: oh! if only!
ob + accusative: on account of, because of
obdūrō, -āre, -āvī, -ātus: be hard, hold out, persist, endure
obiciō, -ere, obiēcī, obiectus: cast, oppose, throw before
oblīviscor, -ī, oblītus sum + genitive: be forgetful of
occīdō, -ere, occīdī, occīsus: strike down, kill
occurrō, -ere, occurrī, occursus + dative: meet with, encounter
ōceanus, -ī, m: the ocean, the sea that surrounds the earth
oculus, -ī, m: eye
ōdī, odisse, ōsus (no first or second principal parts): hate, detest
officium, -iī, n: devotion, duty
omnīnō: entirely, altogether
omnis, -e: each, every, all
onerārius, -a, -um: for freight
oportet, -ēre, oportuit + dative: it is fitting

ops, opis, f: power, strength, wealth; (in plural) riches

optimus, -a, -um (superlative of *bonus*): best

opus, operis, n: work, task, labor

ōra, -ae, f: shore

orbis, -is, m: circle, orb, knob

orior, -īrī, ortus sum: arise, be born

ōs, ōris, n: mouth, face, expression

os, ossis, n: bone

osculum, -ī, n: mouth, kiss

ostendō, -ere, ostendī, ostensus: show, display, promise

ōtium, -iī, n: leisure

palma, -ae, f: hand, prize

pār, paris: equal, like

parens, parentis, m/f: parent

pars, partis, f: part, portion

parvus, -a, -um: little, small

passer, passeris, m: sparrow

pater, patris, m: father

patior, -ī, passus sum: suffer, endure

patria, -ae, f: native land, homeland

patrōnus, -ī, m: patron

paucus, -a, -um: few, little

paulātim: little by little

paulō: a little, a little bit

paulum: a little

pauper, pauperis + genitive: poor (in), scant (in)

pax, pācis, f: peace

pectus, pectoris, n: heart, soul, chest

pecūnia, -ae, f: money

pecus, pecoris, n: flock, herd, cattle

pellis, -is, f: skin, hide

penātēs, -ium, m (plural): the gods of the home, hearth, or family line

pendō, -ere, pependī, pensus: pay, weigh out

penitus: deeply

per + accusative: through

perdō, -ere, perdidī, perditus: lose, destroy, ruin, squander

pereō, -īre, -iī, -itus: die, pass away

perferō, -ferre, pertulī, perlātus: bring, carry through, return

perīculum, -ī, n: danger, risk

permaneō, -ēre, permansī, permansus: continue, hold out, be permanent, remain

perpetuus, -a, -um: continual, everlasting

perturbō, -āre, -āvī, -ātus: disturb thoroughly

perveniō, -īre, pervēnī, perventus: arrive

pēs, pedis, m: foot

pessimus, -a, -um (superlative of *malus*): worst

pestis, -is, f: plague, destruction

petō, -ere, -īvī/iī, -ītus: seek, demand, ask, beg

pharetra, -ae, f: quiver

placeō, -ēre, -uī, -itus + dative: be pleasing, please, be agreeable (to)

placidus, -a, -um: calm, peaceful

plēbēs, -ēī, f: rabble, common people

plēnus, -a, -um + ablative: rich in, full of

plērumque: generally, for the most part

plūrimus, -a, -um (superlative of *plūs*): very many, most

plūs, plūris: several, many, more

poena, -ae, f: punishment, penalty

poēta, -ae, m: poet, artist

polliceor, -ērī, pollicitus sum: promise

pondus, ponderis, n: weight, quantity

pōnō, -ere, posuī, positus: place, put

pontifex, pontificis, m: priest

pontifex maximus, pontificis maximī,
m: chief high priest of Rome

populus, -ī, m: community, people,
population

porta, -ae, f: gate, entrance

possum, posse, potuī: be able, can,
be powerful

post: later, afterward, next, besides

postquam: after

potens, potentis + genitive: strong,
powerful

prae + accusative or ablative: in comparison with, on account of, in
front of

praebeō, -ēre, -uī, -itus: provide,
offer, exhibit, supply

praeda, -ae, f: spoil, plunder, prey

praefectus, -ī, m: prefect, an officer in
the Roman army

praemium, -iī, n: reward

praesum, -esse, praefuī + dative:
be in charge, preside over, have
charge over

praetereā: besides, moreover

praetereō, -īre, -iī, -itus: pass by,
disregard

praetor, -ōris, m: an elected Roman
magistrate

prasinus, -a, -um: green

premō, -ere, pressī, pressus: control,
press, pursue

prīdiē: on the day before

prīmus, -a, -um: first

princeps, principis, m: leader, chieftain, emperor

pristinus, -a, -um: former, original

prīvātus, -ī, m: individual

prīvō, -āre, -āvī, -ātus: rob, deprive

prō + ablative: for, on behalf of, in
place of

probō, -āre, -āvī, -ātus: prove,
approve

procul: at a distance

proelium, -iī, n: battle

proficiscor, -ī, profectus sum: set
out, depart

prōmittō, -ere, prōmīsī, prōmissus:
promise

propinquus, -ī, m: relative

proprius, -a, -um: one's own,
particular

propter + accusative: because of

**prospiciō, -ere, prospexī,
prospectus:** see, look out, take
care, exercise forethought

prōtinus: at once, immediately

prōvideō, -ēre, prōvīdī, prōvīsus:
foresee, provide for, make
provision

prōvincia, -ae, f: duty, command,
province, the backwoods

proximus, -a, -um (superlative of
prope) + dative: closest, next

pūblicus, -a, -um: belonging to the
people, public

pudet, -ēre, puduit: it shames, makes
ashamed

puella, -ae, f: girl

puer, puerī, m: boy

pugna, -ae, f: battle

pugnō, -āre, -āvī, -ātus: fight

pulcher, pulchra, pulchrum: pretty,
noble

putō, -āre, -āvī, -ātus: think

quā: where, in what direction

quaerō, -ere, quaesīvī, quaesītus:
inquire, ask, seek, look for

quam: than, rather than, how

quam prīmum: as soon as possible

quamquam: although

quamvīs: although

quantus, -a, -um: how great, how
much

quārē: why? by what means?
wherefore

quasi: as if

quater: four times

-que: and

queror, -ī, questus sum: complain,
lament

quī, quae, quod: who, what, which

quīcumque, quaecumque, quodcumque: whoever, whatever,
whichever

quid: what? why?

quīdam, quaedam, quoddam: a
certain

quidem: indeed

quiēs, quiētis, f: rest

quiescō, -ere, quiēvī, quiētus: rest,
keep quiet, stop

quīn: but that

quippe: naturally, of course

quis, quid: who? what?

quisquam, quicquam: anyone,
anything

quisquis, quidquid: whoever,
whatever

quō: where

quod: because, the fact that

quondam: formerly, once

quoque: also

quot: how many?

rāmus, -ī, m: branch, twig

rārus, -a, -um: few, scarce, scattered,
loose, thin

ratiō, -ōnis, f: reason, calculation,
reasoning, judgment

recipiō, -ere, recēpī, receptus: hold
back, retain, take back

recitō, -āre, -āvī, -ātus: recite,
declaim

reclīnō, -āre, -āvī, -ātus: lean back

recondō, -ere, recondidī, reconditus:
hide, conceal

reddō, -ere, reddidī, redditus: give
back, return, restore, exchange

redeō, -īre, -iī, -itus: return

redūcō, -ere, reduxī, reductus: bring
back

referō, -ferre, rettulī, relātus:
announce, report, bring back,
carry back, relate, come back

regiō, -ōnis, f: province, district

rēgius, -a, -um: royal, of the king

regnō, -āre, -āvī, -ātus + genitive:
rule

regnum, -ī, n: kingdom

regō, -ere, rexī, rectus: guide, direct,
rule

religiō, -ōnis, f: religious scruple,
observance of a religious
ceremony

relinquō, -ere, relīquī, relictus: leave
behind, abandon

reliquus, -a, -um: remaining, last

rēmus, -ī, m: oar

re(p)periō, -īre, re(p)perī, re(p)per-
tus: find out, discover

requīrō, -ere, requīsīvī, requīsītus:
ask, inquire, seek again, look after,
search for

rēs mīlitāris, rēī mīlitāris, f: warfare

rēs pūblica, rēī pūblicae, f: the state

rēs, rēī, f: action, affair, course of
events, preparation

resistō, -ere, restitī: resist, oppose,
withstand

resolvō, -ere, resolvī, resolūtus:
loosen, release

respiciō, -ere, respexī, respectus: look back

restituō, -ere, restituī, restitūtus: replace, restore

retrō: back

revertor, -ī, reversus sum: go back, return

revocō, -āre, -āvī, -ātus: recall, summon, restore

rex, rēgis, m: king

rīdeō, -ēre, rīsī, rīsus: laugh

rogō, -āre, -āvī, -ātus: ask, ask for, endorse

rota, -ae, f: wheel, chariot

ruīna, -ae, f: downfall, ruin

rūmor, -ōris, m: rumor, murmuring

rumpō, -ere, rūpī, ruptus: break, burst, tear apart

rursus: again

sacer, sacra, sacrum: sacred

sacrificium, -iī, n: offering, sacrifice

sacrum, -ī, n: a holy thing or place, religious rite

saepe: often

saevus, -a, -um: fierce, cruel, violent, savage

sāl, salis, m: salt, cunning; (in plural) wit

salūs, salūtis, f: health, safety, welfare

salvē: hello, greetings

sanctus, -a, -um: holy, sacred, pure

satis: enough

saxum, -ī, n: rock, cliff, crag

scelus, sceleris, n: crime

sciō, -īre, scīvī, scītus: know

scopulus, -ī, m: rock, cliff

scrībō, -ere, scripsī, scriptus: write

sē: himself, herself, itself, themselves

sēcum: with himself, herself, itself, themselves

sed: but

sēdēs, -is, f: base, foundation, seat, home, habitation, region

sēditiō, -ōnis, f: insurrection, rebellion

seges, -etis, f: crop

semper: always

senātus, -ūs, m: Senate

senex, senis, m: old man

sententia, -ae, f: opinion, intention, view, judgment

sentiō, -īre, sensī, sensus: perceive, feel

septem (indeclinable): seven

sepulchrum, -ī, n: grave, tomb

sequor, -ī, secūtus sum: follow

sermō, -ōnis, m: talk, conversation

serviō, -īre, -īvī, -ītus + dative: be a slave to

servō, -āre, -āvī, -ātus: keep, preserve, save, rescue, watch over

sēsē: himself, herself, itself, themselves

seu: or if

sī: if

sibi: to or for himself, herself, itself, themselves

sīc: thus, so, as

sīcut: just as

sīdus, sīderis, n: star, sky

signum, -ī, n: sign, military standard, constellation, zodiac

simul: at the same time

sine + ablative: without

singulāris, -e: alone

sinō, -ere, sīvī, situs: place, set down, allow, permit

situs, -ūs, m: site, structure, inactivity, neglect

socia, -ae, f: companion, partner

socius, -iī, m: ally, follower

sōl, sōlis, m: sun

soleō, -ēre, solitus sum: be accustomed

sōlus, -a, -um: only, alone

solvō, -ere, solvī, solūtus: loosen, free, release, fulfill, weaken

sors, sortis, f: lot, chance

speciēs, -ēī, f: appearance

spectō, -āre, -āvī, -ātus: observe, look at

spēs, spēī, f: hope

spīritus, -ūs, m: breath

sponte: voluntarily, of one's own will

stāgnum, -ī, n: deep water, still water, lake, pool

stella, -ae, f: star, constellation

stirps, stirpis, f: family

stō, stāre, stetī, status: stand

strepitus, -ūs, m: din, noise, racket, uproar

studeō, -ēre, -uī + dative: strive for, be devoted to, pursue

studium, -iī, n: pursuit, eagerness, enthusiasm, devotion, zest, zeal

stupeō, -ēre, stupuī: be amazed

sub + ablative: under

subitō: suddenly

subitus, -a, -um: sudden, unexpected

sublīmis, -e: lofty, elevated, raised up

subsequor, -ī, subsecūtus sum: follow after

sum, esse, fuī, futūrus: be

summus, -a, -um (superlative of *superus, -a, -um*): highest

super + accusative: above, over, upon, on, in addition to

super: more

supplicium, -iī, n: entreaty, supplication, punishment

suspicor, -ārī, -ātus sum: suspect

suus, -a, -um: his/her/its/their own

taceō, -ēre, -uī, -itus: be silent, say nothing

tālis, -e: such, of such a sort, of such a kind, so great

tam: so

tamen: nevertheless, nonetheless, however, but

tangō, -ere, tetigī, tactus: touch, strike

tantum: only

tantus, -a, -um: so great, such

tectum, -ī, n: house, building, shelter, structure, maze

tēcum: with yourself

tegō, -ere, texī, tectus: cover, protect, defend, hide

tellūs, tellūris, f: land, earth

tēlum, -ī, n: weapon, missile, javelin, spear

tempestās, -ātis, f: storm

tempus, -oris, n: time

tendō, -ere, tetendī, tentus: hasten, stretch, strive, exert

teneō, -ēre, -uī, tentus: hold, maintain, detain

tenuis, -e: thin, fine, slight

ter: three times

tergum, -ī, n: back

terra, -ae, f: earth

terror, -ōris, m: fright, dread

tertius, -a, -um: third

timeō, -ēre, -uī: be afraid, fear

timor, -ōris, m: fear, dread

titulus, -ī, m: inscription, notice

tollō, -ere, sustulī, sublātus: lift, raise, take away, remove, steal

tot: so many, such a large number of

totidem: as many

tōtus, -a, -um: all, every, whole, entire

trādō, -ere, tradidī, traditus: hand down

trahō, -ere, traxī, tractus: drag, draw

trānseō, -īre, -iī, -itus: cross over, go across, pass by

tribūtum, -ī, n: tax, tribute

tristis, -e: sad, unhappy, gloomy, sorrowful

tū: you

tueor, -ērī, tuitus sum: protect, look at, watch

tum: then, next, at that time

tumidus, -a, -um: swelling

turba, -ae, f: uproar, disturbance, crowd

turpis, -e: disgraceful, shameful

tuus, -a, -um: yours

ubi/ubī: where, when

ullus, -a, -um: any

umbra, -ae, f: shadow, shade

ūnā: at the same time, together

unda, -ae, f: wave, sea

unde: from the place where, from where

undique: from all sides

unguentum, -ī, n: ointment, perfume

ūniversus, -a, -um: all, every, all together

ūnus, -a, -um: one, alone

urbs, urbis, f: city

ūrō, -ere, ussī, ustus: burn

usque: continuously, without interruption, all the way up to

ūsus, -ūs, m: use, practice, advantage

ut: as, when, like, that, so that

uterque, utraque, utrumque: each (of two), both

ūtor, -ī, ūsus sum + ablative: use, employ, possess

utrimque: on both sides

utrum...an: whether...or

vadum, -ī, n: shallow, shoal

vāgītus, -ūs, m: crying, bleating (of flocks)

vagus, -a, -um: roving, wandering

valeō, -ēre, valuī, valītus: be well, prevail, farewell, good-bye

varius, -a, -um: varied, different, various, diverse

vastus, -a, -um: desolate, vast, enormous, immense, huge, monstrous

-ve: or

vehō, -ere, vexī, vectus: convey, carry

vēnātiō, -ōnis, f: hunting, beast hunt

veniō, -īre, vēnī, ventus: come, arrive, reach

venter, ventris, m: belly, stomach

ventus, -ī, m: breeze, wind

verbum, -ī, n: word

vērē: truly

vereor, -ērī, veritus sum: fear, fear to, be anxious

vērō: indeed

versō, -āre, -āvī, -ātus: turn, twist around, keep turning

vertō, -ere, vertī, versus: turn, convert

vērum: truly, however

vestīgium, -iī, n: footprint, footstep, track, trace

vetus, veteris: old

via, -ae, f: road

viātor, -ōris, m: traveler

victōria, -ae, f: victory

victus, -ūs, m: food

videō, -ēre, vīdī, vīsus: see, look at, watch

videor, -ērī, vīsus sum: seem, seem best

vīlis, -e: of little value, cheap, worthless

vinciō, -īre, vinxī, vinctus: bind, tie, fetter

vincō, -ere, vīcī, victus: conquer, overcome, overpower

vinc(u)lum, -ī, n: chain

vindex, vindicis, m/f: avenger, punisher

vir, -ī, m: husband, man

virgō, virginis, f: girl, maiden, virgin, "Vestal"

virtūs, virtūtis, f: courage, bravery, excellence, manliness, moral excellence, virtue

vīs, vis, f (irregular noun): strength, force, power

viscus, visceris, n: entrails, inner parts

vītō, -āre, -āvī, -ātus: avoid, escape, evade

vīvō, -ere, vixī, victus: live

vocō, -āre, -āvī, -ātus: call, summon

volō, velle, voluī: want, wish, be willing

volvō, -ere, volvī, volūtus: roll, revolve, consider

vōs: you (plural)

vōtum, -ī, n: vow

vox, vōcis, f: voice

vulnus, vulneris, n: wound